So, There I Was…

34 years wearing the badge

Michael S Reeder

ISBN: **978-1-7779816-0-0**

DEDICATION

To my teammates and co-workers (past and present). Thank you for your hard work, devotion, and desire to serve others. You made me a better police officer and person through your example.

To the citizens of Lethbridge, Alberta who've allowed me to serve them for the last 34 years, I'm so thankful for your support and appreciation.

Most importantly, to my wife and son for the sacrifices they've made and worries they've endured through the years. Thank you for your patience and love which allowed me to do something I loved. I am eternally grateful.

CONTENTS

Preface   1

1   How This All Began   5

2   What Have I Gotten Myself Into   12

3   I Guess I Wont Get A Motorbike   19

4   Finally On My Own   27

5   My First Murder And A New Nickname   34

6   Altered Consciousness (And A Magpie)   43

7   Sally And Candace   50

8   Listen To That Still Small Voice   60

9   My Wife Learns I'm A Liar   69

10 Deadly Winter   79

11 Suicide And An Unlikely Hero   88

12 A Knife To The Head And A Long Fall   98

13 Defecation Magnets   107

14 My Next Two Partners   117

15 Murder, Heart Attacks, And A Helicopter   128

16 Negotiator School And My First Call   140

17 Finally, A "Big City Detective"   151

18 Lessons On Interviewing   162

19 Fraud, Incest And Attempted Murder, Oh My!   172

20 The Tryptophan Affair   182

21 Selling A Motorbike, And Other Negotiations   192

22 Team Building And Violent Crimes   200

23 Lana The Killer And Unrequited Love   210

24 Win Some And Lose Some   219

25 Cold Cases   229

26 Unexpected But Needed Change   239

27 Back Where I Started   248

28 Cumulative PTSD   258

ACKNOWLEDGMENTS

Tanner, Jeff, Erin, and Terryl. A current cop, a former cop, a published author, and my sister, the professional editor. Your assistance was excellent and sorely needed. Thank you for slogging through these pages and repressing your glee in pointing out my innumerable mistakes. All remaining flaws are mine.

DISCLAIMER

Although this is not a work of fiction, all names but the author's have been changed to protect the innocent, guilty or just plain stupid. (Coppers included). All incidents described herein are accurate but based on the author's admittedly elderly and self-centred recollections. They may vary slightly from the memories of others present.

PREFACE

One of the many things I've learned over the last 33 years as a police officer is that we love to tell stories. I've been guilty of telling a few over the years, and they usually begin with the phrase "**So, there I was**. . ." In fact, I've shared so many stories, my co-workers, friends, and family, continually tell me I should write a book. (Mostly because they're tired of hearing the same stories, over and over again, I'm sure.) I decided to take their advice and share a few experiences to pull aside the curtain and show what it's like; I mean what it's **REALLY** like, to be a cop.

Over the years, I've had the opportunity to work in a wide and varied cross-section of policing. As a constable, I worked in both Patrol Division as well as a two-year stint in a traffic enforcement car. I was entrusted over the years to train nine new members of the police service. During that time, I was also trained by the Service to facilitate ethics courses for the membership. Fellow officers also voted to have me represent them as a member of the Police Association Board, another name for the police union. As a sergeant, I've worked as a detective in the Economic Crime Section of The Criminal Investigation Division (CID), a detective in the Violent Crimes Section of CID, a Patrol Team Sergeant, a short time in the Recruiting Section and a couple of years in Community Engagement. I also have 18 years of experience as a Crisis Negotiator in our Tactical Support Section (we used to call them Hostage Negotiators.) All but two and a half years of my service as a copper has been spent in an "operational" capacity, so I've seen a few things.

People don't call the police to come to their house, neighbourhood, or business when all is going well. It's always the result of something that they either can't, or don't want to deal with themselves. As a result, police officers usually see folks at their worst, and often on the worst day of their lives. We're expected to solve a problem in ten minutes that usually took years to create. I've spent the majority of my career seeing and dealing with other people's worst day repeatedly. There are also plenty of folks out there that just didn't bother to read the instruction manual on how to be normal, decent human beings.

I read a statistic a few years ago that said an average citizen will suffer through between one and two traumatic or violent incidents over the course of their lives. A police officer sees between 800 and 1,000 of such incidents during a 25-year career. In simpler terms, the worst day of your life is Tuesday for us. That doesn't mean it isn't devastating and/or tragic, but when we're done with helping you through that horrific, possibly life changing incident, we're on to the next call. While you have time to heal, mend, reflect and hopefully learn to cope, we have to go back to work. This isn't a complaint. It's what we volunteered for when we signed up, even though few of us knew the cost at that time.

For the most part, what follows will be some of those incidents. Most of them, I was called to attend, and some I came across on my own. Some are just plain funny, and others only cops (or retired cops) will see that way. Some are sad and others are uplifting. Above all, they really happened. Some of them will make you laugh, and some might make you cry. I tell very few (if any) tales about things I "heard about". I'll share with you only what I've seen, taken part in, or at least had some peripheral involvement. Please remember that we all see or recall things differently, even when witnessing the same thing. (When you interview four witnesses to the same incident and are left wondering if they were even in the same city, you understand the concept.) As a result, there will be stories I tell, which others who were present might not remember the way I have. That's okay; it doesn't mean one of us is lying. There'll be no embellishment or truth bending. The truth will be funny enough. (Or on some occasions sad enough, or scary enough… well you get the general idea).

Although this isn't a true autobiography, it could be considered an autobiography of the work portion of my life. Many cops are guilty of blending the two until they forget their non-work persona, losing a portion of their humanity from time to time. There is also a perception that cops are robots without feelings. This book will hopefully show some of the lighter side of the profession but also the terrible cost we pay for seeing what we repeatedly see and doing what we occasionally have to do. Any copper that tells you the job hasn't changed or damaged them is either a brand new guy (or girl) with little experience on the job, or not being entirely truthful with you. More likely, if a veteran copper says the job hasn't changed him, he isn't being truthful with himself. I know. I suffered from that particular sin for many years until a great friend and co-worker pointed out to me how much I'd changed. I'm happier with the man I am now, but also resigned to the fact that I'm no longer the idealistic person I was in 1988. I'd still do it again but might have done things to handle the stress better, like paying closer attention to what I eat and make regular trips to the gym. That might have helped me to avoid the heart attack I had when I was 38 years old.

A few tidbits of information might be helpful in putting some of the things I'm about to share into perspective. I started policing in the spring of 1988. I chose to work in Lethbridge, Alberta, the third largest city in the Province. The Police Service now has about 170 members, but when I started, there were 89. There weren't computers in the cars. There were no Tasers, pepper spray or collapsible batons issued to us. We had to pay for half of our first Kevlar vest to show that we were "committed to wearing them." I had a .357 calibre revolver with two speed loaders, a total of 18 rounds. (That's the same amount of ammo in my current loaded service pistol, not counting my two spare magazines.) We didn't have a carbine or a shotgun in our cars when I started because, as it was so aptly explained to me at the time, "We don't want the citizens to think we need them." I started policing one generation after constables walked the beat. In fact, mine was the first generation of copper that started after the Charter of Rights and Freedoms was proclaimed. (For you Americans reading this, the rights of Canadian citizens acknowledged in the Charter concerning self-incrimination is somewhat analogous to the Miranda US Supreme Court decision in the 60's in your country.) I graduated from High School in 1982, the same year the Charter became the law of the land. That means, when I started, most of my co-workers had some experience being a "pre-Charter" cop. My first Sergeant became a cop in 1955. My first Station Sergeant (a rank that was eliminated a few years later, to be re-named Staff Sergeant) started the job in 1962.

All the names I use have been changed to protect the innocent, guilty and stupid; cops included. One last thing before I get to it. Please forgive me and my co-workers. Some of the things we find funny are often not normal, to say the least. Being incessantly inundated can cause defence mechanisms to spring up. We sometimes talk about where we might go for lunch while wrapping up a sudden death investigation, even if there's still a dead body on the floor or bed near us. Sometimes we laugh instead of cry but for the most part, we're still human, or at least I hope so. I know that I'm not the same kid I was when I started this adventure, but who is, right? The last chapter in the book is entitled "Cumulative PTSD" for a reason.

So, There I was… 34 years wearing the badge

HOW THIS ALL BEGAN

I never really knew what I wanted to do with my life. I never once thought about a career in policing. I wasn't against the job; it just didn't even cross my mind as an option. I never thought a great deal about school either. Most of my time in High School was spent chasing girls and playing basketball and football. I wasn't bad at schoolwork; I just never really took things like studying seriously. My only goal was to remain eligible to play varsity sports. That meant I had to maintain a 65% average in all my classes without failing any of them. I had a lot of fun, but I never learned the importance of, or even how to study. As I got closer to graduation, I was just going with the flow more than having a plan. I eventually wanted to go to college or university but had no idea where to go or what to study. In short, I was a bit lost and treading water, rather than moving in any specific direction.

I grew up in a religious family. We were (and still are) practicing members of the Church of Jesus Christ of Latter-Day Saints. My hometown was small, having just over 2,000 residents at the time. About 90% of us were members of the church. If you know anything about the Church (or if you've seen the Broadway musical "The Book of Mormon"), you know many of our young people serve a mission for two years. I didn't go right away. Instead, I wasted time after graduation, taking a night shift job as a supervisor for a cleaning company in Lethbridge, just continuing to coast for a few years. When my best friend, (who's also my cousin) left on his mission, all my coasting seemed pointless. Our birthdays are only a month or two apart and he left right after he turned 19 years old, and there I was, working, and just getting by. I finally realized I didn't want that, so I decided I would go on a mission as well. That's how I found myself in the Missionary Training Centre in Provo, Utah two days before my 20th birthday, leaving my friends and family (and girlfriend) behind to serve the Lord.

I was called to serve in the Canada Montreal Mission and asked to serve and teach the people of Quebec in the French language. The problem with that was, I didn't know how to speak French, even though I'd been taking it in school for years. (See above about why those French Lessons were less than 100% effective.) Needless to say, the two months in the Missionary Training Centre before going into the field were difficult. I had no idea how to study and yet I wanted to learn like no other time in my life. I would soon be going to a place that I had to learn how to communicate in a new language to survive. How would I be able to order a cheeseburger at a fast-food restaurant or get directions from a bus driver in an entirely different language? A language that my teachers fooled me into thinking I was about 65% fluent. How on earth would I be able to speak to people about religion? I was in trouble and needed to improve my study habits in a hurry!

When I got to Quebec, I found that I picked up the language quickly. It's amazing what you can do when you are motivated and doing something you really want to do. I grew to love the language and the people. They were my fellow Canadians, but I still felt like I was in a foreign country. I loved it. Even though I was away from family and friends for two years, it wasn't much of a sacrifice, because I lost myself in serving others. There were rough spots where I missed home, but I made life-long friends, and had the opportunity to put myself and my problems aside while helping others. I even managed to learn the language well. All told, it was a great experience, and I stopped worrying or thinking about what I would do with my life when I got home. I even asked and was given permission to stay a few months longer because I loved it so much. At this point, I still wasn't making any plans for my future. Instead, I was just losing myself in the moment, and not worrying about what came next. Then it happened.

There are very few people who can tell you the exact date, time, and location when they decided what they were going to do with their lives. Most police officers don't have an epiphany, telling them to pursue policing as a career. Many have a copper in the family. Some had an excellent School Resource Officer who they admired growing up. Some of them sort of fell into it almost by accident. The fact is most guys and girls that become cops don't remember a time when they *didn't* want to become one. I didn't fall into any of these categories. It took something specific to help me see what I wanted to do when I got home.

So, there I was, June 7th, 1985, in Quebec City, one of the most beautiful cities in North America. I had six months left before I was scheduled to go home, and my partner was a guy I went to high school with. Being partnered with someone you knew growing up is almost unheard of. It rarely happens. At the time we were partners, one of my younger sisters and his brother were dating back home. He and I played on the same high school football team, and we knew each other's parents. We got along very well. I felt like I was in the best city in the mission with the best partner. My language skills were good enough that I no longer struggled or worried about speaking with people about religion, or any other topic for that matter. I was genuinely happy, without a care in the world. Then "Max" came.

I guess I should clarify. "Max" was mission slang for the mail man. In French, the word for Postman is "Facteur". (Get it? Max Factor!) I guess if I need to explain, it isn't as funny as we thought back then. We were still young kids without a TV, radio, or an X-Box. We found our fun where we could. Words like "trunky" (a missionary who is waiting to go home so badly that he's already packed up mentally and is sitting on his trunk) or "plug" (macaroni and cheese) were commonly used, among many other sayings.

So, Max showed up that morning, and we got our mail. Without the internet and before the advent of email, we were entirely reliant on Canada Post to keep us informed about home. Because my partner was from my hometown, we could also share news, and get a bigger, more accurate picture of what was going on while we were gone. Mission rules at the time stated that you could only call home twice a year, on Mother's Day and Christmas Day to speak to your mother. No trunky calls to your girlfriend. "Max" and what he brought us, was very important in our young lives.

One of the letters I got that day was from my girlfriend. I had done the one thing every missionary knows *not* to do. I'd asked her to "wait for me" until I came home. Our communication wasn't as regular as it'd been my first year out, and during that last two or three months, it kind of petered out altogether. Excitedly, I opened the letter and found a wedding invitation. *Her* wedding invitation… to someone else. **She had "Dear John'd" me with a wedding invitation!** It even had a picture of the lovely couple inside, and I knew the guy! He was a good enough guy, but he wasn't *me*! I laughed a bit, then I cried a bit, and then I sat there numb for a bit. Thank heavens my partner knew me longer than just a few months. He let me wallow in my sorrow for a bit and then suggested we get out of the apartment to get my mind off of things. We decided to go out and knock on some doors. At that point anything was better than sitting there staring at the wall (no TV or radio), so off to the bus stop we went.

I'll share a secret with you if you don't tell anyone you heard it from me. Knocking on doors, commonly known as "tracting" or "proselyting" has mixed success at best. Missionaries generally do this only when they don't have anything else to do. You meet a lot of people, and if you are lucky, they'll let you into their home to chat for a while. Even though there is the possibility that the next door you knock on will have that one person searching for the meaning of life, most people are too busy to invite complete strangers into their home to speak about religion.

It was something that would help me get my mind off my troubles, so we prayed and decided to go to Limoilou, a subdivision that's close to the historic old city and one of the older (and at the time, somewhat run down) areas of Quebec City. When we got off the bus, we found a bunch of old "walk-up" apartment buildings right near the bus stop and decided to start there. These buildings were so old that there was no elevator. Instead, there were grey painted steps with a wrought iron railing to hold onto, winding up the outside of the buildings, leading to the upper floors. We went to the first building near the bus stop, walked up the stairs to the top floor and knocked on the first apartment door.

I thought the man who answered the door was old; he was at least 45! He had his arm around the shoulders of a girl who appeared to be about 15 years old, and they were both intoxicated. (In my current job, one of the common descriptors we use for someone in this guy's shape is "floor licking, slobbering drunk.") He was also wearing either a pair of small shorts, or a speedo with his substantial stomach hanging over the top, so at just the right angle, you weren't sure if he was clothed at all. He invited us in, where we found two other young kids about the same age as the girl, in an equally inebriated state. The older man introduced the boy as his son. It was never said, but I got the idea that the son had skipped school and brought two girls home with him to get drunk with his dad. It also appeared to be a situation where he brought his girlfriend home as well as a "friend" for his father. It was my partner's turn to teach so he started in on why we were there, and the message we had to share, but soon realized that they weren't as receptive as we'd first hoped. Some of the things they were saying were relatively disparaging and that they saw us more as entertainment. The father was making fun of my partner while he spoke. I mentioned this to my partner (in English), and he started to wrap it up so we could go somewhere else where our message might be more appreciated. He gave them the "Jesus is love" speech and we said we had to go. That's when things got a bit weird.

As we got up to go, the son shouted out "Dad, Dad, show them Terrible". I wasn't quite sure what that meant and was also fairly sure I didn't want to know. There was a large fish tank by the door that was darkened on the sides so you couldn't see inside. We were standing beside it when the man put his hand out, wanting me to shake it saying, "Are you my friend?" Now if you've had any interaction with missionaries of my faith, you know that we have an autonomic reaction to this. I reached out to shake his hand. I was about to assure him we were his friends, and that we might come by another time, when he took hold of my hand and held it tightly, not letting go. He then reached into the fish tank, which actually turned out to be a terrarium, and pulled out a tarantula that was as big as my head. As he put the giant tarantula on my arm, he again said, "Are you my friend?" I was silently freaking out as the hairy spider slowly walked up my arm. He then scooped it up and said "Ya, you're my friend". He looked at my partner, holding out his hand as if to shake, while a spider the size of a dinner plate was in his other hand and repeated, "Are you my friend?" My esteem went up tenfold for my partner when he looked at the guy holding the huge hairy spider in his hand and said, "You bet I am!" and shook his hand.

After the spider took a walk on my rock star partner's arm, the man asked us both if we wanted a "hit for the road." Now all of this had been in French, and I didn't quite catch what he said, or what it meant and neither did my partner. We asked him what he meant. He said, "You know, a hit for the road!" and pulled out a small bag of white powder. He took his necklace off that had a miniature spoon on it. He snorted a spoonful of the white powder, gave some to his 15-year-old son, and asked us again if we wanted a "hit for the road". I was shocked! Not only had he offered us coke, but he also snorted some in front of us and then gave some to his kid! We declined and left.

I was angry, offended and heart broken, all at the same time. This guy not only wanted to give cocaine to two representatives of the Lord, but he also gave some to his kid, right in front of us, without shame or regret. He was purposefully destroying his own child's life, with a couple of witnesses to the fact. (Not to mention what may or may not have been going on with the two young girls). And this all happened on the day my personal life had taken an unexpected left turn. The girl I asked to wait for me had dumped me, with only six months left before I got home! I looked at my partner and could see he was just as troubled as I was. I told him that the day had been bad enough and that I was in no shape to continue. No good could come from us going into other people's homes, feeling like I felt at that moment. He felt as bad as I did, and agreed, so we decided to go to the mall, or a video arcade, or do our laundry. Anything but what we'd been doing.

As we went down the stairs, I glanced toward the bus stop where we were headed. I saw a guy sitting in a car, close by, looking right at us. The stairs led around the building, and I lost sight of him, but when we went around again, the guy was still looking right at us. As we walked by his car, I could see he had a radio in his lap, and he was still looking at us. I clued in. This had to be a cop! I went over to him to report the crime my partner and I had just witnessed. He looked at me and said:

"Ya, kid, we know. We've been waiting for you to leave. Did you see any drugs?"

He didn't really say it that way. There were a few more curse words mixed in, (some that I had never heard before, proving I wasn't as bilingual as I thought), but I won't share them because I promised this would be as PG-13 as possible. I have since learned that it doesn't matter what language, cops can out-curse almost anyone. He was creative with his adjectives. I didn't even know he was a cop because he didn't identify himself. (Undercover coppers don't do that until they have to.) I just made that leap because of the radio in his lap.

"Yes, Sir, there was a small bag of coke in the living room. He offered us some, and he even gave some to his kid."

What I said didn't shock him. Knowing what I know now, I'm sure he'd seen much worse, but I hadn't, and was still reeling from what I'd seen. I felt this enormous flood of relief. Here were the good guys, waiting for us to leave so they could go in and stop this travesty. They were going to save those three kids from what that man was doing to them. Talk about emotions going up and down and then up again! From what I know now, they were probably waiting for us to leave so they could execute a search warrant.

That was when I knew. I wanted to make a difference like this guy was going to make in those three kids' lives. Heck, he might even be the turning point in that father's life helping him change his ways too. I know it sounds sickeningly idealistic now, but I really did feel those emotions at the time. (When I tell this story to my cop friends now, they laugh or groan at how naïve I was). I knew I wanted to stop people like that guy from preying on the weak and young. That was what I saw that young undercover copper doing when he eventually kicked in that door. I simply *knew* that I would be a cop when I got home. I wanted to help people like those kids. So that's what I decided to do.

****

Two years and nine months later, I was working as a police officer with the

Lethbridge Police Force. (We were still a Force in 1988. They didn't change the name for a few more years to the Lethbridge Police Service.) In those two years and nine months, I finished my mission, went home, and enrolled at the local college, found the girl of my dreams, married her, and got my dream job. That's kind of condensing things a bit, but you know what I mean.

I felt old amongst my fellow college students. It wasn't just because I was three or four years older than most of them. (I was the ripe old age of 22 years old when I started college, going to class with many who'd just finished high school.) It was because I'd left home, lived on my own for a few years, and learned how to take care of myself. I learned another language and experienced another culture. In essence, I'd gotten out of my comfort zone. I'd learned that even though people were different, they were also kind of the same, no matter where you go. I think they call it "growing up", or at least that's what my mother said. I'm glad I had some life experience before starting the job. Nothing can prepare you for what you see as a cop, but it was easier for me to process after seeing things that were outside the experiences I had growing up in a small town. Things were only going to get stranger.

WHAT HAVE I GOTTEN MYSELF INTO?

My official start date with the Lethbridge Police Force was March 27th, 1988. I was still going to school with 6 weeks left to graduate. Part of successfully completing my probation required me to graduate as well as all of the other normal probationary requirements of the job. I had to work six weeks of straight night shift, while going to school during the day. I'd also been married seven months earlier, and although we were both excited, I had a job in my wife's hometown, ensuring our stay in Lethbridge upon graduation, we hardly saw each other for the next six weeks. She was probably relatively happy about that, but I was not pleased at all. To say I am a "reacher" and my wife is a "settler" is an *understatement*. We were happy we didn't have to move away from home and family, and we now knew the direction of our life together. Everything just seemed to have fallen into place for us. These six weeks were short term pain for long term gain.

Two incidents come to mind from that six week stretch worth noting. I was the victim of a prank that taught me never to sleep on the job. This became my introduction into the way jokes were played to increase team morale, while at the same time teaching valuable lessons. Sadly, as the years have passed, fewer practical jokes are played on teammates. I may repeat myself from time to time, but it was a different time, and I miss some of that stuff that might now be considered bullying. (I know I didn't feel bullied.) The other incident was more of an eye opener as to the disparity regarding how the "pre-Charter cops" and my generation would interact with the public. It was also one of the catalysts in my successful application as the ethics facilitator for the police service later in my career.

I was working all night, then going to school all day with, about 5 hours of sleep in between. By about week four, I was starting to get tired. Really tired. The night in question was a relatively non-eventful evening, and my head was bobbing. I had gravel in my eyes, and although I've never been drunk in my life, I'm sure that my speech patterns approached that of a man under the influence. I was paired up with a young cop who had only been on the Force for a couple of years himself. Dylan is one of the smartest cops I've ever worked with, and really good at what we do. I learned a lot from him, not only in the week we were together, but when we went on to be on the same team and then in some of the same units over the coming years. He was sharp and had a great sense of humour. He was also a big guy, and spoke normally, but when he laughed, it came out more like a high-pitched giggle. It was endearing and made whatever he laughed at even funnier, even when I was the target.

There were hardly any calls for service that night. Time was dragging, and so was I. Dylan could tell I was verging on impairment and knew just the thing to do about it. You see, he wasn't married at the time and was trying to get to know a young Corrections Officer who worked at the Lethbridge Young Offender Centre. She happened to be working that night and, because nothing was going on, he decided we should go to that facility and have a coffee with the employees. I was sort of like a third wheel as Dylan got to know her, so he came upon a solution that would solve both of our problems.

"You look dead on your feet. Why don't you have a snooze in the back seat while I go in for coffee." he offered.

I felt guilty for being paid (a grand total of $14.15 per hour at the time) while I slept, but Dylan countered all of my arguments ending with "You could get me killed being this tired!" It was tough to argue with that, so I climbed into the backseat of the patrol vehicle and was probably asleep before he got in the doors of the Young Offender Centre. Those of you who have been in the back of a patrol vehicle are saying, "He fell asleep there? That's just disgusting!" It wasn't like that. We were driving a patrol van, which the older guys called a paddy wagon. (The term comes from a time when the majority of cops in the northeastern states were originally from Ireland, and when the transport van was seen, it was disparagingly referred to as the "Paddy Wagon." Similarly, the term "cop" or "copper" comes from the copper buttons on the coats of Bobby's in 19th century England.) The prisoners transported in the van were placed in the far back where a large after-market compartment with a wooden bench on each side had been constructed. There was a bench seat behind the front driver and passenger seats but in front of the prisoner compartment; a perfect spot for a young copper to lay down for a short nap.

So, there I was, sleeping the sleep of the righteous, without a care in the world. In fact, I was so righteous (or just plain tired), that I didn't hear Dylan get back into the van, start it up, try to wake me without success, and then drive away. He never told me how long he drove around the city with his sleeping partner on the back bench, but it was longer than five minutes. I would like to think that part of the reason he let me sleep was because he felt sorry for what I was going through. Like I said, Dylan is a good guy, and I really looked up to him. Unfortunately, I fear that the real reason he took so long was not entirely altruistic. He may have been driving around the industrial park on the north side of the city, looking for the perfect place to wake me, all the while trying to suppress that high pitched giggle of his.

In the 2700 block of 9th Avenue North, there's a train track crossing the road that was from a small spur line leading to the loading dock of the distillery still operating at the time. The road was less travelled than some in the industrial section, and as a result had a bit of a lip to the pavement at the railway crossing. What I mean to say is, it was a bit of a bump to go over that track *if* you were going the speed limit. If, on the other hand you built up the speed of, say a marked police vehicle, to however fast you wanted on a straight road in the early hours of the morning, where there is no one to complain about how fast a police car might be travelling or why, one might be able to catch some serious air! I can't remember if there was a seat belt on the back bench of that van or not, but I know I wasn't wearing one.

I woke up to my own scream, flying through the air, as if I were an actor in the, not yet released blockbuster Apollo 13. I was weightless and screaming like a six-year-old schoolgirl, to the sounds of the country music radio station, and Dylan giggling like a slightly older, and much more mischievous schoolgirl. We had to be flying at least 100 kilometres per hour in a clearly marked 50 zone! I barely retained the contents of my bladder, and he cured me of ever sleeping in a police car. I've kept that phobia for over 33 years. Dylan also taught me that a well-planned prank could be a team builder, and a morale booster. The team got to rib me over that little episode for years. Even though I was the target, I loved working with that guy. Sadly, the lion's share of those teambuilding moments occurred before political correctness found them to be demeaning and a form of bullying behaviour. That may be true, but it sure was a fun part of my younger days on the job.

****

Some of the less enjoyable things during my younger days revolved around working with the few guys that could not progress from the way they worked in the sixties. One such instance occurred only a few weeks after my start date. I was still working and going to school, while at the same time trying to be a loving and attentive husband. I was obviously not sleeping a lot, and I missed a few things as a result. One of the difficult things about policing is moral or ethical crises arise at the drop of a hat and when you least expect them. You have to be on your toes and be prepared to do the right thing, rather than sail on the direction that someone else has plotted.

On this particular night, I was with a different, much older member of the service. In fact, he'd been employed by a different police service for some time, and then later chose to jump ship and move to Lethbridge. For the most part, he was a pretty good guy, and I learned some valuable things from him, but that night, the copper from the 60's came out.

S o, there I was, in the passenger seat of the patrol van, driving around with an older member of the service, only a couple of weeks after I was hired. He spent a great deal of our time together telling me how I'd made a mistake coming to Lethbridge, and that I should immediately (or as soon as possible) apply to another police service. I made sure I never mentioned to him that I'd been offered jobs by other police services and *chose* to come to Lethbridge. He would've accused me of being as dumb as a box of rocks or a sack of hammers. I never asked, nor did I want to know why he was so unhappy, but over the years, I've noticed that there are always people that will be unhappy in whatever circumstance they are in. I've fallen into that trap from time to time myself. No one is perfect, but I remember this guy when I get too down on myself, the police service, or circumstances that I might be frustrated with.

We were dispatched to a big party and oversized campfire at the large park in the river bottom. There were reported to be over a hundred people there and the party (and fire) might soon get out of hand. My partner spent his time disparaging the dispatcher and the service in general for how we were dispatched and how we responded to the call we were going to.

As we made the turn to go down into the river-bottom park system, we saw a youth (I guessed he was about fourteen or fifteen years old) walking down toward the party. My partner pulled over to the side of the road, and as he was rolling my window down, he told me to tell the kid to beat it. The kid was on my side of the road and when I started to talk to him, I could tell he had been drinking alcohol, but was not too drunk to take care of himself. He was also being polite, so instead of telling him to "beat it" like my partner told me, I asked him where he was going. He told me that he was heading to the party down in the park, but he was going there to find his brother and get a ride to their home which was out of town. I looked over at my partner, who was looking straight ahead, and shaking his head. I asked the kid if he wanted a ride down to the park to see if we could find his brother and help him to get home. The kid looked at me funny but agreed. I got out of the van and opened the far back doors so he could get in. I got back in the

15

vehicle and looked at my partner, who still hadn't said anything to me, and we started down the hill.

There was a small plexiglass window cut into the prisoner box, so that if the driver looked in the rear-view mirror, he could see inside the prisoner box to make sure his passenger was safe and not up to any funny business. There was also a light that shone into the box through that small window. When it was on, the driver could see inside the box better, but it shone brightly enough that the prisoner could not see out. On this occasion, the light was off, so the kid in the back was looking through it. He could see us, and more importantly, the road we were travelling down and the vehicle coming up the hill toward us. It was a bit of a surprise at first, when I started hearing banging on the wall of the back compartment, and the kid start hollering at us to let him out. My partner jammed on the brakes and put it into park even before the vehicle had come to a complete stop. He got out of the van, and started walking to the rear, out of my sight.

I got out and walked to the back of the van just in time to see that the back doors were already open, and my partner had the kid out of the vehicle. He had hold of the collar of the kid's shirt in his left hand, and he was open hand slapping the side of the kid's face with his right. He wasn't saying a word to the kid as he slapped him. I was shocked and didn't act right away but the next blow woke me up, and I stepped in between them. I physically pushed my partner in the chest to separate him from the kid. He just stood there as I spoke to the youth.

I turned to the kid and asked him his name. He told me and kept saying over and over, "That's my brother, I just wanna go home." He wasn't crying but you could tell he was barely holding it together. I asked him if he was alright. He said that he was okay and just wanted to go. I told him my name and asked him if he wanted to make a complaint. He said he really didn't, he just wanted to leave. I asked him where he would go and he pointed up the hill, saying that his grandmother lived close by, and he would go there. I offered to drive him there, but he wanted nothing to do with that. He just wanted to leave. I made sure he repeated my last name back to me, so that he knew who I was, and then let him go. As soon as I let him go, that kid took off up the hill like he was being chased. I had no idea what to do next.

As I said earlier, my partner seemed to be a pretty good guy, even though he had a very poor opinion of our Service. How did a cop on the job for only two or three weeks get in the face of, let alone lay his hands on, someone who had been on the job since before I was born? Although I wouldn't be on his platoon when I finished school, this guy was going to judge me, and more importantly, talk about me to our co-workers with his twist on what had happened. I half expected to get fired when I got back to the station. I also wondered if I could have done more for the kid, but I am pretty sure that forcing him back in our vehicle, when he hadn't been arrested in the first place, was wrong. All these things went through my head in a flash as I walked back to the vehicle. I got in, closed the door, and looked at my partner. He was looking straight ahead and didn't say a word. He just put the van in drive, and we continued down the hill to the park and broke up the party. My partner stood behind me and didn't say a word as I was speaking to people, and they all agreed to leave. (More cop cars and the fire department pumper truck showing up to put the fire out may have helped disperse them too).

****

I'm not sure if my partner ever told anyone the story, but I couldn't let it rest. At the end of the shift, I talked to the day shift Staff Sergeant. He sure didn't seem to think it was that big of a deal, and I was wondering if this was a foreshadowing of what was to come. I was worried that I wouldn't mentally or morally survive the job. They didn't even put me with a different partner for the rest of the week; it was like it never happened. The guy I drove with for that week, never mentioned it. I finally gathered the courage the next week to ask Dylan about it. You know, Dylan, the guy who I learned to trust even after he sent me flying when we caught air like we were in the General Lee in an episode of the Duke's of Hazard? I trusted him, and he helped me a lot. He didn't speak about the other guy's actions, other than to say they were wrong. He told me that times were changing and so were attitudes. I'd done the right thing by stopping the assault and then reporting it, and there was nothing else I could do about it, other than not let this job change me more than I let it.

The kid never came in to complain, and I never heard about the incident again. As for the times changing, well Dylan was right about that. Most of the pre-Charter cops did change, and I learned a lot from them. My permanent FTO was a rock star. I learned so much from him, even though he had been hired long before the Charter came into effect.

I also remember the advice an old detective gave me when I asked him about interviewing and what to do after the subject's lawyer told him not to say anything to the cops. He gave me great advice that was Charter proof. Many years later, long after he had retired, I used that advice to get a homicide suspect to admit to his crime after his lawyer told him to shut his mouth. He went in to graphic detail about how and why he killed his best friend and

17

then went to jail for 16 years. (Don't worry, that story is coming too).

I guess what I'm saying is, there were a few heavy-handed guys that were resistant to change, and one or two bald-faced racists on the job when I started. The good news is, there were far fewer than you might think, and most of them rose to the challenge to learn new things. Sure, there were a few that didn't change with the times, but I bet if you think about it, no matter what you do, and no matter where you are, you work with a couple people that are unfortunately, that way as well.

I GUESS I WON'T GET A MOTORBIKE

Graduation! Finally, I would get to work with the platoon I had been assigned, and work every day with my field training officer, instead of a different one every week. (The platoon name was changed a few years later to "Team.") I had worked with this platoon once during the previous 6 weeks but both my staff sergeant and my FTO had been off on vacation or some sort of training. The way the schedule was laid out, I found myself working nights my first shift after graduation. I was still okay with it though. I finally got to catch up on sleep, and become a normal shift worker, instead of someone who felt like they were working two jobs.

The beginning of shift was the same as it had been the last six weeks, only different. We still sat around a table at the beginning of shift, listening to the platoon sergeant give us an update on what had happened in the last 24 hours, as well as important memos and other information from the other members or units and the administration. My FTO was named Dan and he was the nicest, kindest man I could have worked with. He was one of the only cops from the 80's I knew that had visible tattoos. They looked like prison tats, with a skull that said "born loser" over it on one forearm. I teased him a lot after he met my mom. She took one look at him and then turned to me and said, "Oh Michael, are you going to be alright?" Right in front of him! He laughed about it. He took things like that really well, especially considering he didn't want to train me. He told me later it wasn't *me*, rather some bad experiences he had recently lived through with his last couple of recruits.

It turns out the two new guys he had trained before me had been assigned to him because of perceived problems which needed to be sorted out before they were on their own. (I think they viewed Dan as the "Rookie

Whisperer", capable of straightening out all manner of ineptitude and poor judgement.) It also turns out they thought I might need his skills; however, I was unaware of that fact until a few weeks later when Dan told me. Apparently hiring a return missionary was not something they did every day. They were unsure if I could handle the job and thought I might be too soft. It could also have been there was a touch of dislike for those of my faith.

I got a hint of that during my first job interview before being hired. It was the pre-polygraph interview where questions were asked of me regarding my personal disclosure form in the application package. The man that did the interview was the staff sergeant in charge of the Criminal Investigation Division. I ended up really liking the guy, and almost everyone else in the company really enjoyed working with or for him. He had been involved in two separate police shootings over the years where he had to fire his weapon. He was a really good cop, but all of his frontline policing had been pre-Charter. I think he decided to live on the edge a bit and see how I would react. You could tell, because the first question he asked me showed me that this wouldn't be like any other job interview I'd taken part in. His first question right out of the gate may have been to gauge my reaction.

"Mormon, eh?"

"Yes sir, I am," I said back with confidence, thinking to myself, "Can he ask me that?"

"You know how they pick the prophet, right?" He asked me with a straight face.

"Ya, I am pretty sure, but what have you heard?" I decided to go with it and see where this led.

"You see, they gather up all the men in the Salt Lake Valley that are over 80 years old. They take them all to a freshly plowed field and get them to gear down to nothing. Then they get them on their hands and knees and have them crawl in the freshly plowed dirt. Whoever digs the deepest furrow with his Johnson is their man!" He said with a grin, awaiting my response.

I decided to give him a chuckle and told him that I was pretty sure he had been mis-informed. The rest of the interview went much better. Obviously I did well, as I got the job. He even teased me a bit when he confronted me about never having tried alcohol, drugs, or cigarettes. He told me they would see what they could do to get me to try at least two of the three in the coming years. I found out why a few months later, as I started to hear stories about guys on the job. One struck me as horrific, and I could understand why the non-members of the church might think poorly of us if this guy were any example of what we were like.

This guy was an older member of the Force who, I was told, was always talking about what an observant member of the church he was. He made them feel like they weren't as Christian as he was every time he spoke about religion. This is the same guy, the story goes, who responded as backup to a sudden death of an elderly man. The man was in his late 80's or early 90's and had been married to the same woman for over 60 years. The investigator was taking a statement from her in the kitchen while they waited for the Medical Examiner to attend to authorize the removal of the body as well as determine if it was an unexplained death or one that was expected. Our hero, the second member on scene was not really doing anything, other than walking through the house and being nosy. The deceased was still on the couch in the living room, the man this woman had shared the last 60 years of her life. Her life had clearly changed, and she was trying to come to grips with that when the second cop came into the kitchen.

"Hey, your husband had some great tools in the garage that he clearly won't need anymore. How much d'you want for them?"

This happened before I was a copper, so this may or may not have occurred exactly the way it was explained to me. After getting to know this guy, I have no doubt it happened exactly the way the investigator that was there described it to me. If this was the example of how a member of the Church of Jesus Christ of Latter Day Saints acted, no wonder they had their doubts.

Anyway, back to the reason why they put me with Dan. Even though he might've been seen as the fixer of problems, he was awesome with me. (He must have fixed me quick.) He was a good man who was rough around the edges but took care of me and taught me. That first night, Dan had me sit down at the far end of the table in the line-up room next to him. I soon found out we'd taken seats at the foot of the table because the head of the table was where my sergeant and staff sergeant sat. Those two men did not like each other one bit! I mentally thanked my FTO for keeping me as far away from that fracas as possible while looking at them through the haze of cigarette smoke, arguing about anything and everything. It was definitely not what I'd expected. What I heard next was something I really didn't expect and shocked me to the core!

Now the reason I hadn't previously met my staff sergeant was because he was on holidays the week I had worked with this team. He had a friend who was a cop in South Africa, and I learned that he went there every spring. (Our spring, their fall). Remember, this was 1988, and apartheid was still in full swing, Nelson Mandela was in jail, and the Berlin Wall was still up. With that historical context in mind, the first words I ever heard my staff sergeant say while arguing with his sergeant were, "The dirty kaffirs don't deserve the vote!" As numerous members of the team started to argue with him, I sat there in shock. For those of you who don't know, the term is an extremely offensive and racist descriptor common to South Africa at the time and is the equivalent to the "N" word in western culture. (Perhaps even worse!) I couldn't believe it. I leaned over to my FTO and whispered to him.

"He's kidding, right?"

"Shut up kid, I'll explain later," Dan whispered back.

I was in shock. What had I gotten myself into? The only saving grace was that so many of the guys on the platoon, led by my sergeant, were loudly excoriating the man at length for what he'd said. I left it alone, learning later from my FTO that this was not a man who I wanted to take on head-to-head as a young probationary constable. He and my teammates would do all they could to protect me from him. I just had to do my part and not become a target for him. So, I kept my head down, barely hiding my contempt for the man whose atrocious behaviour was re-enforced later that same night.

So, there I was, with my FTO in the Paddy Wagon, nearing the witching hour. The call load had just started to thin out when we received a "suspicious person" call on the west side of the city. At that time, the west side was mostly residential, with very few businesses, none of which were open after midnight. In fact, very little moved anywhere after midnight. It was like our sleepy bedroom community on the other side of the river. The other thing "suspicious" about the call was, instead of the dispatcher on the radio, it was the staff sergeant. I reached for the mic, as had been my assignment from almost day one. At that time, we had two different types of codes that we had to learn, almost like another language. (10 code, as in 10-4, and a 500 code as in 509, which equated to "arrived on scene", or 519 which meant "out for lunch.") When I reached for the mic, Dan slapped my hand away and while smiling at me said, "I got this kid."

He got on the radio and asked, "What is suspicious about the man, staff?"

"Well, he's black, and he's on the West side!" The staff sergeant responded as if that were more than enough reason to find, identify and uncover why the man was there.

I heard Dan tell the staff to leave the station and check it himself because we weren't. No one else volunteered to go either. I heard later that Max, the sergeant, called the complainant back and told him we wouldn't be going, and to refrain from calling us for that type of thing ever again. Max was a pretty forward thinking, honest sergeant. I learned to appreciate him during those first few months. He protected us all from that racist tyrant sitting in the staff sergeant's office, and I never had a run-in with the man, mostly because of Dan, Max, and the other guys on the team taking care of me. Clearly a change from that behaviour had started long before I got there. Max started policing in 1955.

****

I also learned from Dan and how he talked, that I had grown up in a relatively sheltered environment. It was driven home to me one day while we were driving around on a day shift together.

He said in passing, "Hey you have to introduce me to your wife."

He didn't say it in a creepy manner or anything like that, but I must have had a "What the hell does that mean" look on my face because he started to chuckle. He said he'd had a bad experience with the last recruit that he'd trained. It turns out Dan liked to drive around the downtown core at about 4:00 pm, just as businesses were closing. This gave him the opportunity to check out the young professional ladies going home from work and make the occasional off coloured comment to his partner. He told me he had happened to be driving by a business while training the last guy, when a very attractive redhead exited her place of business. Dan explained to his trainee exactly what he'd like to do with the young lady in question. I am trying to keep this PG-13, so I can't repeat what he said. (I was a grown man of 24 years old and had never even heard anything like that comment before.)

Well, sure enough, the new guy he was training said to him, "Pull on over, and I'll introduce you. That's my wife."

Dan told me that he never wanted to feel that bad again, and that's why he wanted to meet my wife. I laughed until I cried. Poor Danny.

The last thing I still vividly remember from my 4 months with Dan was going to my first car accident and seeing my first badly mangled dead body. Before I get into it, I have to say that when I was young, I was a big fan of driving fast. My cousins and I used to time how fast it took to drive the 38 kilometers from our hometown to Lethbridge, and brag about who had the best time. When I was just about to leave on my mission, my girlfriend, the one who dumped me with the wedding invitation, lived at the next small town over from mine. I got so many speeding tickets going to see her, that my licence was suspended for a month from loss of demerits. The two years I was gone is the only reason I had a clean driver's abstract when I got home. Following the speed theme, I also had a real desire to one day buy a motor bike. I even used to tell my college roommates that the real reason I wanted to become a cop was to drive fast in a car I didn't own and look cool doing it. (Possibly the only way I could ever look cool). Speed was something I loved, right up until that first collision.

S o, there we were, dispatched to an injury accident in the downtown core of the city on 3rd Avenue and 7th Street South. The kid driving the motorbike was 17 years old and had his bike licence for a grand total of ten days. He was driving west on 3rd Avenue on a little Ninja style bike, with a passenger behind him. His speed was later estimated by the skid marks to be at least 105 kilometers per hour in a 50 zone. At the intersection, an impaired driver travelling east on 3rd Avenue, turned north on to 7th Street, right in front of the oncoming motorbike, causing the bike to collide with the passenger door of the vehicle. The bike basically come to an instantaneous stop. The passenger flew over the head of the driver as they hit the car, landing some 10 or 15 meters down the road. He landed on his head, shoulder, hip, and knee, injuring all of them. The good news was, he was still alive. The driver on the other hand, came to a complete stop with his bike, because the handlebars turned sideways and upward upon colliding with the car, and skewered the young driver in the chest. The force of the collision (no doubt exacerbated by the passenger flying over his head, striking the driver's helmet) snapped the straps of the driver's helmet, which flew off his head and landed in the park across the street.

When we got there, I'm sure Dan knew the driver was dead, but the passenger still had a chance. He sent me over to the driver, who was lying on the ground next to his bike to check to see if he was still alive. The kid was on his back, and I still remember three things like it happened yesterday. The driver had a gaping hole in the chest where he was in contact with the handlebars of the motor bike. He'd been wearing running shoes that had come off of his feet as a result of the collision. (It's something that cops, and paramedics often talk about when they see the person's shoes in the middle of the road, like the driver took them off before the collision.) The third thing was the amount of blood. The road he was lying on had four-lanes, two heading east, and two heading west. The huge pool of blood

24

looked like it had started to coagulate, making it look like there were stairs on the road, and the blood was flowing down the stairs and into the storm drain. I didn't know if he was dead but knew that Dan sent me over to the driver because I would be out of his way while he helped the passenger. I knelt down at the driver's head without even thinking about where my knees landed as long as they didn't land on him. I secured his cervical spine with my hands and then knees while I checked for a pulse or breathing. It wasn't until I was sure that he was dead that I noticed where I'd knelt. I was in a pool of blood so deep my pants were soaked from ankles to knees.

I left the dead kid and went over to help Dan restrain the seriously injured passenger, who was in shock and trying to get up to help his dead friend. We held him until the paramedics got there. While we were doing that, another member of the platoon showed up and took the driver of the car who turned in front of the speeding motorbike to have a seat in his patrol car, while he went back to where we were to see if he could help. We didn't know yet that the driver was impaired, until he went back to his car with her in the back seat, that now reeked of intoxicant. He put her on a roadside testing device, and she failed. She eventually blew over the limit and was charged with impaired driving causing death. She was originally found not guilty (I can't remember why), but the Crown appealed, and she was convicted. Her sentence was 18 months to be served on weekends. I am sure she learned her lesson, and the family of the dead kid was satisfied with the outcome. I also learned right out of the chute that if you rely on the court system for your job satisfaction, you will never be happy. That lesson has served me well over the years.

I was a little in shock when we were finished at the scene and left for the station. I only noticed when it was pointed out to me that my pants were soaked in blood from the knees down, and we had to go in and change. What happened next caused me to lose sleep for the next couple of days. I wear white cotton underwear that goes to my knees. When I got to the locker room and took off the ruined pants, the blood had soaked through to my underwear. The blood had wicked three quarters of the way up my underwear to the middle of my thigh. I've since learned to have a "go bag" in my locker containing things like a change of underwear. This early in my career, it never even crossed my mind this would be something that might come in handy. Dan had to drive me home where I could shower and change. My wife wasn't home at the time, so she didn't see the mess. I didn't even bother washing the underwear; I just threw them out. However, she did notice for the next few weeks that I wasn't sleeping very well.

****

I should've told her. In fact, I'm sure that some of the stories I write in this book will be a surprise to her. I haven't shared some of the more difficult or gory incidents. In retrospect this was a HUGE mistake! I felt like I was protecting her from some of the evils in the world that I was seeing, not realizing she is much stronger than I am. This was also a different time. A time where us coppers didn't even talk to each other if something bothered us. There were no such things as Critical Incident Stress Management Teams or Incident Debriefs that are so prevalent on the job now. Post traumatic stress was something that guys got when they went off to war, not cops. No wonder there are so many of us with drinking problems and broken marriages. I have my wife to thank for putting up with me and loving and caring for me during all those years of me suffering in silence, even though she didn't know the specifics of what I'd been seeing over the years. I know now that she suffered as well, but didn't know what the problem was, only that there was one, as she slowly watched me change from the person she married. When I told her this story, she said to me that she remembered a stretch of time when I first got hired that I wasn't sleeping very well and suffered from bad dreams. Now she knows, 33 years later.

If you are reading this and thinking about a career in law enforcement, or if you're a young guy or girl just starting out on the job, think about it this way. When you marry someone, you promise to take on each other's burdens. You trust him or her with everything else, so maybe trust him or her with how you feel about something, or how something has affected you. If I'd done this, I would probably still have the same feelings and issues that I've had over the years but wouldn't have felt like I had to handle them by myself.

FINALLY ON MY OWN

My time with Dan lasted about 4 months. I learned a lot in that time, including some things that surprised me, although I'm not sure why. Dan's personality type was not even close to mine. I'm intense, with a need to always moving, doing, or learning something. It's difficult for me to sit back and let things come, and Dan couldn't be more the opposite. He was patient and kind, even to drunks and those that abused him verbally, without being a push over. In later years when I became a Crisis Negotiator, I tried to emulate some of those personality traits. I did it so much and so often, that they became natural. Of course, I'm still pretty intense, but I learned patience on the job from Dan.

I was on my own in September of 1988, and soon thrown into the deep end, expected to take any call in my beat. I still asked a ton of questions of my teammates. It probably got to the point where I'm sure they thought I'd never get it. I was learning, and enjoying myself, and soon forgiven for the incessant questions. I wasn't even the youngest guy on the platoon anymore. They'd just hired another recruit class that September, so there was a new guy on our team with his FTO. When he was finally on his own, I would no longer be assigned to drive the van. Things were looking up. I didn't even mind my stint as a Front Desk Constable. Their responsibility was to answer any questions the general public might have, either as in person walk-ins, or on the phone, when they called the general complaints line. The Front Desk Constable was also required to answer the "Crime Stoppers" phone and take anonymous tips from the public. It was while I was working the desk one day that my career took a turn I didn't ask for, didn't want, and certainly didn't expect so soon.

In those days, when you walked into the front doors of the station, you went up a few stairs, and then down a long hallway to the front counter where the Desk Constable worked. There was a sliding glass door directly to the left of the Desk Constable's workstation, that led into the dispatch area, where another constable and a civilian dispatcher worked. The sliding glass door was usually left open, so when it was slow at the front, the desk constable could go in and help, or just talk to the two employees working in that office. I was in dispatch when a discussion occurred on the radio that would directly affect my career path and I wasn't even involved.

There were three traffic enforcement cars that worked on our platoon. Their primary function was to enforce traffic laws and respond to collisions. They were also allowed to back up patrol guys when needed but didn't take on the larger investigations, as it would get in the way of their primary function. I had absolutely no desire to work in the traffic unit. I wanted to learn the larger and more complex investigations. It has been my experience that there are very few cops who say to themselves, "I want to be a cop," and leave it at that. As they learn more about the job, most have a more specific goal, such as "I want to be a K-9 cop", or "I want to be in the Tactical Unit, or Forensic Identification Unit." It had been my goal since going to college to not just become a cop, but one day work as a detective in the Homicide Unit. It didn't matter that Lethbridge didn't have a "Homicide Unit" at the time. When a homicide occurred, the Criminal Investigation Division (CID) got the file, and that's what I wanted to do. I didn't think working a traffic car for a couple of years would help me achieve that goal.

S o, there I was, in dispatch chatting with our Dispatch Constable, when a traffic related complaint came in. He contacted one of the traffic cars on the team and assigned him to the call for service. The traffic member declined. He didn't give a reason why he wouldn't or couldn't go, he just said he wasn't going. The two guys started getting into a pretty heated argument about whether the dispatcher could tell the traffic guy what to do or not. It finally got so bad that they started swearing at each other over the radio. The argument came to a screeching halt when the patrol staff sergeant got on the radio and ordered both of them to report to his office immediately. That ended the argument, and as soon as the traffic guy booked off at the station, I tried to do two jobs while the Dispatch Constable followed him into the staff's office.

Now this wasn't our platoon staff sergeant (called a station sergeant at the time). The patrol staff sergeant was kind of like the executive officer for the inspector in charge of Patrol Division. He started policing in the late 50's

28

or early 60's and dealt with things the way my mother might have. He didn't put up with a lot of crap. When he spoke, it was as if the inspector spoke, and all were required to listen, salute smartly, and do what they were told! About ten minutes after the meeting started, I was called into the office. I was scared to death, and I hadn't done anything other than witness the fracas. Clearly the staff didn't need a witness. He called the two of them into his office without anyone calling the issue to his attention, so it was obvious he'd heard it on the radio. I went into the office with a great deal of trepidation and made sure I said nothing that would get me in trouble.

"Reeder, how long have you been with us now?" he asked out of the blue. The two other constables were not sitting. They were both standing at attention at the front of his desk, looking straight ahead.

"Eight months now, sir," I said, as steadily as I could.

"That is more than enough time in," he replied. He then turned to the traffic member and said, "Go out to your car, get all of your belongings out of it and then give him your keys," while pointing at me. "You are now in traffic. Please leave us."

I could hear the staff yelling at my two boneheaded teammates as I left. "Until I say otherwise, you will replace him as the desk constable. Don't bother requesting a transfer to either a different section or a different platoon. Both of you will learn to get along and be respectful!" I kept walking so I couldn't hear any more.

****

It's funny how things have changed. Nowadays, we have a Human Resources unit involved in these decisions and one must apply to a posting for lateral transfer. It is designed so everyone in the Service meeting the identified criteria of the posting has the opportunity to apply. I didn't want to go to traffic, and the other two guys REALLY didn't want to work together. The staff sergeant's decision would probably not teach those two guys to get along, but it did teach them to work together. It also had the added benefit of broadcasting to anyone who might have a desire to act unprofessionally at work, that there was an immediate and uncomfortable repercussion. Both of those members ended up at those jobs for just over a year. Voltaire's edict *"Pour encourage les autre"* (to encourage others) comes to mind. No one else wanted that long of a stint in either job. It was only a couple years of my career. Knowing what I know now, there were things I learned while in Traffic that I could use when I was back on Patrols. After all, it was while I was in traffic that I responded to my first attempted murder.

S o, there I was, sitting in the station doing some paperwork a couple months later when I was called by dispatch to attend a domestic-type dispute. She said there was no one else available and needed me to go even though I was a traffic car. I was being asked to go across the rear parking lot of the station to a senior citizen apartment building. The caller reported she had seen a man in the hallway on the 8th floor threaten a woman with a small knife. The caller stated they now had the knife, and the woman was safe in her apartment. The man in question was still in the hallway. I acknowledged the call; told dispatch I was on my way and decided to just walk across the lot to deal with the matter, leaving my car parked where it was. As I was walking across the lot, the sergeant in charge of the Training Unit was just pulling into the lot, and he called dispatch and told them that he would go with me. Reggie was the sergeant in question, and he was not only the Training Sergeant, but also a member of the Tactical Unit at the time. I ended up being very thankful he was there with me.

In retrospect, we should've taken the elevator to the floor below or above, got off and then taken the stairs to the floor where the bad guy was. We were told he had a weapon. This would be doubly important if the bad guy was in the hallway of the building. He could hear the bell of the elevator arriving and set up an ambush. Reggie and I talked about it later and admitted to each other that we were both a bit complacent because it was a senior's building, and the caller told dispatch they'd disarmed the subject. I learned one of the golden rules of policing as a result of this call. If it is a matter of your safety, expect the worst, and don't ever take the caller's word, or the dispatcher's interpretation of what the caller said, as gospel!

We got on the elevator and headed up to the 8th floor, pleasantly chatting about how our day was going, and him asking me how I was settling into the job. It was warm, and I'd taken my hat off and held it in my left hand. When the elevator doors opened, I could smell burnt gunpowder. There's nothing like that smell, and even though I'd been on the pistol range a lot in the last year, I would've recognized the smell anyway. Most small-town kids in Southern Alberta at that time owned at least a .22 rifle and did some serious damage to the gopher population on the closest farmer's back forty. (My grandfather had horses, so he hated gophers. Gopher holes break horse legs. He used to pay us kids twenty-five cents a tail for each dead rodent when I was young.) Reggie could smell it as well. He quickly moved his head out into the hallway and back in again, all while having his hand over the slot the elevator door slides into. I just stupidly stuck my head out into the hallway and sort of froze for a second. It felt like I stood there for a minute or two, when in fact it was probably less than a second, but time does not act normal in situations like what we had suddenly found ourselves.

I saw an old man standing in front of a closed door about 5 meters down the hall to my left. He held a small (we later found it to be a .22 calibre), bolt action rifle in his hands, pointed at the door with smoke lazily curling out of the open breach. He was looking down at his feet at the ammunition he had spilled all over the hallway floor. I saw there were a couple of visible bullet holes in the metal door to the apartment in front of him. (We later learned he had fired five rounds into the door before we got there and spilled his ammunition on the floor while trying to reload. He was looking down and in the process of reloading when we showed up.) My decision seemed to take forever. Reggie later told me that it was the right decision though, and I made it quickly enough that he didn't have to even tell me what to do. The hall was too narrow for both of us to go down, so he held the door open with his body as he knelt down, gun drawn and ready to shoot the old guy, using the side of the elevator door to steady his aim. I moved out of the elevator to the far wall of the hallway, pointing my gun down range, moving slowly toward the man with the gun. (I went toward him because I was scared that he would go into the door he was shooting at and hurt whoever was inside before we could stop him.) While I was moving, Reggie and I were both shouting at the old man to drop the gun.

I have found myself in similar situation several times since, but this was the first time I'd ever contemplated shooting another human being. Actually, I wasn't really thinking about it. I did what I had been taught. In my mind, I drew a line that I would not let him cross before I fired. That line for me was if the bad guy either turned the barrel of his weapon down the hallway toward us, or if he reached to open the door handle in front of him. I was also "double staged" on my revolver. The Smith and Wesson .357 that I carried had an interesting idiosyncrasy. I don't know if this was by design, or just happened that way because I'm not one of those guys who knows a lot about firearms. You could hear a click as you started to pull the trigger back, and then a second sort of click when the trigger got to the point that the hammer was almost all the way back. (First and second stage.) All you had to do was breathe a little heavier to get the trigger to pull hard enough at this point to let the round go down range. Thankfully, the man looked up from the floor right at me as I was coming toward him, put the rifle down against the wall in front of him and backed away from it with his hands in the air.

Huge relief, right? Except right at that moment, when I was about two meters away from him, the door he had been shooting at swung open, and a short older woman in a cotton dressing gown came out of the door. The dressing gown was covered in blood from the neck of the garment all the way down. There was so much blood in fact that I was later teased by my good buddy Dylan, because when I was eventually able to call for an ambulance, I got tongue tied about the injuries, and stumbled out "There's just blood every where!" Anyhow, when she came out, my decision tree changed again. I tried to holster my pistol as I lunged for the old man. He was between me and the victim. I wanted to put myself between him and the gun and the lady. Even though he no longer had the gun in his hand, I didn't know if he had a knife, if there even was a knife, or if he had another weapon of some sort. I couldn't get my weapon holstered so I grabbed the shoulder portion of the old man's coat with my left hand and threw him back toward my partner. Reggie had already exited the elevator and started running toward us when the lady came out. I pushed the injured woman back into her apartment to get her clear of the bad guy. Reggie teased me later because that old man caught some serious air. At the time I was 6'1" and about 230 lbs, and this guy was barely five feet, about 110 lbs and about 85 years old. Reggie told me he had to catch the old guy before he landed and broke a hip. Cops and their dark humour. I've since learned this is one of the reasons that we use dark humour. This was a pretty intense situation, and I'd never experienced anything like it before. The humour had a calming affect, and also made me feel like part of the team.

I didn't see Reggie with the old man, and I was now concentrating on trying to find the injuries to the lady. She was about 70 years old or so, and the front of her dressing gown was soaked in blood. I kept trying to pull the garment away from her chest, trying to find out where she'd been shot. She kept batting my hands away, trying to be modest and not allow me to see what was under her dressing gown. I kept moving her hands away, thinking she had to be in shock. Then she kind of turned to her side. I thought she was turning away from me, but then I saw the back of her neck. She had a very large horizontal cut to the back of her neck, obviously the source of the blood on her dressing gown. She still wasn't talking much other than saying "thank you" over and over again, in a pleasant, cultured British accent. When I was on the radio asking for an ambulance, I saw an old man walk toward us inside the apartment using one of those four legged walkers. He was wearing a white button up shirt and had two splashes of red on the front. I later learned they were stab wounds as well.

After the cavalry arrived (more cops, paramedics, detectives, and a forensic identification unit member), I started to wind down a bit. This is when the requisite teasing happens and I learned that if they tease you, they think you did pretty good. It's when they don't say anything to you, or worse, your boss lets you have it, you know you screwed up. We later learned the old man was 85 years old, and he had met the much younger 75-year-old lady in the hallway or cafeteria of the building. He was from central Europe and she from England. After they got to know each other a bit, she invited him to her apartment for tea. He thought she meant a romantic liaison instead of just tea. When he showed up, he found her walker bound 80-year-old husband and he realized he had misunderstood her invitation. He became a little angrier than one might expect and pulled out his 3-inch lock blade knife from his pocket. He opened the knife up and then grabbed the lady by her hair with his left hand while facing her, and then reached behind her head, and cut the back of her neck in a horizontal motion with the knife in his right hand. He didn't have enough arm and hand strength to cut her bad enough to kill her. He may have also been distracted by the 80-year-old man with the four-legged walker who attacked him for stabbing his wife. Hence the two stab wounds in her husband's chest.

****

I was worried for a while because I missed a few things. The boys teasing me really did help me to put things into perspective. When Reggie kept going on about how badly I mangled my hat when I made a fist with the hand holding it at the smell of gunpowder, I couldn't help it, it just slipped out. I asked him if he had been thinking about his own age when trying to catch the old man. Both of their hips could have broken, and then I would have had to call a second ambulance. Everyone then lit Reggie up about elderly 40 year old's, doing a young man's job. It was at that point I truly felt like I belonged, like I was good enough to do this job. I was now one of the guys. It was a really good feeling and drowned out the fear I'd felt. I was then able to think about how I reacted, how I could've done better, and what I should've done differently. I was also encouraged that some of the good decisions I'd made that day were not thought out, rather made by instinct. Apparently, I was getting the hang of the job, and I fit in. Most importantly, I realized I usually wouldn't have to face these types of calls by myself. There were a good bunch of guys and girls I worked with that would have my back, as I had theirs while we charged toward danger instead of running away from it. This concept was reinforced when I responded to my first murder a couple of months later.

MY FIRST MURDER AND A NEW NICKNAME

There are many things in life we can't control, and one of them is getting a nickname. Thankfully, most don't last forever, and I've successfully outlived the nickname I gained in my early years. I think it's because it happened so early in my career, and all the coppers who gave me such an auspicious *nom de guerre* have long since retired. The story, and therefore the reason for the nickname has died the death it deserved. I'm taking a small risk in telling you this story, but if one must have a nickname assigned by others, I guess "Blue Eyes" isn't as bad as it could've been.

So, **there I was,** the winter of 1989, freezing every time I got out of my car. There was a lot of snow on the ground, and the snow removal equipment for the city was having a hard time keeping up. There were even ruts through the hard packed snow on the main thoroughfares like Mayor Magrath Drive. The good news was really bad driving was so much easier to see. Impaired drivers are especially obvious during poor driving conditions. That night, I found a car driving northbound on Mayor Magrath Drive that fit the criteria. He was driving so poorly that even with only months on the job, I could tell the driver was probably impaired.

I stopped the car and walked up to the lone occupant and asked him for his documents. The man was a fumbling mess and obviously impaired. (He later blew a reading on the old Borkenstein 900A breathalyzer of 240 mg%. A whopping three times the legal limit.) He couldn't find his wallet, let alone his driver's licence. He smelled so strongly of an intoxicant that I didn't even have to put my head near the window. He couldn't even figure out how to turn off his own vehicle when I asked. When I told him to exit the car, he stumbled and fell as he got out. When he stood up, I handcuffed him, and read him his Charter rights, the police caution, and the breathalyzer demand. He claimed he understood and wanted to talk to a lawyer. I asked one of my teammates to tow his car for me, and we were off to the station so he could talk to counsel and then I could get breath samples from him.

Sounds normal, right? Like every other impaired driver a cop arrests over a career spanning three decades. This one was a little different. When the man, who we will call Dieter spoke to me, I thought he was messing with me at first. He was speaking in the stereotypical, only in the movies version of what a gay man might sound like. This man was acting over the top as if he was trying to make me uncomfortable. (Or at least that's how it looked.) When he first got out of the car, he stood up (after falling down) and put his right hand on his hip, fingers pointing backward, thumb to the front, and cocked his hip before he asked me why I stopped him. He was dressed entirely inappropriately for the weather. Dieter had black pointed low rise boots that zipped up the sides, with pink socks, folded over the tops. He was wearing skin-tight black leather pants that had laces going up the outer seam, from ankle to hip bone. The lacings were like shoes laces, and there was no backing behind them, so you could see his skin all the way up the sides of both of his legs. He wore no coat; instead he had on a big blousy black sweater, and his blond hair was long and permed. Except for the hair, Dieter looked just like the Dieter character made famous by Mike Meyers on the Saturday Night Live recurring comedy sketch "Sprockets". (Hence the false name.) From Dieter's speech patterns, it was like he was trying to perform his own interpretation of the TV character, without the German accent.

So, when my backup came to tow the car, we were off to the station. Dieter was quiet on the way, so I still wasn't sure if he was just messing with me, or if that was really the way he talked. (I found out the truth years later from one of my detective buddies who had dealings with him on a much bigger scale than my impaired charge. Dieter talked that way even when he was sober.) When we got back to the station, I took him to the interview room to search him more thoroughly. I brought him a telephone and gave him some privacy. This was at the old police station on 5th Avenue South. There were only two interview rooms on the patrol floor of the building and another two on the CID floor, one flight up. Unfortunately, those doors opened directly into the work area for the Patrol Constables to do their paperwork. (We had no holding cells either. These interview rooms did double duty). Kris, a guy from my recruit class, was the only one in the patrol area when I took Dieter in to the interview room. I left the door open, so Kris could be a witness for me if Dieter later claimed I had done something inappropriate. (This was long before video cameras were mounted on the walls in each room of the building).

When I went to search Dieter, I first asked him to put his hands on the wall so I could check his pockets. He exaggerated putting his buttocks out toward me and arched his back when I went to search him. At that point I knew it was going to be one of those nights. I started to search him while wearing latex gloves. His pants were so tight that I couldn't get my hands in his front pockets, so I asked him to empty his pockets for me.

"No, you do it," he lisped, trying for sultry, but missing the mark by a wide margin.

I was starting to get frustrated, because I thought he was messing with me. I said, "Look man, I have to empty your pockets. If you won't help me, I will take this pocket knife of yours and cut your pockets open."

"Okay, okay. Don't be such a bitch!" he responded.

I didn't rise to the bait. I finished searching him without cutting his pockets, and then sat him at the table. It was my habit to read a person their rights to talk to counsel again when we arrived at the station just before they used the phone, so they knew why they were there, and what they were using the phone for.

"You have the right to retain and instruct counsel, without delay." And then I paused,

Dieter reached across the table, touched my arm, and said, "Don't be silly".

I looked at him, and then kept reading. Every time I paused, he would reach across the table and touch my arm and say, "Don't be silly", "You silly goose" or," Of course, silly" all in that breathy, attempt at sultry.

When I got to the end of the caution card and the breath demand, I was pretty tired of him touching me, especially if he was messing with me. (I was starting to think that he wasn't at this point.) So, when he touched my arm and spoke to me a final time, I'd had just about enough. I leaned in, put my pointer finger in his face, stared him in the eye and said,

"If you touch me again, we're going to have a problem."

His response followed me for years. He paused, looked me in the eyes, and slurred in his poor attempt at a sexy, effeminate accent,

"You know, you've got the prettiest blue eyes."

I blinked. He got me and there was nothing I could do about it. I couldn't punch him in the face because he complimented me. I stood up and decided to leave him alone until it was time to take him to the breath tech to get breath samples. I forgot one thing. When I turned around and looked at the open interview room door, there, sitting at a desk not 15 feet away was my teammate Kris. He was pointing at me with a big smile on his face, clearly having heard the whole conversation. As I exited, Kris blew me a kiss. I was doomed. It would spread like wildfire. Asking Kris to keep his trap shut would only make it worse. I just walked by, trying to laugh it off, but Krissy knew. . . I was doomed.

Dieter was done with the breathalyzer, but his readings were so high that we took him out to the Lethbridge Correctional Centre (LCC) to hold him until he was sober enough to release. (They had a nurse on duty in case there were any medical issues due to the amount of alcohol he had ingested.) When we walked in to the Admit and Discharge section of LCC, I saw the CO3 (Corrections Officer 3, the rough equivalent of a Sergeant) who I'd gotten to know pretty well. When he looked at me and started to speak, I knew this would follow me for years to come. He said,

"How ya doin' blue eyes?"

****

The next summer, I responded to my first murder. Although I was too young and lacking in experience, this type of investigation was what I'd wanted to do since going to college a few years before. I was so young that most of what the detectives did was a mystery to me. It was much later when I became a detective myself that I learned how in-depth and complex these things could become. I know now that there are often hundreds of tasks, big and small, that must be completed. At the time, I was just happy to be able to help out with some of the more menial tasks assigned at the front end. It showed me the depth and scope needed to bring these files to a successful conclusion and would one day help me achieve my ultimate goal of becoming a homicide investigator.

So, there I was, in my traffic car on my way to the station on an afternoon shift to finish up some paperwork. I was almost there when a general call came over the radio of shots fired and a man with a gun in the parking lot of the Park Place Mall. I was only a few blocks away, and headed that way, hoping that more information would be shared soon. It was nine o'clock at night on a Thursday, so the mall was just closing except for one door, which led in to the theatre. When the call came out over the air my friend Steve just happened to be in the mall parking lot. We'd been in college together, but he'd just finished his FTO training and was on his own, in the van. He was at the other end of the parking lot, with his vehicle pointed away from where the shooting occurred. It was really windy that evening (Lethbridge, go figure), and he heard the gunshot but didn't recognize it as a shot. He thought it was a gust of wind that had hit the back of his van. The caller told dispatch that a woman had been shot and was lying at the north west end of the mall parking lot. I was only a short distance away, in an unmarked car on the west side of the mall, driving slowly, in hopes of seeing the shooter before he saw me. I heard Steve book out over the radio as having the victim in the north west side of the parking lot just to the north of the Sears store. He confirmed that she'd been shot.

Things sped up at that point. Jake, another one of my traffic co-workers, was just a short distance away when Steve told us that he couldn't see an assailant, and there were two bullet holes in the victim. There were a lot of people in that mall, either leaving work or leaving after an evening of shopping. It was the biggest mall in the city, with the largest theatre. People who weren't shopping, were leaving the early movie, or going to a late one - lots of targets, and only three coppers.

I was directed to the corner of the building where I waited for Jake, so we could go in to the mall together, looking for the bad guy. When I got there, I looked over to the marked patrol van that was parked between where the victim lay, next to a kneeling Steve, and the north walls of the mall. I could see he was trying to do first aid on the victim but put it from my mind when I saw another patrol car pull up next to him. Jake got there next to me about the same time. There were now four of us, so it was time to go find the bad guy.

We were standing at one of the north doors into the mall waiting for word from the boss to go in, when Jake said something to me that I didn't hear. We had just started working together, and I didn't really know him yet, but he became a great friend over the years, eventually becoming my inspector when I was in the Criminal Investigation Division the first time. He repeated what he said to me with a wry smile on his face when I looked at him like I was deaf or stupid.

"Hey kid, I think you might need your gun out for this one."

"Oh, ya. Sorry" I said as I drew the revolver out of my holster.

We started checking every person that was exiting the mall through the doors we were at, one covering the person, while the other checked in a cursory fashion for weapons and got their names. (Bearing in mind, it was closing time, and we were at the largest mall in the city.) We pointed our guns at a lot of people for the next ten or so minutes, when all of a sudden, we received a call of an intrusion alarm for one of the jewelry stores inside. Change of plans according to the boss. There were a bunch of us there by then. Five of us ran into the mall through the theatre entrance door, running past people waiting in line for their movie, our weapons in hand and heading to the alarm. The reasoning was that the bad guy might be in there shooting or threatening folks, and some fast-thinking victim had set off the alarm to get the cops there. When we all ran up to the jewelry store with our guns out, breathing hard, we saw a lone employee pulling the sliding doors to his business closed.

"Sorry fellas did the alarm go off? I was sure I gave myself enough time to close the door." He sounded pretty sheepish. Then he saw all five of us with our guns out, his eyes went so wide they might have fallen out of his head with any fast movement.

One copper stayed with the store owner to question him a bit to see if he knew anything about what had happened. The rest of us started back toward the parking lot. It was at that point that we got a call on the radio, saying a second body had been found, and this one had a gun. His injuries appeared to be self inflicted.

We went back to the north doors of the mall and were directed to do specific tasks. Mine was to go to where the second body was and keep that area secure until the Forensic Identification Unit and detectives arrived. When I got there, I saw a guy, lying face down. His head looked as if it was in a pothole buried to the ears. There was no pothole. He had placed the rifle under his chin and shot himself. This caused the front of his head, including most of his face, to basically disappear. The wind blew most of what he shot off to the east of him, landing on numerous parked cars.

Now you don't go from that kind of adrenaline to nothing at the drop of a hat. When I got there and took over the scene, there was a Lethbridge

Herald photographer trying to get as close as possible to do his job. I asked him to move back and move his vehicle. He started out with a hard no, until I got my handcuffs out and began walking toward him. It was at this point that he determined discretion was the better part of valor. At first, I thought I might get in trouble, until I saw one of the shell casings on the pavement directly under his car, and the remnants of the shooter's face on cars farther to the east of the reporter. At least I was justified in moving him, as he had inadvertently tampered with the crime scene. I was ramped up quite a bit, but he knew I was right.

****

This incident sparked my interest in the investigation of domestic violence based crimes. It turns out that the perpetrator and the victim lived in RCMP jurisdiction, and communication between police agencies back then wasn't nearly as good as it is now. The couple had been going through a messy divorce the preceding year, and the wife had finally gained some traction with a judge to either freeze her abuser's bank accounts, or something like that. He was not happy at all and decided to show her who was boss one last time. He knew she worked at Sears and went to the mall just before 9:00 pm when she got off work. He was waiting for her near her vehicle but when he saw her walking toward her car, he also saw a security guard walking with her. This was not part of the plan, so he went to his car, got a hunting rifle out and walked toward her.

While he was doing this, there was a young girl driving her car toward him on the ring road on the outside of the mall parking lot. He walked right in front of her moving vehicle, held up his left hand, rifle in his right, and motioned for her to stop her car. The man then put his elbow on the hood of her car to steady his aim and let a round go, all while this young girl watched in horror through her windshield. The round hit his estranged wife in the chest, dropping her to the ground. As he was racking a second round into the chamber, the young girl got out of her car and ran for help. She ran almost six blocks to the police station to report the incident. She would mentally beat herself up when she later realized that she could have run him over instead. That would not have helped the victim anyway. The first shot to the chest was fatal. He hit her with the second round as well, but it skipped off the pavement and struck her already supine body in the pelvis area. When Steve got to her, he thought at first that the security guard had been hit as well, but the kid was just playing possum. He really didn't have any other choice, short of taking his chances and running. Steve later told me he'd tried to give her mouth to mouth using a Brooks airway. When he put it in and blew into her, nothing but bubbles and froth came out of her chest, spraying him with her blood. She had no pulse and was probably dead before Steve even got to her.

This call helped narrow my focus and increase my intensity when taking a call of a criminal nature. One day I wanted to be a detective and figured I needed to be ready when the opportunity arose. I realized at that point I could improve my investigative skills while still a constable responding to everyday occurrences. (After all, if you look at it from a fairly basic point of view, a murder is just an assault that went bad.) More importantly, I became hyper vigilant about domestic violence incidents. At that time, we had to talk the victim into signing a statement regarding the abuse she was subjected to by her domestic partner. The Province eventually changed the guidelines on how to investigate domestic violence. One of the things they did was remind the police that they could arrest upon reasonable and probable grounds that an offence occurred, with or without a statement from the victim. There also needed to be a major shift in thinking by police officers. If a cop went to a call of a fight in front of a bar, he would arrest the dominant aggressor, but for some reason, that wasn't done when going to a call of a couple fighting in their home. Before that change in policy, I don't remember how many times I'd gone to a domestic dispute, knew he was abusing her and was unsuccessful trying to convince her to provide a statement. It really sucks to know deep in your bones that the moment your police car is no longer in sight, she is going to take another beating, and there is nothing you can do about it because you can't stay parked in front of her house.

It's funny how you don't think of motivations or timelines when you decide to actively change how you do something. What it also helped me see, was the need to get better at interviewing victims as well as perpetrators. I began to actively seek out co-workers who could help me improve that skill. If I could get to the truth of an incident and the motivators of the perpetrator (and sometimes the victim), it would help me to become a successful detective and hold the bad guys accountable for what they'd done. It would also help to possibly intervene before it became as tragic as this incident was.

Seeking guidance in becoming a better interviewer was a step toward my goal of working as a detective. It was also surprisingly, one of the steps down the path of one day being a Crisis Negotiator. A skilled negotiator is often times a very good interviewer as well. The necessity of rapport building, the appropriate use of themes, and smoothly inserting them into conversation, or the use of the Law of reciprocity, which is the life blood of a good interviewer. (And a good negotiator, I would later learn.) I didn't even know what all of that meant at the time, but it was time to learn. Later in my career, I was given the opportunity to attend the Canadian Police College in Ottawa on numerous occasions. (Seven or eight times, they all kind of blur together after a while.) One of those courses was called Forensic Interviewing. It was a two-week course on how to interview bad guys, with an emphasis on homicide suspects. When I went on the original Negotiator course, I found the subject matter so similar that if it were university course curriculum, Forensic Interviewing would be the first-year course and the Crisis Negotiator course would be the next. Turn the page to learn more about my early, weak attempts to interview bad guys.

ALTERED CONSCIOUSNESS (AND A MAGPIE)

It was the beginning of 1991 and finally, freedom was here. No more traffic calls and writing handfuls of tickets. I could finally get my career back on track. I'd learned some new skills, but in the end, I started to have a conscience. When I went into Traffic, I was told to write a certain number of tickets per day (10 per day on a 10-hour shift). By the end, I was struggling with writing tickets to citizens who just happened to be late for church. (Not exactly, but you know what I mean.) In the first 18 months, my ticket numbers were in the top three in the Service every month. By the end, they were nowhere near that. Instead, I decided to spend the last 6 months looking for impaired drivers. I became pretty good at it, replacing my low ticket numbers with criminal charges, ensuring no one could complain that I was lazy. Traffic also made me very confident in giving evidence in court. Back then, traffic tickets were heard in normal Provincial Court, not a Traffic Court, as happens now. When people pled not guilty, I was giving evidence in front of the same judges who would later hear my criminal cases.

A couple of months before I was done in Traffic, I charged a fellow named Adam for impaired driving and refusal to provide a breath sample. He was one motivated individual who went well past normal attempts to avoid giving breath samples. There is more case law provided in the Criminal Code for these types of offences than any other. This shows how many people go to trial when charged with impaired driving, and how many loop holes and technicalities exist. If the investigator isn't "switched on", he allows the offender innumerable ways to escape conviction. Later in my career, I became a breath technician, and the two-week course involved more science and memorization than I had in any other course. The long and the short of it is, if you are arrested for impaired driving, and a breath sample is demanded, give the sample. There are a lot of technicalities your lawyer can try to use to possibly land an acquittal. Conversely, there are only two reasons given in the Criminal Code to justify refusing a demand for breath samples. The first is to hope a judge determines that the sample was demanded without grounds to do so by the officer. (An iffy proposition, and quite a gamble). The other is that you are physically incapable of providing the sample. (i.e., you have been in a collision and your injuries make it very difficult or impossible to provide breath.) The following is a lesson of what not to do when trying to avoid providing breath samples.

So, there I was, stopping a car driven by a fellow named Adam, who was well known to the police in Lethbridge. He had a substance abuse problems, seldom had an active drivers licence, and usually took his frustrations out on whatever girlfriend he happened to be with at the time. Even though I was relatively new, I'd already dealt with Adam on many occasions. Back then, we were taught not to use the roadside testing device unless you couldn't form the grounds to arrest without one. (Exactly the opposite of how we work now.) I didn't need a roadside testing device to form my grounds for arrest because of his obvious impairment. I knew him when he was sober, and he wasn't that night. Adam was soon in the back of my car, in handcuffs, being explained his rights to counsel and the breathalyser demand. He claimed he understood and wanted to talk to a lawyer. He then sat back, laid his head against the seat, closed his eyes, and would not answer another question or query from me. Adam was usually a mouthy jerk when arrested, so I welcomed the silence.

When we got to the station, he still had his head back, but now he wouldn't stand up, nor would he speak. He acted like he was unconscious. I called my Sergeant down to the bay where we brought our prisoners into the building. We tended not to call paramedics for everything back then like we do now, so my boss checked and saw Adam was breathing fine and had a good strong pulse. He told me to transport him to the hospital to be checked out. Adam stayed silent with his eyes closed on the way to the hospital, but it was obvious he was awake. I saw in my rear-view mirror when we hit a bump or went around a corner that his body didn't react the way an unconscious person's would. I was pretty sure he was faking it to avoid giving breath samples but, a doctor had to give a professional opinion before I charged him with refusal.

I drove us into an ambulance bay and got a wheelchair. The police were up at the hospital quite a bit and I already knew most of the nurses by name. I asked one if she would follow me out to the bay where I could collect my prisoner. She agreed and went with me, where I lifted poor Adam out of the car and put him in the chair. (He was just a little guy, and easy to pick up and put where I needed him.) I wheeled him into the Emergency department and to the exam room the nurse had pointed out. I lifted him from the chair and put him on the bed. Adam and I waited together for the doctor to arrive. All this time, he didn't say a word, nor did he help me in any way when I lifted him up and moved him around. I could have used pain compliance, like a thumb to the mandibular angle (bottom of his jaw) or the mastoid (behind the lower ear), but since I wanted to get breath samples from him, I didn't want to start our interactions with pain compliance techniques. It turns out that sometimes, hospital visits can be painful.

The doctor entered the room, and I introduced myself because we hadn't met yet. She was a sharp, no nonsense kind of professional who was easy to work with. I told her why I was there, what my prisoner had been arrested for, what had happened leading up to getting to the station, (nothing), and how he acted when I got there, (asleep). They checked his pulse and blood pressure and all the other normal things they do to new patients. Then the tests to determine his level of consciousness started. The doctor explained each test as she performed it, and how an unconscious person would react compared to one who was faking.

She first lifted his arm up above his head and dropped it. As it fell, the arm landed above his head. The doctor explained to me that an unconscious person would not think to move the path of his arm as it fell, and it would've hit him in the face. She then decided to check his blink reflex. To do this, she opened his eye by using her finger and thumb to pull apart the upper and lower eyelids, and with her other hand, placed a cotton ball right on the exposed eyeball. She explained that an unconscious person would not try to close his eyelid to cover the eyeball with the cotton ball on it, like poor Adam was desperately trying to do as she spoke. As soon as she took the cotton ball away, his face no longer scrunched up in pain, and he stopped trying to close his eye. Finally, she took a clamp and placed it on the cartilage that separates the nostrils right above a person's upper lip. She calmly explained to me that this was called the Columella and was sensitive to pain that an unconscious person would not feel. She then applied pressure to the clamp. Poor Adam's feet came off the gurney, then his back arched, and his face scrunched up even worse than before. That had to hurt! As soon as pressure was taken off, he went back to his pretend unconscious state. That's when he made his next big blunder.

With all that alcohol on board, he must have needed to use the washroom. He just decided to urinate, right there laying on the gurney, faking unconsciousness, taking the doctor's valuable time away from real patients, just so he could avoid criminal responsibility for an action he had chosen. He must have really had to go – the entire gurney and the floor under it were soaked with urine by the time he was done. The doctor was not pleased and ordered the nurse to catheterize poor Adam. I was not quite sure what that meant, until I saw the nurse bring back tubing that looked to be the diameter of a garden hose. (It wasn't near that big, but considering where she inserted it, it may as well have been!) The nurse inserted the garden hose into the urinary tract of poor Adam. (And there was only one place, short of surgical intervention, to insert said garden hose to get it there!) I couldn't help it, and involuntarily bent forward and put my hand over my junk, like any guy reading this just did. It is an autonomic, sympathetic reaction! Good old Adam was game though. That was the only test I saw them perform where he didn't flinch. (That might be because I was too busy flinching myself to see if he did.)

The doctor checked his blood pressure, pulse, and oxygen saturation again, then told me that in her medical opinion, Adam was wide awake and faking a lower level of consciousness. I asked her if he could understand when I spoke to him. She said that if he could understand me speaking to him before, he was still able. I knew Adam was a bit of a half-wit, but we had conversed on many occasions, and he understood me every time we talked, including when I originally arrested him. I read him the warning for refusing to provide samples of his breath. He didn't answer, still feigning unconsciousness. I thanked the hospital staff and took him to jail, charging him with refusing to provide breath samples. The good news was that he made a miraculous recovery, just as we were driving into the bay of the Correctional Centre. He made a great show of wondering how we had ended up at the jail and why I wouldn't let him provide breath samples. He even asked what had happened to his pants, which were now soaked in his own urine. When the jail staff booked him in, he was even able to meander off to the drunk tank under his own power.

Fast forward a few months to Adam's day in court. He had pled not guilty and decided to act as his own lawyer. There is an old saying out there. "A defendant who acts as his own lawyer, has a fool for a client." It would seem as though this saying is based on fact. The judge tried to have Adam avail himself of legal aid, but he would have none of it. He said he was prepared to go to trial, so we started down that path.

I gave evidence first, describing for the court the driving pattern, and signs of impairment displayed by the accused. I stated that I had seen him sober in the past, so was able to make a comparison. I spoke of our detour to the hospital, and what had occurred there. Poor Adam had no real questions for me. Then they called the nurse who described what had occurred. Lastly, the Crown called the doctor to the stand who described the tests she performed and the results she observed. In cross examination, Adam tried to get the doctor to admit that she tortured him instead of trying to learn if he was unconscious or having a seizure. She went through each test again, why she performed them, and how she determined that he was conscious through the entire proceeding. The doctor was finally excused, and that's when the show got even better. It was short but funny, nonetheless. During poor Adam's closing argument to the judge, he put forward the argument that he'd been tortured while in the hospital, and as such, should be let go for the sake of principle.

"I am going to stop you right there, sir. I have one question for you." the judge interrupted. "If you were unconscious during your time in the Emergency room, how do you know you were being tortured?"

While Adam searched for the answer to that impossible question, the judge interrupted his poor attempts at manufacturing an excuse and found him guilty of both impaired driving and refusal to provide breath samples. Adam sat down defeated and listened to what his punishment would be. The prosecutor had to actually turn his back on the judge for a moment to avoid being caught stifling his laughter. I have to admit, I was suppressing a laugh myself. Humour is important in this job, and you have to take it where you can find it. Otherwise, we might be overcome by the horrific things we see. That might be the basis of the pranks we play on each other; tension relief.

****

I mentioned earlier that I would share very few stories or incidents where I wasn't present or involved. There are just too many of those stories to not share a few of them. What follows is an incident that I wasn't there to witness, but have verified from multiple sources, including the "victim". When I say victim, I mean to say one of the most prolific pranksters of my generation of coppers, who just got a taste of his own medicine. Here's a guy who, when tired of a janitor using the phone in the locker room to call home as the cops were changing, came up with a plan to correct that behaviour. Instead of talking to the guy about it (a viable option, but rather pedestrian for our hero), he made sure he was naked as the day he was born when the victim in question came down to use the phone. . . like clockwork at eight, every morning. When that didn't work, he took to practicing his quick draw in the large mirror in the bathroom, which was in plain view of the wall mounted telephone, dressed the same way. When I say dressed the same way, I mean not a stitch of clothing other than his issued duty belt, unloaded firearm, and forage cap on his head at a rakish angle. Every time the poor janitor came down to use the phone, there Jay was, standing in front of the mirror with nothing on but a smile, his hat, and his duty belt, practicing quick draws while growling, "Go ahead, make my day" as if he were a shorter, unclothed Clint Eastwood. The janitor soon picked another phone to use.

Jay is also the guy who once went with me to a mental health call, where a troubled person was at a downtown fast food restaurant, begging to be taken to jail. I was doing my best to tell him that he was a good person, and we took people like him to the hospital. We only took bad guys to jail. (Weak I know, but the best I could do on short notice.) Jay was there with me, and I could tell he was getting bored. He may have also thought that this fellow was suffering from an acute need for attention, rather than a real mental health crisis. So after about five minutes of this, he finally interrupted me and said, "You know, if you punch this officer, he will take you to jail."

Like I said, Jay was a pretty deserving guy to get a bit of payback. My friend Dylan was just the guy to do it. Dylan was not just another pretty face who drove around so fast he would launch his sleeping partner into the lower atmosphere while they drove together in their patrol van. No, Dylan was a trained professional. He was an experienced Explosives Disposal Technician, and he was always looking to increase his skills. He was really good buddies with Jay, and they were always messing with each other, to our constant amusement.

It was decided that young Jay must be made to pay, and the only thing he would understand was pain. The guys needed to make it hurt enough for Jay to know that there were consequences to his actions. The plot must have been conceived and planned out at an EDU training day. (There is no proof of this, but it was so elaborate, combined with the tools and explosives needed, you couldn't just whip this prank up in a couple of minutes.) The plan was to covertly gain entry to Jay's locker and set the small explosive charge so that it went off only when they wanted. Collateral damage was bad, but people getting hurt was secondary. This was war after all, and sacrifices had to be made for the greater good. You see, Jay had a stuffed and mounted magpie hanging from a string at the top of his locker. The thing was old, and dusty and he had clearly got it for a loonie at a garage sale, or more likely took it from someone's trash, and put it in his locker for comedic relief. He would sometimes fling his locker open to make the dead, stuffed bird "fly" out of his locker. He would even occasionally make the sound of a majestic magpie in flight because the poor, dead bird no longer could.

The lockers in the old station were very easy to enter. They were so old that even though you had to use a key to enter, any key would do. You just had to jiggle it up and down enough, and you were in. Dylan and his buddy Roy, another EDU tech, wired the poor hapless bird with a squib, and then connected that to a contact switch. When the contact was broken, the squib went off, causing a very small, "hardly noticeable" explosion.

I am told it was quite the sight to behold. Jay the master prankster strolled into the locker room, full of vim and vigor, ready to fight crime and/or evil for another day. He may have had a brief conversation with someone before he went to his own locker down by the entrance to the showers. He took out his key and, with a mischievous flourish, turned it and opened the door. It was universally thought by those who knew Jay well, the only flaw in the plan was to set this up overnight so that the charge went off in the morning. Jay was much less likely to have swagger when coming in at 6:30 am, compared to how he would at 5:00 pm. The beginning of an afternoon shift might have seen him jauntily swinging the locker open with a mighty "CAW-CAW" as the stuffed bird swung out. As it was, he sedately opened his locker, broke the contact switch, and set off the squib. The poor old bird was instantaneously transformed from the majestic black and white king (or queen, we weren't sure) of scavenger birds, into nothing but feathers, drifting slowly down from the roof of the locker room, softly settling on Jay's shoulders. The bonus was that the feathers would have to be cleaned up by the janitor that Jay scared out of the locker room with his naked antics. Of course, back then, this was just good clean fun (until someone lost an eye, as my mother used to say). Nowadays, setting off an explosive in a locker room would most likely result in an ASIRT investigation and year long suspensions. (ASIRT is the Provincial watchdog for police misconduct.) The late 80's and early 90's were a wonderful time to be alive fighting crime and evil.

SALLY AND CANDACE

Crimes against persons are the most serious offences we investigate as police officers, whether they are street level assaults, or more serious incidents requiring a detective to take over the investigation. I try not to judge people; I was raised to "Judge not." That flies in the face of the fact that every time I lay a criminal charge, I am swearing under oath that I believe the person I am charging committed that crime; some would say "judging" them. That is quite a feat considering I grew up believing there is only one person who can judge our actions, and it's not me. It's a difficult high wire to balance upon. One slip and you fall to places you don't want to be.

This is doubly the case for sex crimes and domestic violence offences. Both are a manifestation of control and subjugation. They are attempts to physically and/or mentally control the victim, usually by the application of force, and (in the case of domestic violence) by an offender who claims to love and care for the victim. I know there are various psychological reasons why offenders do these things, but I'm not a psychiatrist. I'm the poor guy who sees the end result and the human cost. I see what the act does to the victims, usually for the rest of their lives, and often causing a ripple effect on the victim's children. It's imperative to keep your emotions out of the mix as an investigator. If you are biased while gathering and interpreting evidence, your emotion and lack of impartiality could be fatal to the investigation. Easy, right? Just ask yourself what you would do and how you would feel if you were the 25-year-old cop that found yourself in this next situation. I also have to warn you, although true, this story is heartbreakingly graphic and disturbing. I have to tell it this way because it happened this way. I'm stuck with the images in my head, but you don't have to be.

So, there I was, on my way to my first real sexual assault investigation. I'd been involved in a few with my FTO, but I felt totally unprepared, nervous as heck, and scared to death of making a mistake. The victim was a twelve-year-old girl, and the caller was her mother. They were waiting for me at the hospital. I was a nervous wreck the entire way. I was trying to remember the things I had learned in training and in college, but that wasn't real life, and this clearly was. I'm not going to lie; I did a bit of praying on the way there. I didn't want to be emotional, but had to connect with this little kid, who had just been taught a lesson about life that no one at any age should have to learn. I had a sister who was only a year or two younger than this little girl.

I got to the hospital and spoke with the doctor. He told me that the victim was a young Indigenous twelve-year-old girl who had been brought in to the hospital by her mother. He told me the mother was currently in the hospital cafeteria. When I learned of the injuries the little girl had suffered, my blood boiled. She hadn't been beaten, nor would she suffer from any permanent physical injuries although there was some significant tearing. The doctor said that the tearing was partly due to the fact that little Sally was pre-pubescent and very small for her age. He also told me that she was on the fetal alcohol spectrum and had some fairly significant cognitive difficulties as a result. She would have difficulty with things like seeing the cause and effect of choices, and long-term thinking or planning, to name a few. In essence, she kind of understood what happened to her, but couldn't figure out why. I gave him the sex crimes kit, and he told me the pediatrician would be in shortly to do a more in-depth exam. He or she would gather the evidence needed for the courts, place the samples seized in the kit, then give the kit to me to send to the crime lab if needed. It would later be entered in court. Her mother still wasn't there, so I went in to the victim's room to introduce myself.

Sally was a cute kid, who didn't seem to have an aversion to cops in uniform like some young kids. She said she lived on the west side of the city and lived there with her mom and older brother. He was a couple years older than she was. I knew her mother because we'd been to their house on innumerable occasions for noise and disturbance calls. Sally couldn't remember their address. I even told her about my little sister who was close to the same age as her. (This is something you're not supposed to do, but I was new, and didn't know any better.)

After I asked her some general questions to help her feel comfortable with me talking to her, I inquired about what happened the night before. Sally told me she went to sleep in her bedroom while her mom was still out. She told me she woke up to an older man on her bed lifting up her nightie; it was a white one that was kind of like a dress, and he lifted it right off of her, over her head. He took her underwear off, and then got on top of her. I won't go into further detail, other than to say that Sally asked him to stop, and he ignored her, so she put up with the pain until he was done. I asked her if there were any marks or tattoos on the person that did this to her, and she described a very distinctive tattoo on his ribcage. She went on to speak about what the man smelled like, and some of the things he said. She said he didn't take his boots or pants all the way off and passed out in a drunken stupor next to her, pants still around his knees. (As an aside I have learned over the years what I didn't know then. When a victim talks about sounds or smells or adds tidbits of seemingly unnecessary and unsolicited information like "he didn't take his boots off because his feet always smell really bad" without prompting, they are usually true statements that add to the overall veracity of the statement). Sally told me she got up and put her nightie on and went to find her mother after her attacker had passed out. She couldn't get her mom to wake up, so she went to the room of her fourteen-year-old brother and climbed into bed next to him. She told me she didn't know she was bleeding until she woke up in the morning. When I asked Sally if she knew who had done this to her, she told me his name. I asked her how she knew the guy, and she told me he was a friend of her mom's and that she thought he was related to them.

I called my sergeant and told him what I'd learned to that point. He sent another cop to the house, to see if anyone was there, and to keep continuity in case we needed to write a search warrant. In my own little world, I thought that was going a little far. I was sure the mother would co-operate, and that we wouldn't have to get a warrant to search the crime scene. What mother would stand in the way of the cops searching for and prosecuting the rapist of their twelve-year-old daughter? Proving again how young and naïve I was. Clearly my boss knew some things I didn't. I went looking for mom to find out what she knew and ask for her help with the case.

I found her in the cafeteria, and she had just finished eating. She said she needed a smoke, so we went outside, and I asked her what had happened. She told me she'd been at the bar the night before and had invited some friends to her house at closing time. She claimed that those people invited more people unknown to her. She told me that when she got up in the morning, the first thing she did was check on her children. She said she'd discovered a "white man" who she didn't know in her daughters bed. She went in search of her daughter and found her in bed with her brother. She told me there was blood on her daughter's nightie, and at first, she just thought it was Sally's first step toward entering into womanhood. When she woke her daughter up, she learned what happened the night before. The mother said the white man she found in Sally's bed was gone when she went to confront him. She then took her daughter to the hospital. I asked her to provide a list of names of the people that she had invited home from the bar, and she gave me a rather lengthy list, and it included the name of the man that Sally had identified as her assailant. At the end of the interview, I told her that Child Welfare would be contacting her. She seemed angry at that, but I told her it was protocol for all such incidents involving children. I don't know why, but I didn't tell her that her daughter had given me the name of the man who'd done this, and that she not only knew him, but identified him as a relative. It might have been because of how she went on and on about what she would do to "that white man" if she found him and "you better find him first." I knew I needed to talk to my boss about what my concern was before I told the mother what I knew.

After getting statements from both the victim and her mother as well as permission from the mother for the release of the medical records, I went back to the station and spoke with my boss. He had me start working on a search warrant for the victim's house, to obtain the bedding, clothing, and other physical evidence to assist the investigation. This is where I quickly got in over my head. I like to write as a hobby (obviously). I finished my first novel only a few years after this occurred. Writing a technical document is different than fiction, especially if it becomes something that might harm or be fatal to an investigation regarding the rape of a twelve-year-old girl if not done exactly right. No pressure, right? I tried, but soon found I was out of my depth. A more senior copper from the oncoming shift helped me out, (I like to say he helped me out, but in fact he was the guy that wrote it while I held his coat. I really didn't know what I was doing).

A bit of humour in a rather serious incident happened that made me laugh, but also taught me a lot about how search warrants work. When "we" were finished with the warrant (actually, when Chris was finished with the warrant), we went to the home of a Provincial Court Judge to have the information sworn and the warrant signed. The process works like this. The copper or "affiant" writes out exactly what occurred, where they want to search, what they want to obtain by executing the search warrant, why they believe the things they are searching for are in the place they want to enter, and why it can't be done in a less invasive way (and sometimes why it has to be done at night). Most importantly, if the information to obtain the search warrant is deficient in any way, the judge refuses to sign, and you either have to go back to the drawing board and add the information needed and try again, try to figure out how to get what you need legally and without warrant, or proceed without the evidence you were seeking. The judge we were going to speak to was so old and had been on the bench for so long, that he retired soon after this incident. It was after hours, so we went to his house and were sitting in his kitchen while the judge read the information to obtain the warrant. Every now and then, he would stop and ask Chris a question about the file. Every time he did this, Chris pulled out his notebook and wrote something in it, answered the judge's question and then wrote something down again. After the third or fourth time this happened, the judge asked him what he was doing.

"If the information provided in the document isn't sufficient to obtain the warrant on it's own, and I have to give you more information to justify granting it, I have to be able to testify on the stand what extra information you used to decide to grant or deny the warrant, Your Honour."

The judge turned red, looked down, looked back up again as if to say something, then turned over to the last page of the information to obtain, and signed it without comment (or reading the rest of the document). When we were safely in the car, Chris started to laugh, and admitted he had wanted to do that to that judge for some time but hadn't because he was worried what the judge might think or do the next time he had to testify in front of him.

We went to the house and executed the search warrant and obtained what we needed in about an hour. Mom wasn't home yet, and her son was very helpful when we told him why we were there. (He hadn't turned to a life of crime yet, or at least not much). A member of the Forensic Identification Unit came with us and took the bedding and the white nightie she was wearing. The ident copper also took photos of the residence. We were done at the scene, and it was on to the next step of the investigation. Hunting down all the names of the people Sally's mom brought home from the bar to obtain statements from them about what they remember and if they had seen or heard about what had happened to Sally.

It took what seemed like forever to track down the eleven or twelve people who were at the bar and had come home with mom. Three of four of them gave me the story of an unknown white guy who had come over when the bar shut down, but none could provide a name, who he came with, or how he got there. The majority of those I spoke with however, told me there wasn't a white guy with them at all, and claimed they would have noticed. They saw the same guy that Sally identified as her rapist there and added that he was really drunk. One of the witnesses even told me that the rapist had told him that he was really tired and was going to crash in one of the rooms in the house. The witness described to me the door he went into when he left to "crash". Because I had photos of the inside of the residence, I knew he was describing the door to Sally's room. The only thing left to do was track down the bad guy, arrest him, and then see if he would admit to the crime.

I am pretty good with that last part now. I have been able to get confessions for minor assaults and break and enters, right up to multi-million-dollar fraud schemes and murders. I was given a hand by others as I matured as a copper, learning from some really talented interviewers over the years. I wasn't very good at it back then but wanted to give it a try instead of having someone else do it. I figured even without a confession I had enough evidence to convict anyway. I soon learned never to think that way.

It took me about a week, but I finally found the guy, arrested him, and brought him in to give him his chance to tell me his side of the story. After talking to his lawyer, he told me that he would not give me any kind of statement. Cops in Canada are given much more leeway about interviewing bad guys than our brothers and sisters to the south. I see TV shows from the States that show the cops not able to talk to the bad guy when he says he wants a lawyer. We don't have to do that here. In this instance, I replied to my suspect with, "fine, you don't have to say a thing. Just sit there and listen to what I have to say." Nowadays, I can usually get them involved in the conversation, and soon have them give at least a partial inculpatory statement. Back then, I didn't know what I was doing, and I got frustrated easily. (I think it has something to do with age and inexperience.) Anyhow, when he told me his lawyer advised him not to say a word to me, I was just fine with that. I told him that I had enough without his statement and charged him that night. (He even had a tattoo just like Sally had described on his rib cage.) Due to his criminal record, (he had a lengthy one, including other sex offences), and the fact that he was related to the victim, I was able to argue to the Justice of the Peace that the safety of the victim was in jeopardy if he was released. He was remanded into custody, and I prepared my court documents. I was proud of myself for bringing this file to a successful conclusion. It was a lot of hard work, and was frustrating at times, but I'd removed this sex offender from the street and knew the judge would teach him what happens to those who hurt little girls.

Perfect, right? Not so much. I guess I should've kept in contact with Sally and her mom. If I had, I might've at least seen the train coming, but I didn't, and got run over by it the day the trial was scheduled. It didn't even go to trial. The Crown called it quits when Sally and her mom both said I'd charged the wrong guy. The Crown saw all the work I'd done, and reviewed all the witnesses, including those who'd seen my bad guy go into a room to "sleep." They also believed he'd done the crime but had no reasonable expectation of a conviction without the mother and the victim telling the court at least a semblance of the truth.

I was devastated, but I don't blame Sally. She was just a little kid with enough problems to float a boat. She also had to live with that harridan of a mother. A mother that had bald face lied about what happened when told that her daughter had been raped, and then provided the police with misinformation in hopes of deterring us from finding the identity of the perpetrator. This, from a parent that cared so little for her children that she left them alone to go to the bar until closing time, then brought most of the patrons back to her house, and promptly passed out, giving the offender unfettered access to her innocent, twelve-year-old child. I have no words.

****

It isn't always family members or outside forces that screw up a file like this. Sometimes we are responsible as well. I never thought I would be so angry about an investigation and how it went off the rails again, until I investigated this second sexual assault.

So, there I was a few years later, older, wiser, and a little more patient. I was in the station for some reason or other, when a woman came in to the front counter to report that her foster child had been sexually assaulted. I was asked to investigate the matter and I spoke to the foster parent first. She told me she recently had a twelve-year-old girl placed in her home named Candace. She said Candace had gone out one evening to find out what sex was like. Candace had no problem telling anyone about what happened, and thought it was perfectly fine.

I spoke to Candace, and she told me what happened; actually, kind of bragged about what happened. She said she'd wondered for some time what sex would be like and decided to go find out for herself. She told her foster mom she was going out for the afternoon to meet with some friends and headed downtown. She went to the mall and started looking for a likely candidate. She saw a young man who she thought was attractive and went up to him and told him what she wanted to do with him. She told me the man was twenty-four-years old and he had a great car. (She described the car in great detail). He agreed and took her to his house. They went into the basement where his room was, and she took her clothes off. Although she was starting to develop, it was obvious to the man she was young, because he asked her how old she was. She told him the truth, that she was twelve. She said he laughed at that, stating he was twenty-four and joked about being twice her age. He took his clothes off as well and they had sex. She made no bones about the fact that she enjoyed it, and even said she was pretty sure he wore a condom, because she could smell the latex like smell. (See above about unsolicited smells and sounds causing the veracity of the statement to be more likely). When they were done, she got a ride back to the mall, where she promptly got on the bus and went back to her foster home and told her foster mother.

Candace remembered the man's name, his address, and what kind of car he drove. She even remembered that the man's father had the same name as his son, because she met him before they went downstairs for sex. Candace honestly didn't see the problem with what had happened. She had made a choice and was okay with it. I told her a bit about the Criminal Code's definition of the age of consent. At that time, the age of consent was fourteen years of age. (Unless the older party was a person of authority, like a cop or teacher etc.) After I told her about the age of consent, I left her alone in the interview room. As I was leaving, she asked me for pen and paper so she could doodle. I did that and went to speak to her foster parent.

I spoke to the foster parent and then told her that Candace had been very open and honest. I encouraged her to go get checked at the hospital, had her sign a medical release form, and went and got Candace so she could go home. When I went back to the interview room, Candace said she had a present for me. It was a childish drawing of a princess in a big blue gown, wearing a crown, and holding a magic wand. Written across the top of the page, it said "Thank you Constable Reeder". That was a clear indication of how old Candace really was. She drew me a picture like a little kid would. That's because she *was* a little kid, regardless of what she'd set out to do. She could no more form consent than Sally had. She had no idea what she was consenting to.

So, after a few weeks of looking for the bad guy, including going to his house to try (unsuccessfully) to take a statement from his father, I learned the guy had fled to Seattle where he had relatives and friends. After the father told me exactly what I could do with my attempt at a statement, and the attempted arrest of his son for that matter, I got a warrant for the son's arrest. I asked the Crown's office if they would extend the warrant so we could attempt to extradite him from the United States, but they wouldn't, citing cost.

Fast forward a few years, where my warrants were executed in Calgary, and the subject was brought to Lethbridge for the trial. It turns out that while he was in the United States, he had developed some interesting friends, and had started to deal drugs in our fair city. (The last time I saw him, many years later, he was arrested with over a kilogram of cocaine. Upstanding citizen!) When the trial date arrived, I looked forward to talking to Candace again. She'd moved shortly after the incident to the northern part of the province, and I hadn't seen her since. When I did, I couldn't believe the change. She was living on her own now and looked like a young adult. She was on track to graduate high school that year and was thinking about going to university. She was one of those success stories of the foster care system that you always hear about, but seldom see. I took her in to meet with the prosecutor and while they talked, I went and spoke to the foster parent who brought her into the station five years earlier.

Almost an hour later the Crown Prosecutor came to me and told me the case had been dealt with and that I was excused. I asked him what the sentence was, and he said he had withdrawn the charge. I was flabbergasted but had learned to keep my temper in check. I asked him if there was something wrong with the file or if I'd done something that made the matter un-prosecutable. He rather flippantly said I'd done nothing wrong but just didn't think he could convince a judge the victim had ever been twelve years old. Other than the obvious retort, "Everyone has been twelve at one point in their life", I referred him to the drawing Candace made me while waiting for me in the interview room. I'd attached it to the file to show where Candace was mentally at the time of the offence. He said "Ya, I saw it, but did you see her rack? I would never be able to get the judge to see past that." He smiled at me and walked away. Again, I have no words.

****

I never saw Candace again, but I saw Sally almost every week for years as we both got older. She dropped out of school at about fourteen or fifteen, started to drink pretty hard and got into drugs. It wasn't long before she was turning tricks downtown to pay for her habits. Every time I see her, it breaks my heart. In fact, I am shedding a few tears right now while writing about this. I can't say that things would've worked out differently for her. She was pretty damaged by Fetal Alcohol Syndrome, and then when she started using drugs and alcohol, she did more damage to herself. Would she have still ended up hooking on the streets if things had gone different in court? I am not idealistic enough to think that this outcome could have been prevented. Would a mother who cared enough for her to take a friend to task for raping her daughter have made a difference? I am not sure.

However, I *do* believe things would have been different if Sally had a mother who had cared enough about her to abstain from drinking while this young girl was in her womb. That investigation has stayed with me for over 30 years now and was a very formative thing in my career.

In 2017 I was deemed to be a Subject Matter Expert on the investigation of sexual assaults and asked to teach the recruit class that year. It was a two-day course on the do's and don'ts of a correct sexual assault investigation. The easiest way I could do that was to provide a case study for each concept I was trying to teach. The first case study I used was Sally's.

LISTEN TO THAT STILL, SMALL VOICE

Policing is dangerous enough without poisoning the well of goodwill provided by the citizens who might otherwise help us. Poor decisions or outright criminal behaviour of a small number within our ranks poison that well more than anything else. (Those that beat Rodney King or killed George Floyd are examples of criminals within our ranks.) It doesn't matter if Rodney King was or wasn't a criminal, or Floyd was convicted of horrendous things prior to the day he died and was lawfully arrested just prior to his death. The fact of the matter is, once caught, they should be treated with as much dignity and respect as possible. A copper can't always protect himself from all the threats that surround him. He has to rely on his teammates and the community. If you lose the trust in one or the other, it is a mighty lonely feeling dealing with some of the things we deal with. I also believe there's a "still, small voice" inside each of us that, when we listen for it, can help keep us safe. Call it what you like, intuition or spiritualism, but I have experienced it and cannot deny that it exists. Back in 1991, listening to that "feeling" saved my life and probably that of Drew, one of my teammates.

S o, there I was, coming to a stop at 43rd Street heading back into town on Highway 512, otherwise known as the Jail Road. It was about 3 o'clock in the morning, and I'd been at the jail dropping prisoners off. I'd been out of communication for the previous hour or so. (Our radios at that time did not function very well in the Correctional Centre.) I was following a vehicle west on highway 512 that was coming to a stop at the T intersection at 43rd Street. The vehicle was going the exact speed limit, so he was either aware of the cop behind him, he was impaired, or both. Our light to enter onto 43rd Street was red, and I sat behind the vehicle and queried the licence plate in front of me. I was concentrating pretty hard on the actions of the driver and the way the vehicle was moving to notice anything else around. It's a long light at that intersection and when it finally turned green, the driver in front sat there and didn't move for at least two or three seconds. The vehicle suddenly gunned it and went through the intersection in a hurry, turning south on 43rd. Now, I'm a pretty "A" type personality and tend to follow my gut and make decisions quickly, so it was my intention to immediately follow the vehicle and stop it as soon as it was safe. I was pretty sure the driver was impaired. Then I paused, as if someone had whispered the word "wait" in my ear.

I'm not saying I heard a voice telling me to wait, because I didn't. What I am saying is, that for some reason, I didn't do what I normally would've done and gunned the engine of my car to follow and then stop the vehicle, driven by someone I thought might be impaired. It was almost like I felt confused or stupid for about a half of a second. So, I didn't hit the gas right away, and it saved my life. My buddy Drew was travelling north on 43rd Street coming up to my intersection and doing at least 100 kilometers per hour with his emergency lights on. (It was 3 o'clock in the morning, so he didn't have his siren on.) He obviously thought that I saw him and knew where he was going to so fast with his emergency lights on, because he went through that intersection against his red light without touching his brakes. I hadn't heard anything on the radio while in the jail and had been target fixated on the vehicle in front of me. Drew would've hit me square in the driver's door at about 100 km/h. That momentary "feeling" saved my life.

I followed Drew north on 43rd and got to the traffic collision he was dispatched. It was a single vehicle roll-over, where the vehicle had been travelling way too fast on a gravel road back into the city, and lost control. When we got there, we found a single vehicle in the ditch, on it's roof, with two people on the ground, having obviously been ejected from the car. I went to one person in the ditch, and Drew went to the other. My guy was still alive, and Drew's was dead. I recognized my guy as a person I'd arrested maybe a month before for a couple of residential break and enters. He knew me by name, and as soon as I knelt down beside him, I asked Joseph how he was doing. He recognized me, called me Mike, and asked about his friend. I claimed I didn't know anything about the other guy (who was his usual partner in crime) because I'd come to see him instead. He admitted to me he'd been driving, and they were coming into town from Coaldale (to the east of the city) on the back roads because they had been drinking. His buddy was dead, and his life was ruined because of a bad decision, or not listening to his conscience, or whatever you want to call it. I was still alive because I had listened. Life (and death) hinge on listening to our conscience, or that still small voice. I promised myself while still a "young" cop that I would pay more attention to things going on around me so I could make it to being an old cop. I guess it worked, because as I write this, I am the definition of an old cop.

****

In '91, the Lethbridge Police Service began to experiment with dash cameras for our police cars, partially as a result of the assault of Rodney King in Los Angeles earlier that year. Most of our traffic cars had a camera system mounted on the dash, with a VCR recorder in the trunk and a monitor between the front seats. (You see kids, back in the olden days there were these things called Video Cassette Recorders. They were about the size of a paperback book, wait. . . so a paperback book was. . . Oh, just Google it!) Anyhow, these dashcam recorders were ahead of their time for recording things, but the disclosure laws in Canada made it too difficult at the time. We have to store the video evidence for years and on every interaction recorded, not just incidents used as evidence of a crime. That would have been a lot of VCR tapes, and we would've needed a special room in the exhibits locker just for all the videotapes. (The problem was solved many years later with the advent of digital storage and hard drive size.) Although this experiment was a bust in the short term, there were a few incidents that made the experiment worthwhile.

The first thing we learned was that it started recording as soon as you hit the record button, or more importantly when you turned your emergency lights on. The audio also turned on and continued to record until it was manually turned off. So even if you turned the red and blue lights off, the tape kept recording until you turned it off. The audio remained on, even if you weren't in the car and the car engine was off. These important technological advances took some getting used to and caused the embarrassment of a few of my brothers and sisters in blue.

One night shift, a more enterprising member of the Service decided to see if he could watch a movie in his car. He went to Blockbuster and rented a movie. (You see kids, back in the olden days. . .. oh, never mind!) My buddy decided watching a movie while enforcing the traffic laws might be just the thing, so he put the rented movie in the VCR recorder in the trunk and sat in a high traffic area to watch a movie on the little six or eight inch black and white monitor between the front seats. It wasn't like he was goofing off - he had proof he was doing his job! About three minutes into the movie, he stopped a speeding car, warned the driver, and then went back to watch more of the movie. He forgot the first rule of "Dash cam video rules" … "When you turn the red and blue lights on, the recording starts, no matter what kind of tape." At the end of his shift, he went to Blockbuster and diligently turned the rented tape in. He even rewound the tape for the next user like you were asked to - (Be kind, rewind). The next guy who rented the same tape took it home and sat down that evening to watch the show. He must've been astounded when he saw the movie cut away at just over the three minute mark, to a different movie altogether. There was the time and date stamp, PC (Patrol Car) number, and the "Lethbridge Police Service" on the top of the screen. The video showed a vehicle stopped in front of the dash of an obvious police car. It showed our hero walk up to the offending vehicle, shake his finger sternly at the driver, then walk back to his car, as the offending vehicle drove away. When the officer got back into his car, he must have diligently turned the recorder off, probably out of habit, because the movie turned back on, without interruption.

A side note to this story is also an indictment on our current "gotcha" society. The guy who rented the movie after my buddy, took the tape to the media instead of back to Blockbuster. They decided it was not a story they wanted to run and brought it to the Police Administration to deal with instead. Nowadays, that would've led on the six o'clock news and eventually gone viral. I know the officer that did this, and I can assure you, the punishment meted out was such that it would never happen again, not just by him, but any of us.

Another thing a lot of the guys found out quite quickly, was that the Traffic Staff Sergeant reviewed each of the tapes from the day before. He was required to write a report as to their efficacy, and whether the Service should purchase more to install in all the cars. The staff in question was my first boss. He was the one I mentioned earlier who liked to travel to South Africa before it was cool and didn't think people of colour should be allowed to freely walk on the west side of the city without the police checking up on them, let alone given their franchise to vote as they saw fit. He was roundly disliked by almost every copper on the job, and it was widely believed the real reason he was reviewing the tapes was to see if he could catch any coppers who might have done something he thought was wrong. That situation, combined with a bunch of cops with some time on their hands, as well as means, and opportunity, lead to a bad time for that staff sergeant.

For example, I give you Tyler, and Rick, a couple of coppers who stopped in for their morning coffee at one of the local Tim Hortons restaurants. One of them had a traffic car and had been busy that morning. So busy in fact, he'd forgotten that the car was still recording both video and audio. As they sat there chatting about their lives and all the other things that coppers speak about with their buddies over coffee, the camera was diligently recording the brick wall of the restaurant. The audio, however, was picking up every word that both men spoke, including disparaging (but mostly truthful) opinions about the current Traffic Staff Sergeant. Tyler mentioned he already had his ten tickets for the day, and he planned to do nothing else but drive around aimlessly in a car he didn't own, burning gas he didn't pay for. (His exact words were "I got my quota beat by 10:00 am and I am F*@#in' golden for the rest of the day!") It was only ten in the morning, and shift ended at five o'clock in the evening. That would be a colossal amount of goofing off.

What's worse than bragging about some impressive goofing off skills, was how Rick responded. He spent a great deal of time speaking about the perceived short comings of his current boss, (our hero the Traffic Staff Sergeant), to the point that those of us who later heard the tape, commented on his skill, acumen, and overall mastery of the English language on calling the old guy down. I mean he was a master, waxing rhapsodic about the foibles of all old cops in general, but specifically with "old bohunks that could not rub two coherent thoughts together, even if he could recognize them, which was doubtful." Even though I put those words in quotation marks, they aren't direct quotes. It was so long ago that I can't remember exactly what he said and would not do his diatribe proper justice from a 30-year-old memory. Suffice it to say, we all thought it poetry, or at least the best prose we uneducated knuckle draggers had heard in many a year.

The next day, Rick was called in to the staff sergeant's office and yelled at, threatened, and excoriated for longer than you would think a guy could keep up a head of steam to yell at a person. (They taught me years later when I was at negotiator school that people who are mentally unhinged and yelling usually cannot keep angry and yelling forever. The negotiator need only wait them out. My teachers clearly never met this boss.) At the end of the lengthy and at times very personal, spiteful, and mean-spirited dressing down, Rick was asked by the boss what he had to say for himself before the boss wrote up the charges under the Police Act. Rick looked the old man square in the eye, then at the screen, showing a great recording of the brick wall, and back again at the boss and said words to the effect "That is a lovely recording of a brick wall. Can you put a name to that voice?" He didn't receive a reply so continued, "if there is nothing else sir, I have to go write my ten tickets for the day." And left the office.

An avalanche of pranks on video for the old Traffic Staff Sergeant to begin his day with ensued! We were all guilty of getting one or more of our regular homeless people to come over and say hello to the staff sergeant on camera. Most were willing to do it, and some even displayed hand gestures to show what they thought of him. (These hand signals were not encouraged, I assure you.) I'm told there was even a clip floating around of one of our regular customers smiling and waving happily into the camera, saying an intoxicated hello, while wearing a Lethbridge Police Service forage cap that looked surprisingly like one that hung in the traffic office. I never saw it, so can't speak to the veracity of that rumour, but whoever thought it up was a genius. Pure comedic gold!

The final straw for pranks on video was one that had been very well planned, rather elaborate, and funnier than heck (and probably a step or two over the proverbial line). There is no audio to it, but I still have this clip somewhere. It took place in the lane behind the Bridge Inn and Wally Lee's Restaurant on 1st Avenue South in the 300 block. Both buildings have long since been torn down but at the time the Bridge was a local watering hole where the second and third floor had monthly rented rooms, usually paid for by the Provincial Government for those on welfare or other forms of income support. It was next to Wally Lee's Restaurant; another "must attend" for the discerning cop for breakfast food and witty banter in a very thick Chinese accent. Wally loved us and loved to tease us as well. (A few years before I was hired, a Sergeant forgot his radio in Wally's fine establishment, and all who were working that day heard a very thick Chinese accent on the radio saying "Sergeant, Sergeant, you forgot your radio!) Anyway, from the lane behind these two businesses, there was an alcove that was a windbreak, but you could not enter either of the businesses. The perfect stage for the show.

The video shows a young man wearing a dark hoody with the hood up and a letterman's jacket from one of the local high schools, running full tilt into this alcove. His exit is quickly blocked by the arrival of the police car with emergency lights blazing, recording the action for all to see, (especially the boss the next day). Another cop car parked on the other side of the same entrance, effectively blocking the young ne'er do well's safe getaway. Three cops can then be seen exiting the cars and running into the alcove following the suspect, where the camera of the one car is suspiciously placed to perfectly frame the action of the entire encounter. (George Lucas could have done no better!)

The three cops are seen capturing and then beating the crap out of the kid with the hood still over his head, until he falls to the ground. They then continue to kick him while he's down, laying in what appears to be an unconscious heap. They laugh over his inert body, then go back and kick him some more for good measure. They drag his limp body toward the hood of the car that is recording the encounter, the head of the perpetrator hanging down and hidden by the hood. When they get to the car, framed only a few feet in front of the camera, one of the coppers pulls the hood off, grabs the hair of the offender and holds it up for all to see, including the staff sergeant watching the action the next day. It was the smiling face of an off-duty copper who happened to be in the station and agreed to participate in the prank. Needless to say, that was the end of any pranks using the dash cam recorders directed at our poor old staff sergeant. A short time later, those cameras were removed from the cars. They told us it had to do with the problem I mentioned earlier, storage space and disclosure for the numerous videos. Some of us think the boss just got tired of being made fun of and gave up, wrote a report to the administration saying it was impractical and cost prohibitive at that time, and would not work until technology changed or the laws of disclosure for Canadian Courts did. It was a good run while it lasted and could not have happened to a nicer guy.

Speaking of the Bridge Inn reminds me of a story from back in the day that taught me never to put money in my mouth. I am reluctant to tell it because it is pretty gross, but I figure that you bought this book to share a bit of what we experience, even if it is a bit disgusting. It happened around the spring or early summer of '91 or '92 and has been burned into my memory. I am sorry for doing this to you, but misery loves company, or forewarned is fore-armed or something like that. You've all been warned!

So, there I was, called to the Bridge Inn for a dispute over money. I happened to be driving on 1st Avenue South, and arrived about 30 seconds after the call came in. When I got there, I saw a girl I knew well from previous dealings, and a young man I had never met before, arguing in the hotel lobby. He was demanding his money and she was saying she didn't have it. I could see this coming from a mile away. The reason I knew the young lady was because she was a prostitute who frequented the downtown core. She was also a little hard to mistake for someone else. She was about 250 pounds, even with one leg amputated at the thigh, so she got around using crutches. (She used the crutches until she was too intoxicated, and then she usually fell where she was. We would then pick her up and take her to jail to keep her safe until she could care for herself.) I separated the parties and then got the story first from him, then from her.

The young man admitted that he'd purchased her affections for the evening, after they had agreed upon a price which was well above the going rate. (Clearly his first Rodeo, but not hers). They retired to the Bridge Inn where he sprang for a room, over and above the amount they'd agreed upon and got busy. Shortly after the deed was done, the young fella had what is commonly called a PON, (post orgasmic nap). Whilst he was napping, the young lady decided to leave, but even though he had paid her up front, she felt she'd given her all to the performance, and deserved more (or was just greedy, even though she had already gouged him to excess) and went through his pockets. There she found a large wad of cash in mostly 20's and 50's. He had recently been paid, or had his taxes back, I can't remember. Either way, he had upwards of $3,000 in his pocket, over and above what he'd already paid her. Now, she wasn't greedy, leaving him some of his money in his pocket, but she did take three or four extra 50's for her trouble, and decided to leave before he woke up. The problem was, when she left, it was to the distinctive "thump-stomp" sound, caused by her using the crutch combined with her prodigious weight.

This noise woke the young gentleman up. It would seem he was getting wise to the ways of the world, because even though he could hear her leave, the first thing that came to his mind was not the love of his life leaving without saying goodbye; rather, he was concerned that the money he had in his pocket might have found it's way into her not so trendy purse. When he found himself a couple hundred short, he raced out of his room, forgetting his shoes, and confronted her in the lobby in front of the proprietor of the fine establishment. When the owner realized an assault might occur shortly, he called police. Fortuitously (or not, depending on your point of view), I was just up the street and therefore "Johnny on the spot" when the call came in.

Like King Solomon of old, I wisely came to a decision, and asked the young man if he was more interested in getting his stolen money back, or if he wished to pursue the matter in a court of law. His starting position was that he wanted all of his money back, including the exorbitant amount he'd paid for her time. I told him this was a non-starter and taught him a bit of Latin, Caveat emptor. He finally agreed that if the stolen money was returned, he would retreat, lesson learned, and live to fight another day, poorer for seeing the perfidy of others, but richer in life experience.

At first the young lady was having none of it, claiming her innocence (she was anything but innocent, I can assure you), and that she'd not only not stolen the money, but also took umbrage with the accusation that she would allow her affections to be purchased in the first place. This was an impossible position to hold, as she had been caught almost in the act (on both counts). The money still had to be on her person, and I told her that if I had to, I would arrest her for the theft, and have a female officer search her for the stolen money. I explained once we went down that path, there was no turning back from criminal charges. Not wishing to scar my poor female co-worker permanently, I used all of my considerable charm and power of persuasion to encourage the young lady to choose door number one and forgo any criminal charges being laid. Our young lady agreed, turned her back to me, reached into the crotch of her pants and brought out the missing money.

Disturbing but not too bad so far, right? Well wait, there's more. It turns out that this young lady was at the point in her menstrual cycle where she required a feminine hygiene product. I don't know if she had a pad on or not, but if she did, the money had been placed between her person and the pad, causing those fifty dollar bills to turn a great deal redder than they were when she put them there. (Canadian 50 dollar bills are red.) In fact, she was having what you might call a "heavy flow day." When the young man grabbed the money from her hand, I noticed a short time later that there was blood dripping from his elbow. To add insult to injury, she believed she'd performed so well that she deserved extra money for a cab. This young man was so happy to have his money back that he agreed. He transferred the money from his right hand to his left, licked his bloody thumb, peeled off the top fifty and gave it to her. She left, went outside, and paid the cabby with the money that had recently been used as a feminine hygiene product. For all I know that fifty is still in circulation. Never put money in your mouth!

MY WIFE LEARNS I'M A LIAR

My first transfer to a different patrol team happened around my third or fourth year on the job. This used to happen quite often, especially with the younger members of the service. I don't know what the reasoning was, only that it was common place to be moved every three or four years. Nowadays there are so many places for young coppers to transfer in a lateral position that they seldom spend more than their first five or six years in patrol division at a single stretch. Back then, unless you wanted to work in K9, School Resource, Ident, or Drugs, you basically stayed in patrols. I was a patrol cop for 16 years (including a two year traffic detour), before I was moved to Criminal Investigation Division, and that was because I got promoted. There were two non promoted positions in all of CID when I went there, and they had only been created the year before. Now there are nineteen different positions in CID alone that a young copper can apply to laterally transfer without being promoted. I may never have applied for promotion had the same opportunities been available when I was young. That is a long-winded way of saying that I had to wait a few years longer back then to achieve my goal. In the mean time, we got moved around a lot, from one patrol team to the next.

My new team had a bunch of really good guys on it, and I enjoyed it immensely. The new staff sergeant was not a racist like my last one, he was just an Asshole. (You note that I capitalized that word. It was on purpose.) Part of the reason that the man didn't like me was my own fault, or rather his fault for being an asshole, and me telling another sergeant that I was going to arrest "that asshole."

The local cop bar was right across the street from the police station in those days, at the Army and Navy Club. (We were in the 400 block of 5th Avenue South, and the Army and Navy Club was in the 500 block.) Early in my sojourn on that team, the boss took a day off for some sort of party for old cops at the club. There was another guy I didn't know working for him that night. I was on the road, and my friend Jake (the guy that told me that I might need my gun when we were at the murder at the mall a few years before) was working the front desk. It was really cold out and our boss (who I hardly knew) came to the front counter and asked Jake for some lock de-icer for his car door. He was quite intoxicated when he asked for it, and Jake mentioned in a friendly way that he could arrange a ride home for him instead of him having to worry about even being in care and control of his truck while he was impaired. The boss turned Jake's offer down cold, got the lock de-icer, and went back out the front doors.

S o, there I was, out on the street, minding my own business when Jake put out a general call on the radio to let us know that there were members of the service who might need a ride home from the club. There was no accusation in his message, and no names were mentioned. It was a simple and well intentioned request to drive by and see if we could get some of our co-workers home safely. I was close, so I drove by. As I got to the front of the building, I could see another guy there being yelled at by my new boss in the middle of 5th Avenue South. I rolled up and said, "Hey fellas, anyone need a ride?"

The new boss looked at me and said "F#%@ you, Rookie!" and then continued to argue the other copper. I looked at my team mate talking with the drunk boss, and he waved his hand at me in a gesture to tell me to get out of there, and he would talk to the boss. I left the area and went back in to the station through the back doors. When I got there, I discovered the drunken boss had come back into the station and started yelling at my buddy Jake for telling other guys that he needed a ride, and that it was none of his business. While he was yelling at Jake, he was poking him in the chest (his Kevlar vest) with his finger to emphasize each syllable. That is, until Jake had had enough, caught the finger poking him, and applied a bit of pressure to it. This caught the boss by surprise, but it also shut him up. Jake told me this, and I got pretty angry. I went over to the guy that had volunteered to work for my new boss that night and said,

"You should get the number of the Inspector handy. I'm gonna go and sit on his truck and arrest him if he is stupid enough to drive in that shape."."

Policy stated that for a situation like that, a member of higher rank than the copper under arrest needed to be in the loop, and usually present. The acting boss tried to talk me out of it, but I would have none of it. I left the building and went to a parking lot a block away and looked back towards my staff sergeant's personal truck. It was already running, without anyone in it. That angered me more. If he had started the vehicle, he had been impaired while in care or control of it when he did, already breaking the law. I sat there, waiting for the man who had received offers of a ride home by two of my co-workers, who were also his own men! He then had the temerity to go into the station and assault another one of his men who had only tried to arrange his safe trip home. I waited for about twenty minutes, looking at the truck that was still running, with no one in it, until a woman I later learned was his wife, pulled up. She shut the truck off, kept the keys and went into the bar and retrieved her drunken asshole husband, and took him home.

The only thing that ever happened to the boss was that he was made to apologize to Jake for poking him in the chest. Jake told me later it wasn't even a half-assed apology. I thought he got away with one, but that it was over now, and I moved on. Unfortunately, a few months later my wife was diagnosed with Cancer. (It doesn't seem like one piece of information has anything to do with the other, but I'm getting there.)

We had to have our yearly vacation selections in on January 10th of that year. I was lucky that year, as I got some really good holidays in the summer. Holidays are selected on a seniority basis, and I was pretty junior, but there were a lot of big game hunters on this new team, so the fall was booked up before the summer was. Of course, all of that good luck didn't seem to be much luck at all when we got the news about my wife's illness a week later. I had learned that my 28-year-old wife had cancer and would require ten weeks of radiation therapy in Calgary that spring. We found out on the 16th of January. I went in to the boss and told him my problem. I had the holiday selections of the entire team with me, and there was room for me to change my holidays so I could be with her for the lion's share of her treatment. He sat there while I explained my predicament until I asked him if it were possible to change my holiday selections so I could be there for my wife. He wouldn't even look me in the eye when he said "Nope, they are set in stone."

Knowing what I know now, that is, of course, a line of garbage. Had I gone to his boss, the Inspector in charge of Patrol Division, and told him the same story, he probably would have just told me to go, and put me on administrative leave. But I was young and didn't know any better. For six of the ten weeks my wife was in Calgary, sicker than sick, thinking she might die, with her mother there instead of me. I'm sure that my mind wasn't in the right place for that entire year, especially when she was gone, but we worked through it. I am Christian and supposed to forgive everyone, but I'm still working on that one. I am sure that he was angry at me for threatening to arrest him and looking for an excuse to show me *he* was the boss. I probably was a bit over the top about how I said it, but I don't regret going to sit on his vehicle and would still do the same thing today. I know in my heart what my reason was. I sat on his car to save his, or someone else's life, not for petty revenge for poking my friend in the chest. He can't say the same thing about denying me the ability to change my holidays to other available days so I could be with my sick wife in her time of need.

That staff sergeant retired four or five years later but actually showed up at my promotional party years later. (Ironically, at that same bar). We only had one interaction that night, and it shows what kind of fellow he really is. He walked up to me, holding a beer that I'd paid for, and drunkenly slurred, "Now you're going to find out what it is like to have assholes like you, working for you." And walked off. Even though he ranks up there in the top two or three jerks that I have ever worked for, I am eternally grateful to him for the lesson in leadership he unknowingly gave me. I was promoted in 2004 and for the last 17 years, I have been blessed to lead men and women in uniform. I make sure that I **<u>NEVER</u>** treat them the way I was treated by that man.

****

A funny thing happened shortly after my wife's treatments. Well, I think it's funny, and so does my wife now, but at the time, it was a shock to her system. It turns out that she didn't even know me at all, or at least that's what she said when she saw me in action eight or nine months later. She finished her treatments and is still with me to this day. We had some scary days (and weeks and months), but it brought us closer together. When she got back home from Calgary, she decided as she got better (and was no longer throwing up every day) that she wanted to go to work with me. We used to have a ride-along program for spouses. She obviously knew about my boss, so we picked a day that he was off, and then I brought her in for the only ride-along she's ever had with me in over 33 years of policing. We picked a weekday dayshift, and she came in for shift briefing and everything.

Back then, smoking was still allowed in the building, but the smokers on my team refrained from lighting up when she was around, for fear of making her sick. The coppers on my team were a great bunch. So much so, that I soon figured out when we were on the road, they were also jumping my calls. (I confronted my best buddy on that team later, and he told me that she looked so sick that it shocked them all. She was about 90 pounds at the time. They had talked amongst themselves and decided they just wanted us to spend time together. They hatched a plot to make sure we got to just be together and talk and look at houses. Like I said, they were all great guys.) In fact, there was only one call they couldn't steal from me that day, because they were all busy.

So, there we were, my fearless wife (all 5'1" and 90 lbs) and I, going to a call of a landlord tenant dispute. When we got there, the landlord told me that he was just concerned for his tenant. She had mental health issues that seemed to be getting worse. Before we went up to the door, I gave some very specific instruction on what to do for every possibility that I could think of. I could tell that what I do for a living suddenly became very real to my wife, when I started telling her what I wanted her to do if the person got violent. Her green eyes got bigger as I spoke, but she nodded her head and I knocked on the door.

An old lady answered the door. (I thought she was ancient then, but really, she was only about 65 or so.) She was even smaller than my wife. She immediately invited us in and acted as if it was a relief that I was there. Her English was accented, but easy to understand. She told me her name, and then demanded that I arrest all the farmers in the area for trying to kill us all. When asked some questions about this statement, she went off about the amount of "chemical toxins" Canadian farmers use when they grow food. She said it was a conspiracy and it was slowly killing us all. I found out later she was a retired professor who taught at either the college or university, and she also worked at the Agricultural Research Station run by the federal government just on the outskirts of Lethbridge. She had clearly "slipped a cog," but was very knowledgeable about this particular issue, and there was no way that I could just talk her out of her beliefs. The other problem was she really wasn't a danger to herself, or anyone else, she was just not well mentally, and probably without any professional help for that very reason. She was too sick to function well in society by herself, but her illness didn't meet the severity threshold to get her the supports she needed. If you count addiction as a mental illness (and it is), this issue is the largest drain on public resources. It exponentially beats whatever is in second place.

I had this troubled lady explain more about what her concerns were, as my wife stood by the door, silently listening to every word. Then I realized how I could help her and get us out of there without promising her I would arrest every farmer in the area.

"I notice that you have some bags over by your pantry. What's in them?" I asked her.

She told me they were five-pound bags of rice that she'd purchased from an Asian market in town. She went on to say that the rice she got from that market was safe and I should eat it as well, as it would probably save my life.

"Didn't they tell you when you worked at the research station?" I asked with feigned shock and surprise.

She asked me what secret they hadn't shared with her and so I told her.

"That rice is like a scrubbing agent that acts like a filter. All you have to do is take a small amount and pour it out on the window sills and by the door. When the wind carries the toxins in, the rice filters it out, leaving you with fresh air. You don't need very much, and you have to change it at least once a month." I instructed her. "Make sure you clean it really well, and throw that used rice out, because it will have filtered all the toxins."

She looked like she was going to cry. She reached out for my hand with both of hers and said thank you about 20 times. She assured me that she would do what I told her. I encouraged her to call the police if she had any more problems and we left.

When we got to the car, my wife was quiet for longer than I expected. I thought she was feeling empathetic for this poor old lady suffering from mental illness. I let her think about it for a bit, and then she said the most astonishing thing.

"You lied to her." She didn't accuse me of anything, and she wasn't mad. It was a statement but came out like she had just discovered something.

"Of course I did." I started with a bit of a laugh. I was going to explain all about my motives, and how I couldn't arrest the poor lady, but she interrupted me.

"No, what I mean is, you were really good at lying to her."

Now she sounded like she was thinking about every conversation we'd *ever* had, to determine if I was telling the truth or not. All I could do was laugh. That may be the real reason she has only been on one ride-along. I think

74

that if she knew the "work me" it might shock her too much.

****

We would never victimize anyone in our circle of friends or family outside of the job like we did to our co-workers back then. The pranks have truly calmed down a lot compared to my first five or ten years on the job. I'm not sure why that is, but there are probably a number of factors. First off, most of the pranks we played then would be so over the line now that neither the members nor the administration would accept that behaviour. It is probably for the better though, as we certainly got out of hand on occasion. For example, I remember taking a statement from someone one night shift in front of the bar, and when I had the witness sit in my passenger seat, I turned the light on, and something caught the corner of my eye. I turned to look in the back seat and found a large cardboard box that had been strapped in to the seat with the seatbelt. In the box, angled so the occupant(s) of the front seat of my PC could see was a huge pig's head facing us. It's pretty tough to explain to the witness of a crime why there was a pig's head in the back seat. Of course, that pig's head made the rounds for the next week to the cars and lockers of assorted co-workers until it started to smell. Fairly juvenile when it happens to you, but kind of funny when it happens to others. Other pranks, however, are a bit further over the line, and have much longer reaching effects.

What follows is one of those stories that I mentioned where, although I wasn't there, I confirmed it actually happened with all of those involved, except the poor fellow who had to clean the car. I didn't have the guts to ask him how he felt. He still works with us and has been here longer, and probably knows more secrets than I do. He was the ultimate victim in this incident. The entire prank is an example of sophomoric half-wits going a bit too far.

So, there was this guy on another team named Ty who used to always leave his patrol car unlocked at the back of the station when he went inside. (I probably should confess, that even though they told us all to lock them, hardly any of us ever did.) Now Ty was relatively new on the job, but he was one of those guys who was never really "new." He was young, but nothing seemed to bother him. He followed the rules that were important to him, or that he knew would get him jammed if he disobeyed them, but those that he thought were stupid, or less important, he tended to "forget." He figured there wasn't a safer place in the city than the parking lot of the police station, so why should he have to lock his doors. Sounds logical, or at least you would think so, unless you worked with predators like Steve and

Kris. They decided they needed to teach Ty the error of his ways. So, they went to the meat packing plant on the east edge of the city.

Any young person who grows up in Southern Alberta, or in any other ranching area, knows that cattle don't like to be shipped in trucks. They become a bit nervous and agitated, and as a result, when they defecate, the product they make tends to be less solid, and more or a soupy or chili-like consistency. (Descriptors chosen on purpose; think about this the next time you eat chilli.) Our two heroes showed up at the plant just as a truck driver had finished dropping off a load of cattle and was cleaning the floor of his trailer. He was using a long snow shovel and scooping out loads of soupy cow excrement as two coppers in uniform in marked police cars showed up to the rear of his trailer. They asked him if he would be so kind as to fill up the handy dandy garbage bag, which they just happened to have with them, with what he happened to be shovelling. I often wonder what kind of look the truck driver must have given these two young coppers before he shrugged his shoulders and began scooping that soupy cow dung into the garbage bag they were delicately holding open, hoping none of the contents slopped on their uniforms.

When the bag was about a third full, they decided that was more than enough to make their point and thanked the kind man for his effort. I know Steve pretty well, and I believe he is the kind of guy who would have offered to pay the truck driver for his time, but I can't be certain that he did. It's just something that he would probably do. With their bag of slop, the two hurried back to the station in hopes of finding their prey.

As luck would have it, good ol' Ty was parked in the back lot of the station, and upon checking his wheels, they discovered the poor rube had left his car unlocked again. Really! When would he learn? These two fellas probably thought they were doing the sergeant a favour. If they could teach Ty to follow policy and lock his car, that would be one less thing for the boss to worry about. It would also be something that Ty would probably eventually appreciate. A simple reminder that he forgot to lock his wheels. Heck if the lesson took, maybe they would save Ty from having his car stolen in the future. These two guys were saints and actually helping everyone out by teaching this short, sharp lesson.

They opened up the back door of the patrol vehicle and took out the garbage bag full of soupy cow dung from the trunk of their own car. (It would be too stinky in the back seat of **their** car!) They then counted to three as they swung the awkward bag of cow dung into the back seat of the car. As they let go of the bag at the count of three, they both realized their mistake at just about the same moment.

You see, in those days, the city did not have a professional company install all of the extra requirements in a marked police car. When they bought a new car, they took it to the radio "line shop" and had them install the radio and when they needed other things put in, they took it to the appropriate city department where the needed equipment was added. Unfortunately, they had city employees install things like the silent patrolman in the back seat. (That is the metal and plexiglass barrier between front and back seat so when the good guy puts the bad guy in the back seat, he doesn't have a shower of bad guy spit to clean out of his hair, among other obvious reasons.) Each silent patrolman was different, as they were just "make worked" into their spot. There were usually little bolts sticking out or other idiosyncrasies with each car. Ty's silent patrolman had a lone bolt that stuck out just a bit further than either man could see in the dark. It snagged the plastic bag and ripped it as if being cut by a knife. This of course, caused the soupy contents of the bag to splash all over the backseat and floor. Another thing they may have miscalculated, was the amount of soupy dung they'd "borrowed". It turns out they overestimated the amount needed to make the backseat area smell a little bit. The soupy contents went to the floor and then flowed to the front floor boards by travelling under the front seats.

I don't know if Kris and Steve felt shame or joy as they saw their prank go sideways right in front of them, but both were real troopers, and would not let something like this spoil their night. (In fairness, I am pretty sure they didn't know that the "crap soup" had gone under the driver's seat and was now in the front half of the vehicle floor as well.) They both settled in to watch Ty get into his car. Their wait soon paid off as Ty come out to his car, opened his door, and put his long right leg in first then slide into the seat, only to jump right back out of the car again. It was just the reaction they were hoping for and felt vindicated that they had a small part in teaching a teammate to follow the rules without appearing preachy. It was all well and good until Steve noticed the back leg of Ty's pants. Anyone who has grown up in Canada knows that during the winter, getting in and out of a car causes the driver to track mud, snow and sometimes road salt into the vehicle, where it accumulates on the floor mat. If the vehicle has been running for a while, the snow and slush melts, causing a slurry of mud, water, and salt to lie there, and sometimes soaks up the back of the driver's pant leg. It looks like a salty white triangle on the back of your dark pants if you let your leg rest where the pantleg can touch the water. Now imagine what happens to your pant leg if it has been in soupy cow manure for even a second or two. Ty was not happy, nor were the bosses, or the poor fella who had to clean the car. As a side note, it should be mentioned that the goal our two (until now, unknown) conspirators set out to achieve was a great success. We ALL locked our cars after that escapade.

DEADLY WINTER

One thing that surprised me about this job is the amount of death we see. I'm not talking about the gory car accidents or the murders, although we see a lot of those as well. No, I am talking about your everyday, run of the mill, person who has given up the ghost. We call them "Sudden Death Investigations" although there is usually nothing sudden about them. If a person dies at home we attend, even if they were sent home from the hospital to spend their last days with their family. When we go, we're supposed to treat each like a potential homicide until that possibility is ruled out. In the old days, we called the Medical Examiner (ME) to the scene. There were a few Doctors who were on-call and did this job over and above their practice. That has since changed, and we now call an ME investigator in Calgary. We describe what we can see and voice our concerns if any. They then decide whether an autopsy is required, or if the death was expected.

When I first started, and for a few years thereafter, even if the ME determined the death was expected, an autopsy was performed. In essence almost everyone who died, was "posted", (short for Post Mortem Examination, I think). Now the ME's office only calls for an autopsy when the cause of death is undetermined, unexpected, or a possible homicide. (There are a few other reasons, but these are the three that are most often the case.) When I was a young copper, there was a policy from the Inspector in charge of the Criminal Investigation Division, that if you responded to a sudden death, you were also required to attend the post mortem exam, including the autopsy which was done at the morgue at Regional Hospital in Lethbridge. Now autopsies are all done in Calgary, then the body is transported back when the exam is finished. I won't get into describing an autopsy, but suffice it to say, they are not my favourite thing to attend.

So, there I was, working a Sunday day shift. I was a little bored, so I was running radar on the west side of the city for speeders. It was a normal day and there were a few offenders to be found, but Sunday is a bad day for me when it comes to writing tickets. I generally give out a lot of warnings, unless the driver shows me that he doesn't deserve a break, or the offence is so egregious that I have to do something about it. The latter occurred at about ten o'clock in the morning on University Drive. It was the main north-south route on the west side at that time, and the young driver appeared to be attempting a land speed record. I finally got him stopped near a church, and he pulled into the parking lot to get off the main road. The driver proved to me that he deserved the ticket when we talked (pointing out how I should be out there finding real criminals), and I went back to my car to write his ticket. I was almost finished when I saw a bit of a disturbance at the door of the church in my rear-view mirror. A lady came running out and came straight for my car. I got out before she got there and asked her what I could do for her. She asked me if I knew first aid. That was a pretty broad question, but I told her I did. She told me she needed me to come with her. I told the young kid driving that I would be right back, called dispatch on my radio about what was going on, and went with her into the church.

Inside, I found a guy lying on his back on the floor in the chapel, with a group of people around him. There was one guy kneeling next to him that I kind of recognized. I knew he was an RCMP officer from the Lethbridge Detachment, but I couldn't remember his name. He was performing mouth-to-mouth on the man who was lying on the ground. When I got there, he asked me if I knew how to do chest compressions for a person whose heart had stopped. I told him I did, knelt down with him, then after checking for a pulse and landmarking, away I went. Back then, they taught 5 chest compressions to one breath, so we started doing that, while waiting for the paramedics to get there.

I was lost in the act of doing compressions, when I noticed an older lady standing to the side, watching us while weeping quietly and being held by the priest. I guessed that I was trying to bring back a man from the other side who probably wasn't going to make it and doing so in front of his spouse. Even though we tried, the man passed away. When the ME showed up, I had to ask him some questions. Apparently, an older person has less muscle mass, and their bones that are often more brittle than someone younger. So, when the person dies, what muscle the deceased had is no longer contracted and protecting the more brittle rib cage. The moment the person dies, the muscles stop contracting, eliminating the small amount of protection. That amount of force used before death, now breaks them. I was in the middle of a set of five when I heard a loud crunching noise coming from the man we were working on, and my hands went almost to his spine. I had broken some of the bones in his chest, and everyone there, including his wife, heard it. In first aid class, you're taught to keep going if this happens, so I did, but it felt a lot different than it had before.

He died in church surrounded by his friends and family. He was also in his late 70's or early 80's. Overall, not a bad time or place in life to go out. It was hard on his spouse, but there was a lot she could use as a positive as she learned to cope with his death, if that's even possible when you see the person you've been married to for two or three times as many years as you haven't, suddenly taken from you. I don't know how she felt, but I have only been married 34 years, and I know how *I* would feel. It took me a long time to get past the feeling that when I broke his ribs, I had a part in his death - even when doctors tell you that simply isn't the case. I am not sure that the ME wasn't just saying those things to make me feel better and they weren't there when his wife heard me break them.

Two things happened to me as a result of this incident. The first resulted in me giving the boys at the station some more ammunition to tease me. As I was kneeling, doing chest compressions, and raising a bit of a sweat, one of my buddies who came to back me up stuck his head in to the chapel and asked me what I wanted done with the young man that I had stopped. Without thinking I said, "Give him the yellow copy." It all started later with the traffic sergeant coming up to me and asking if I was interested in a transfer to his unit. I said I wasn't, and he said it was a shame since I had the wherewithal to ensure I got a ticket served on an offender, even as I was killing an old man in a church. It was a different time. Teasing like that seldom happens now.

The second thing was an award offered to me by the St John's Ambulance organization. It was called, ironically enough, the "Life Saver" award. I don't know if the Mountie, who was also given the award, showed up for the presentation of the medal, but I didn't. I sure didn't feel like accepting an award after what happened.

****

We coppers used to spend a lot of our downtime at the Lethbridge Regional

Hospital. They don't even go by that name any more. It is now the Chinook Regional Hospital. When it was still LRH, we would go up to the Emergency Unit on nights when it was slow and have coffee with the nurses and doctors. (I don't drink it, but you know what I mean). I've always been of the opinion that if I go into the hospital with a sucking chest wound, I want the staff to know me well enough to at least know my wife's name if I don't make it. We suffer through many shared experiences, from simple things like working holidays as essential workers, to the more serious things like seeing trauma and wondering how people can do the things they do to each other. Both topics were roundly discussed on a regular basis in the nurse's lounge on those slow nights that happen from time to time. (Those slow nights don't happen at all now, but it was a different time.)

So, there I was, with a co-worker in the emergency department of LRH on Christmas Eve. We were in a very deep discussion with the nurses and the on-duty doctor about such non-issue issues as how freaking cold it was this year, right up to and including what was wrong with the world. We all came to the agreement that either Santa needed to succeed in changing the hearts of men, or that God had the right idea with that whole flood thing - as long as we were allowed on the ark, and the flood should start as soon as it warmed up enough for the water to not turn to FREAKING ICE! I think I mentioned it was cold. While we were discussing these weighty issues, a security guard ran into the lounge and told us all to come quick, as there was a fellow freezing to death outside.

The guard led us out the south doors of the hospital, down the stairs to the sidewalk. There, next to a bus stop, we found a man who presented to be about 30 years old. He was sitting on the cold sidewalk, no coat on and his pants and underwear were around his ankles. His hands were on the sidewalk next to him, and he was trying to use them to lift himself off the sidewalk and propel him forward a few feet. The trail in the snow showed that this was how he had been moving for at least the last fifteen or twenty feet. I mentioned it was cold earlier, but to be specific, it was about -40 degrees Celsius, and had been for almost a full week. It was like living in a freezer. I mention this because parts of this guy's skin looked like meat that'd been in the freezer too long. My buddy and I scooped him up and carried him into the front doors of the hospital where a few nurses and a doctor were waiting with a wheelchair. We threw him into it and wheeled him as fast as possible to Emerg. When we got there, they had someone else get him on to an exam bed and we stood out of their way.

It was kind of a chaotic ballet, with each person assigned to a task that was beneficial or necessary with the goal of bringing this guy around. There was no doubt he was in trouble. He was unable to speak and looked like he was unconscious. They tried to get him to give them a name at first, but soon gave up when they saw he was not responding. At one point, I saw a nurse try to stick something into his rectum but heard a distinct "thunking" sound. It sounded like when you clap your hands, but instead of the palms striking each other, you curl your fingers in to the palms, and hit your knuckles together from the second knuckle down. An horrific sound, considering it was someone's body that was that frozen. He had no identification on him and was not even wearing a coat. The only thing my partner and I could think to do was to follow his tracks in the snow. The problem was some of the people living around the hospital had found the time that day to shovel their walks. With no fresh snow to leave tracks in, this seemed like a fool's errand. We kept trying though, sometimes following tracks, and sometimes guessing.

When we finally found his house, it was kind of a no-brainer. It was only a block away from the hospital, and more importantly, the door was wide open, with the lights all on and no one else around. When we went in, it was apparent that two men lived in the place, because of the pictures, and a few bills with either one man's name on it or another. We narrowed our patient down to two names, but still didn't know who he was. We guessed that the other roommate was out right now, possibly looking for the fellow in the hospital, or hadn't been there when he left. Either way, I left a note with my name, why we were there, and asked him to call the hospital or me at the station.

We went back to the hospital to tell what we had learned. They told us the guy we brought in was in pretty rough shape. Even if he did live, there were some significant life changes coming his way. They would have to remove a great deal of his dead and frozen muscle tissue around his buttocks and the back of his thighs. He may have to lose both hands, but the doctor told us that this was less likely, as they were getting some promising signs of blood flow there. Either way, the doc said his life had just changed. He asked if we found out any further information to bring it to them if we were able. We promised to do so and then went out and finished our shift.

We didn't find his friend that night. My buddy Drew found him the next day, about six or seven blocks east of where we had searched. The man had grown tired (most likely due to onset hypothermia), crawled under a fir tree, curled himself around the trunk, and froze to death. Detectives later learned from the guy who lived, that he was in a romantic relationship with the man who'd died. He said that they'd both been drinking a lot and began to argue over some petty little thing. Both decided to walk out on the other, one going east and the other west. Neither took their coats, and neither expected to be out more than a walk around the block. The survivor got to the front of the hospital and decided that he needed to urinate. He pulled his pants down, all the way to his ankles, and while he was relieving himself, and due to his intoxicated state, fell over and couldn't get back up. He saw how close he was to the hospital, so he began to crab walk and slide his butt cheeks along the sidewalk in hopes of making it to the doors before he froze to the concrete. He was heartbroken, and I don't blame him. The thing they argued about was so inconsequential it would've been a one-minute disagreement if the two were sober. He was scared about what would happen to him in the future, especially from a health perspective, but he was much more devastated for losing his husband. I couldn't imagine losing my wife in such an awful way, while knowing that the reason we argued, cost one life, and changed the other. It was all so senseless.

It was either that same Christmas season or the next year when a similar death occurred. (All these incidents seem to run together as the years go by.) It was about noon, and again, bitterly cold out when we received a call of a person kneeling in the parking lot of a hotel on the south side of the city. The person looked like they were praying, but not moving. When the caller went to check on the person, they found her dead. When I got there, I was sort of disgusted with my fellow human beings. This young girl was kneeling on the pavement of a hotel parking lot, with her forehead and nose right on the pavement. I get why people might be reluctant to interrupt or look to see if she was okay, except for the fact that it was so cold that anyone with their face on the pavement for longer than a few seconds must not be doing okay! As it turned out, she died like that, with her forehead and nose frozen to the pavement. She also had vomit coming out of her mouth which was frozen from inside her mouth, right to the pavement. She had to have been there a while for that to happen. We had to go into the hotel and ask them for a few pots full of hot water so we could thaw her forehead and nose enough to get it off the pavement. I find it hard to believe that no one saw this young girl in the parking lot all night long, and if they did see her, didn't check on her. That was a sad notification of next of kin. Even with all her problems with drugs and alcohol and other unknown demons, no one deserves to die that way.

Are you sensing a theme? We see a lot of crappy stuff and have to deal with it like it's part of a normal day. (It actually **is** a normal day for us.) It's no wonder that the majority of us have issues. I once investigated three sudden deaths in two days, and the last one was on Thanksgiving, at an extended care facility for the aged. That is quite a treat, watching the curious residents walking by the room to see who it was, and how it happened. All the while, the look in their eyes, as if asking themselves, "Am I next?" Parts of this job suck.

****

No one likes to go to the "check on the wellbeing" call. It often means there is a dead person within, and most likely they've been that way for a while, because people generally don't call the police to check on someone the first day they're worried. They tend to think it is a bother, or they are overreacting, so they wait and wait until they can no longer soothe their own conscience without some sort of action. That action is usually to call police, and often too late for us to help.

I wasn't there for this, but it encapsulates why we don't like going to these types of calls very much. This happened like 23 or 24 years ago, and we still tease them about it. Jordan and Alec roll up to this place, and they can't get anyone to answer the door. In situations like this, unless you hear someone calling for help (which has happened to all of us at least once), you can't just kick the door in. Usually a neighbour has a key, or you call a locksmith as a last resort. In this set of circumstances, the slimmer of the two (more like the junior guy, because Alec and Jordan were both slender) try to crawl through a window. When Jordan got in, he could smell an awful stench, and thought that the person they were looking for must be dead. He was new and hadn't yet experienced the smell of human remains that have been decomposing for days, weeks or months. There is nothing like it, and you can't mistake it for anything else. He got in and opened the door for his partner. They followed their noses and found an emaciated body of an elderly lady on the bed in her bedroom. She smelled of feces and she has clearly been there a while. When Jordan got on the radio to call it in, she opened her eyes, and croaked "What are you doing here?" It turns out that she had broken her hip and somehow climbed back into her bed, and then couldn't get out again. She had no phone and so lay there in her own excrement waiting to die, or someone to find her. Alec told me that Jordan's fingernails are still in the ceiling where he jumped up like a cat, clinging to the roof until Alec told him it was safe to come down. He also had to assure the old lady that all would be well. She heard him scream like a twelve-year-old schoolgirl and thought that something was wrong with him.

Sometimes, even though the situation sucks, we are able to save a person's life like Alec and Jordan did. Sometimes it is too late. When I think of that, I automatically think of a call I attended where the complainant was a thirteen-year-old girl. She was worried about her next-door neighbour who wasn't answering the door. She said the windows were all black, and even though she had a key, she was too scared to go in, so she called us.

S o, there I was, rolling up to the house on the north side of the city that the young girl had identified as her neighbour's. The kid was waiting out on the front sidewalk, and she told me her neighbour was an older lady from the old country (she didn't know which old country), who drank a lot. She hired my complainant to come over every couple days and do her dishes and laundry and sometimes just sit and talk with her. The kid told me she went over to check on her and do the dishes (and pick up all the empty vodka bottles that were left around all the time) but no one answered the door. She also noticed the windows were all black, but on the inside. I had seen the movie "Backdraft" and immediately got a little nervous. I went to the front window and sure enough, it looked like soot on the inside of the windows. The window was not hot to the touch, but I wasn't gonna open that door. I called Fire HQ to attend, and when they got there, they immediately told me to take the kid farther back, confirming my suspicion.

I saw the fire guys break out a window at the side of the house, but nothing happened. The glass did have soot on the inside of it. They went in and then called me a short time later and told me that it was safe to come in. It turns out, this older lady had accidently started a fire in her living room, by dropping some sort of open flame or burning cigarette into an area that was saturated with high proof alcohol. The fire went on for a while, until it ran out of oxygen. (This old north side house was solidly built.) The old lady was obviously dead, and it looked to be accidental. The cause of the fire would determine a lot. If the fire was accidental, then it was likely that the death was as well, but if it was set on purpose, it was an insurance fraud gone wrong at the very least, right up to suicide, or even possibly a murder. Murderers tend to not have moral qualms about trying to burn the evidence of their crime. Either way, I had to pass this off to CID.

When I talked to the little kid, I went out of my way to praise her, in front of her parents who were unaware of the arrangement she had with the old lady and were not as impressed with the situation as they might have been. That kid was smart enough to call us rather than try the door or find a parent to get permission to call. It is a possibility that she, or her parents would have seen a backdraft explosion up close and personal if they'd tried to check it out themselves. The other thing my boss and the detective were quite pleased with was the statement I'd taken from the kid. It was one of those things you hear the kid say that doesn't really mean anything at the time, but then becomes important later on.

When I asked the young girl why she was over there to help so often, she told me the old lady was in pretty rough shape and had no family to help her. Bad enough, that sometimes she couldn't walk, so she would scoot around in a sitting position on the floor, using her hands and feet to propel her. She was often in night clothes and gave herself rug burns on the back of her legs and buttocks. I added this to the statement just for the sake of being thorough. It turns out that this was quite important. The ME was concerned with the scar tissue and repeated rug burns she found on the deceased that could not be explained. When the detective read the statement I'd taken from the girl to the ME, they realized that this was an accidental death. Without that small tid-bit, those poor detectives would have had to expend a lot of energy, possibly thinking that this woman had been dragged around in her house prior to it burning down. I learned a valuable lesson from that. No matter how seemingly inconsequential something is, it might be that small detail that points you in the right direction and gets to the truth. Even if it doesn't seem to matter now, it might later. Something I tell every young copper who starts out on the job. Be curious about everything. Never take anything at face value.

SUICIDE AND AN UNLIKELY HERO

I'm a firm believer that almost everything we do has unintended consequences. Negative consequences are going to happen to us all from time to time. We're all imperfect beings and make mistakes. We just have to keep the number of screw-ups to a minimum. We have an opportunity to make up for our mistakes by doing as much good as possible, all in hopes of keeping that cosmic balance sheet in the black. I often tell this story to younger members of the service to make a point. It is a perfect example of doing something good without worrying about getting something back as a result, and then seeing a serendipitous return on that investment. I should tell you all of my co-workers have done things like this (and often on a much larger scale) without expectation of a return. We deal with so much human indignity and pain that we would be inhuman or dead inside if we didn't try to help out from time to time.

So, there I was, working a quiet Sunday morning shift. I'd started at 7 o'clock in the morning, and as usual on dayshifts, I was running a bit behind while getting ready for work, so I ended up going without breakfast. After shift briefing, and checking out my equipment, I hit the road and went through a drive-thru as soon as I was able. It was a sleepy Sunday so there were no calls waiting, giving me time to get my Croissandwich and eat it while driving around. (That is something a copper gets good at, eating while driving.) After my first sandwich, I was full. I started looking for an alley where I could find a garbage can and throw the second sandwich out when I saw an opportunity.

As I was driving past the park in the downtown core, I saw the shuttle bus from the correctional center had just dropped off the prisoners who had been released from custody, most having spent the night in the drunk tank. This was still back in the day when there were hardly any hard drug related problems on the streets. The majority of those with addiction problems were alcohol related. Over the course of a day, we would find people who were intoxicated and causing problems, and lodge them at the correctional centre until they were sober. There was often no charge laid, rather a prevention of the continued breach of the peace. When sober, and therefore less likely to continue the behaviour they had been arrested for in the first place, the person was brought back into the city by a shuttle van provided by the correctional centre, where they were dropped off at a central place.

These were relatively sober people (now) who'd spent the night in the drunk tank. They were heading their separate ways from the park. As I drove up to the intersection of 5th Street and 5th Avenue South, I had the green light, but a guy who I immediately recognized as Albert was walking against the light in the crosswalk. He stepped out right in front of me, causing me to stop. I thought for a minute about giving him grief, or even a ticket for walking against the light, but then I looked at him a little closer. I'm not sure he even saw my marked PC coming toward him, or if he would have cared if I ran him over. He had no coat on, and even though it wasn't that cold out, he was shivering quite a bit. It couldn't be just the cold he was having a hard time with, so instead of jacking him up, I let him pass. I then pulled up beside him in the middle of the road and rolled my window down.

"Hey Albert, you alright?" I asked.

"Ya boss, just a rough night. I need a drink" he responded.

I asked him when the last time he'd eaten, and he actually stopped and thought for a minute, and then said, "Thursday or Friday, I guess." I decided I was gonna throw my sandwich out anyway, so I offered it to him. At first, I am sure he thought I was screwing with him, because he gave me that look. I told him I had just eaten one and showed him the empty wrapper. I said that I just didn't want the other one and was going to throw it out if he didn't want it. He thanked me and ate it in three bites, still standing in the crosswalk on 5th Street South. I told him he needed to get off the street, and then said I would see him later (no doubt, I probably would) and drove off. He didn't say thank you, but his mouth was full, and I could tell he appreciated it. My good deed for the day was done, and I didn't think about it again for months, until we started looking for Albert when he tried to kill a guy named Rory.

Rory was a pretty big man, standing at least 6'4" and was about 250lbs if he was an ounce. I'd never had to arrest him for anything. He drank a lot but even when he was drinking, he was very respectful with the police, and didn't mean anyone any harm that I knew about. I'd heard a rumor that he was so strong he'd once lifted an engine block out of the box of a half ton truck, but I find that hard to believe. He was a big, strong man though, and people must have talked about his feats of strength for a reason. Rory was also very skilled with the ladies. He was a good talker, as long as he wasn't too drunk, and was always in the company of a young lady, and many times not his wife. Sometimes it was the wife of another man, and that's where he and poor Albert's paths crossed.

Albert had a common law spouse named Sharon. She had a wandering eye, especially when she'd been drinking. Unfortunately for Rory and Albert, that was just about every day. She was usually in the Bridge Inn, and from time to time, she even offered a romantic liaison with someone if they were willing to pay her. (She sometimes had a greater thirst than her purse could pay for.) When she was with Rory, she didn't charge him, and he was nice enough to buy her a drink every time he had one. That was good enough for her and I had no doubt she probably showed her thanks regarding his generosity in a physical way on occasion. What Albert didn't know wouldn't hurt him. The problem was that Albert found out, and he was a jealous man. He was also a chronic repeat offender when it came to domestic violence. He often smacked Sharon around (sometimes worse) when he found out she'd been unfaithful, and then often went looking for the other fella who had shared her affections.

Rumour had it Albert beat on Sharon pretty badly when he found out she'd been with Rory. He decided that this was an indignity he could not abide, stole a pitching wedge (golf club) from the back of a truck that he happened upon in the downtown core, and went looking for Rory. He went into every bar in the downtown core, pronouncing loudly upon entry that he intended to kill Rory for his perfidy as soon as he could find him. He did this whilst waving a graphite shaft pitching wedge in his hand and threatening those around him who might try to disarm him.

Albert had almost exhausted his search, arriving at the last bar in the downtown area, the Alec Arms. He went in the side door with club in hand, announcing his goal to all those who would listen. Unfortunately, Rory had just left through the other door to the same establishment, and some drunk in the place, probably for shear entertainment value, gave Rory up to the now very drunk, and still very angry Albert. He went outside and found

Rory waiting for a cab on the corner of 5th Street and 4th Avenue South. (A block south of where I'd given him the sandwich months before.) He confronted Rory about his lecherous ways showing more anger and poor judgement than a small man should. It was at that point Rory made a tactical error. He laughed at the very drunk, and considerably smaller Albert, and turned his back on him to get in to the cab that was rolling up. Albert saw his chance and swung the club.

Now, I've never played golf in my life, but I'm told that it's very difficult to break a graphite shaft on a golf club. Some have even told me that the feat is impossible, but I've seen it. If one very angry drunk hits another in the back of the head, hard enough and at just the right angle, not only does the shaft break, but so does the skull of the intended target. I was the first to respond to the call, and found Rory lying on the sidewalk in front of the Alec Arms with blood all over the sidewalk and a hole in the back of his head that you could park my car in. He was breathing and his heart appeared to be strong, so I waited for paramedics, called my sergeant, and started talking to members of the crowd to learn what had happened.

The clientele of the Alec Arms were not likely to help the police on a regular basis, but the victim was a guy everyone liked, so there was soon a glut of people willing to provide statements. They were even surprisingly similar enough to be believable. I was shocked. When my boss got there, he told me he'd already called for our CID detectives to come and assume the file but assigned me to go to the hospital in the ambulance with the victim. I told him what I'd learned so far, then hopped into the ambulance with the medics and we were off to LRH. Usually one of us goes in the rig with the victim to see if he will say anything about what happened, or to record any dying declaration the victim might make before passing from this life to the next. (My partner worked a murder years later when I was in the Violent Crimes Unit, where a woman gave over ten dying declarations to different people about the fact that her daughter had stabbed her in the chest, before she died on the operating table. That was a pretty easy murder to solve even though it was heartbreaking.) There was no declaration from this victim, because Rory was unconscious all the way to Emerg.

He stayed that way for his assessment in Emerg and the trip to Medical Imaging for the CAT scan, where I got to follow and see the test as it occurred. The guy doing the test even explained it to me as it went along - it was the coolest thing, considering it was taking pictures inside Rory's melon. There was even a really cool, but shocking picture of the perfect shape of where the pitching wedge had gone into the base of his skull, with bone exploding inward. That is when Rory had his first seizure, right in the middle of the CAT scan, and things got serious. (As if they weren't already.) It turns out Rory came very close to dying and was never the same again. He was partially paralyzed on the left side of his body and needed a cane to walk for the remaining 15 years of his life.

While I was at the hospital, the detective assigned to the case gave me a call. I told him what was going on, and the condition Rory was in. He told me they had obtained statements from people at the Alec Arms about what happened, but also from a couple people from every bar in town that said the same thing. The hunt was on for Albert, and the charge was attempted murder. My boss let me work with the detective, because it was originally my call. Patrol guys are usually along for the ride just to hold the coat of the BCD (Big City Detective), but in doing so, they get to see how one of these files is worked and gain experience for the time when they become the BCD and work the big case. Kent was an excellent teacher. I also learned a bit of humility and about using the right tool for the job, but I am coming to that part.

So, we went on the hunt for Albert and learned he was holed up at a friend's house on the west side of the city. (I discovered the value of Confidential Informants from that.) We went to arrest Albert and took him into custody without incident. Well there was one incident. As soon as we got the bracelets on him, and Kent read him his rights, Albert said "I won't say S#%@ to you, but I will talk to him", pointing at me with his chin because his hands were behind his back in cuffs. It turns out he was willing to tell me his entire story, incriminate himself in an attempted murder, because I'd given him a free sandwich three or four months earlier. When we got to the station, I told Kent the story. I sat in for part of the interview with Albert until he got comfortable enough with Kent that I could leave the room and go watch the rest of it on the monitor. It was one of the coolest experiences of my young career and re-affirmed that this was what I wanted to do eventually; to take on investigations like this. At the end of the investigation, Kent told me how important giving Albert that sandwich was. It is just happenstance that Albert was the accused, but even if he was just a witness, treating him well might be the difference of getting that key piece of information needed to put the whole investigation together. It was an important and formative investigation in my career. I later went on to work in CID on two separate occasions and had the opportunity to work from million-dollar frauds right up to and including murder investigations. I learned a lot from Kent and others like him and loved that part of the job.

****

Before the Columbine School shooting in 1999, police didn't think as much about mass casualty incidents or how to respond to them as we have to now. I think there was (and may still be) a certain hubris that Canadians have, thinking that those problems are distinctly American. They are not. Eight days after Columbine, there was a school shooting in Taber, Alberta. Taber is only about 50 kilometers east of Lethbridge. When a call comes in that sounds like a mass shooting or a mass casualty event, there is already a certain pucker factor. Consider how bad it was for those of us responding to a mass casualty event prior to those two formative incidents in policing. No one thought to train us for that sort of thing, other than cordon it off and call the Tactical Unit. That is, until after Columbine.

So, there I was, responding to a "shots fired" complaint at the Lethbridge Regional Hospital. Our dispatcher had taken a call from a nurse at the Emerg department who reported that she was hiding under the table in the nurse's lounge and had heard three gun shots. From a cop's perspective, one shot might be a crazy person going up there to kill themselves. Three rounds expended had to mean something much more ominous. I kicked my Crown Vic into light speed while hoping for more information on the radio. As I mentioned in one of the previous chapters, we used to spend a lot of time in that nurse's lounge chatting with the nurses and doctors - they were our friends. Some of them were even spouses of my co-workers. (That old saying about cops and nurses.) Then the call got worse. Dispatch identified the complainant (the nurse hiding under the table) as a cop's wife. She was the spouse of Reggie, the copper who helped me with the old person domestic where he was shooting into the door after stabbing her and her husband. Reggie also happened to be working that day, and I later learned he ignored his boss and came up to the hospital against orders. Luckily, we'd already dealt with the matter, but I am getting ahead of myself.

I pulled up near the Emerg entrance, without lights and sirens on to prevent any bad guy from hearing my approach. Bobby, the acting sergeant had arrived moments ahead of me but was waiting for me to go in the door with him. You never do this sort of thing alone. On the way there, I'd been thinking about what we'd be doing when I got there, realizing we could not surround the hospital and wait for the tactical unit. We had to go in. Then I started doing "what if" scenarios in my mind. The hostage scenario was the most troublesome, and especially scary considering the identity of the caller. It would be me and Bobby, going in with guns drawn, hoping we could keep a lid on the situation without the loss of life (and fervently hoping that there hadn't been any yet). These situations were scary enough without knowing the people who were in jeopardy.

Security for the hospital approached us and waved us into the ward itself, saying it was safe until we got past the door leading into Emerg. They told us that it was a lone gunman with a revolver of unknown calibre. No rounds had been fired at them, but they had heard four come from inside the ward itself. They hadn't seen the gun in the man's hand but pieced it together from those that got a chance to leave Emerg when the guy came in. They had no weapons and couldn't be expected to deal with this sort of thing. They were there to prevent the occasional drunk from wandering into the path of a physician or to enforce visiting hours or keep tabs on a person waiting for a bed in the psych unit.

Bobby and I went in together, guns out and clearing each corridor slowly as we went, cutting a "piece of the pie" of each room we came to until we knew that they were clear. The halls were empty, but there was no sign of shots being fired or any blood on the walls or floor. The Emergency Department was set up somewhat like jail units without the lockdown ability. There was a central island where the staff worked and had their phones, monitors, and computers. Radiating out to three sides from that hub, there were curtained off areas that form the "rooms" where the patients were treated. When the curtains were drawn back to the walls, it was a semi-circular room surrounding the staff work area. When they were pulled forward, the area was segmented off into many small rooms with a central area connecting them all. Off to one side there were also two "hard" rooms, or rooms that have walls and a door. These were where the psychiatric patients go for physician assessment in private. It was also easier to restrain and hold them there if necessary.

When we entered this area, we found no one there, not even patients. We had to clear each small enclosure one by one. By now there were more police members on scene, so it went quickly. Bobby and I were there first, so we were leading the search. We soon cleared all but the two psyche rooms without encountering anyone. These were more difficult. They came off a narrow hallway and were problematic to clear without giving up cover. I was about to slowly go past the first door with as wide an arc as I could allowing me to gradually see what was inside, when one of the other guys saw a video camera on the roof at the entrance to the rooms.

He came back a few moments later and told us he could see everything in the room from the camera. He said that there was a lone male, lying on the floor with a pool of dark liquid underneath him that looked like blood. The second room was empty. Bobby decided to clear this last room slowly as well. The guy was probably dead, but we were incredibly careful about betting our lives on something that we couldn't confirm.

We cleared the last two rooms and found what we were looking for. Lying in a large pool of blood was a lone male, with a .357 Magnum on the ground next to his lifeless hand. From what was left of the back of his head, it was obvious he had placed the barrel in his mouth and pulled the trigger. Then I paused when I saw the dead man's face. "That's Tim!" I said, immediately recognizing the man. I'd been to his house for supper. His wife and mine were close friends. My wife and I were the godparents to their two children. His younger brother was a cop in the neighbouring agency to our east. I suddenly thought about his wife and their two children, fervently praying they were alright, and that Tim had just decided to end his own life and not take anyone else with him.

As these thoughts were going through my mind, Dr. Joel approached us. He told us Tim had come into the ER in an agitated state, brandishing the weapon and saying he needed help. Dr. Joel explained how he took him into the room we had found him in and asked him what he could do for him, as if Tim was suffering from a cold. It was with awe that I realized this small, balding, soft-spoken man was one of the bravest I'd ever met. I go to work with a 9 mm and 46 rounds, a Kevlar vest, and assorted other offensive and defensive weapons. This man had nothing other than his voice and a stethoscope on him and he purposefully took Tim, an armed, psychotic man, into a room so the other doctors and nurses could evacuate the ER. He'd given himself up as a hostage for the safety of all the others in the ward. To this day, I can think of nothing braver or more loving than what Joel did, not just for those he worked with and the patients he cared for, but for Tim as well. He is still truly one of my heroes.

Dr Joel went on as if what he had done was no big deal. He said that Tim had simply told him he planned on taking his own life. He then extracted a promise from the doctor that there would be no attempts to resuscitate him once the deed had been done. Joel then asked Tim if he wanted to be alone while he did this or if he needed him to stay behind. Tim said "No, you can leave", and Joel did so. As he was walking down the corridor out of the ER, he heard three shots, one right after another. (What must have gone through his mind when he heard those gunshots, and how close he had just come to meeting his maker!) There was a pause and then a fourth and final shot rang out. (We later found that Tim had fired three rounds into the ceiling before getting up the nerve to put the fourth one into his head).

By this time, there was sheer bedlam. Reggie had been reunited with his wife, the nurse who had originally called us. There were tears shed and hugs exchanged. Most of us went back to work. After asking me about a hundred times if I was alright to continue because of my friendship with Tim, I was assigned to go do notification to his wife. His brother had already been notified by the Chief of Police in the neighbouring jurisdiction where he worked. It was with a considerable degree of trepidation that I went to Tim's family home. Tim's wife Dana and my wife were best friends. We'd gone to supper at their house on countless occasions. I knew they'd been having problems because of Tim's diagnosed mental health issues but was unsure why this had happened after being married for over fifteen years. They had been high school sweethearts and had two great kids.

As I pulled up, I saw Dana sitting on her front porch with a lost look on her face. She was holding a notebook in her hand that I later found to be a twenty-one page suicide note. As soon as she saw the police car, she realized what I was there for, but then recognized me. She ran to me, hugged me, and kept telling me that she was sorry. Although she had been living with Tim's mental illness for so many years, her first thoughts were of me and the fact that I had to be the one to find him.

I sat her down and told her what had happened and then asked her if there was anything I could do for her. No matter how hard you try to do your job and be detached from it, when the person in front of you is a person you know, the job is so much more difficult. We cried together and then I asked her if she wanted me to help explain it to the kids. Thankfully, she said she would have family do that with her. (Although I don't consider myself a coward, I sure felt like one when I felt relief in not having to explain to their six-year-old son and three-year-old daughter why their father wasn't coming home).

Dana eventually remarried and moved to the United States with her kids. It took me a while to get past the difficult time of seeing someone I knew lying in a pool of his own blood, the back of his head splattered all over the wall of a room. I'm thankful now that I was the one who spoke to Dana. Even though I didn't look forward to it at the time, I'm glad I could help my friend through such a difficult time. There are many things about this that bother me, and it's a brick I have had to carry around in the backpack God gave us, but it could have been much worse.

Our society teaches us men don't cry, especially big tough cops. I am certainly thankful I've never believed that. We see situations like this in our line of work. They leach away at the soul, especially if you don't find a way to cleanse yourself from time to time. One of those ways is through your faith or talking them through with a spouse, trusted friend, co-worker, or counsellor. It's no wonder that alcoholism and other personal problems are so prevalent in the police culture and PTSD is so under diagnosed. What we do is tough, and we tend to think that getting help is not something a "tough guy" does. Times are changing though. I look back on this and still hold on to what Dr Joel did and thank the Lord above for men like him. Talk about a hero! That small statured giant, with nothing but a desire to help the sick and afflicted, put his life on the line, not only to help possible victims who might be in the path of a person with a gun, but also help the guy with the gun! He restores my faith in mankind.

A KNIFE TO THE HEAD AND A LONG FALL

In the mid to late 90's the Lethbridge Police Service started to grow. When I started in 1988, we had just under 90 coppers, and right now our authorized strength is almost double that, at just over 170. The city was growing, and the service needed to keep up to meet those needs. We started having recruit classes that were larger than they'd been in the past. They had to scrape the bottom of the barrel for Field Training Officers as a result. That is where I came in. When they got to the bottom of the barrel, there I was.

The probationary process had changed a great deal from the time I got hired to the time I trained my first recruit nine years later. When I was hired, there was no in-house training other than a familiarization with the pistol they issued. They relied entirely on what the college taught. These new recruits who were coming to us all had college degrees but were also spending time in an in-house training period, prior to getting out on the road with their FTO's. These young people had a minimum 2-year associate degree from a college, or previous police experience. They then went through an in-house course that was three months prior to hitting the street with their FTO. I won't go through the requirements of that training, but suffice it to say, they were better trained before hitting the road than I'd been.

My first partner (I don't like the rookie word; it seems demeaning to me.) was a young guy named Chase. He was the same age I was when I got hired. He was engaged to be married, and a religious guy to boot. We were cookie cutters of each other at the time, other than the fact I was way handsomer than he was. What he gave up in looks he more than made up for in smarts. Soon *he* was training *me* in some things. (In fairness, he was also better looking than me. I just didn't want him to think he had me beat in every category if he reads this.) We got along very well, and he became really good, really fast. Soon, Chase was doing most of the talking (when I learned to shut my mouth and let him do his job, which was more difficult than I thought it would be), as well as most of the writing. I almost felt guilty sitting in the passenger seat and letting him do all the work. Almost. He was on his own soon enough, and I was back to having to do my own work.

The only really "good" story I can remember while working with Chase was responding to a sudden death on the side of a highway leading out of town. The lone occupant pulled over for a sleep at the side of the road before continuing his journey. He fell asleep in his parked, running car, and accidently killed himself with carbon monoxide. The car was very old, and it was cold outside. The exhaust leaked, as did the floor boards, and carbon monoxide accumulated inside the car until there was enough to kill him. I have never seen anything like it before or since. (The accidental thing, not the gassing thing. I have seen lots of those.)

The reason I remember it was because when we were leaving the scene, I saw that the Forensic Ident guy was trying to take a candid picture of us as we left in our patrol car. I had previously informed Chase that Ident members were not to be trusted. Never let them take your picture. (I love them but know exactly what they would do with my picture. There is a great morphed photo floating around somewhere with my face on Yoda's body.) I leaned over from the passenger seat and politely gave the Ident guy the finger with a big smile on my face. Later that same year, my wife added that picture to the photo album we prepared to give to a potential birth mother as we went through the adoption process. He had snapped the picture just before I gave him the finger, so it looked like I was waving, and we both had stupid grins on our faces. My wife loved the picture, and I didn't have the heart to tell her there was a dead guy in a car, not fifteen feet behind the photographer, and he almost got the finger instead of a wave. I guess the cat is out of the bag now. The photo album worked so well that the birth mother picked my wife and I, and we adopted our son that December.

I really enjoyed training, mostly because I liked having a partner in the car. I've since trained nine recruits as a primary trainer, and almost all of them have been awesome experiences. (At least for me they were.) Each one of the nine I trained during those years taught me a few new things that I used from that point on. Chase taught me the importance of staying calm and communicating clearly. I learned to keep my temper in check with the public from his example. (He was way better at that than I was.) That experience with Chase was also a step along the way to my eventual desire to become a Crisis Negotiator. Shortly after Chase was on his own, I was dispatched to what was originally a domestic dispute and turned in to an attempted murder-suicide. He thought he killed her, then killed himself.

So, there I was, on my way to a domestic in progress, like I'd been a hundred times before. I rolled up and was about to stop a door or two down from the dispatched address to wait for my back-up, when I noticed something that immediately drew my attention and caused me to go right to the house without waiting. It was the middle of the summer it was quite warm out. There was a girl, sitting on the step with a nine-inch bread knife stuck in her forehead. She was holding the blade of the knife in her right hand as it protruded from her head while talking to herself as she rocked back and forth. Blood was dripping down her face and onto her jeans and pooling on the porch. As I walked up to her and she looked at me, still holding onto the knife sticking out of her head (either out of shock or an attempt to keep it from moving) she said "That Bart is an asshole. He's raisin' hell in my house, and I want him out." She didn't shout or scream. It was so matter of fact and even-toned that it would have been comical, save for the knife sticking out of her forehead, waving like a diving board after someone had jumped off into the deep end.

I called my back up and told them to expedite, then asked dispatch for an ambulance and told them what was happening. I asked the woman if she knew who'd done this to her and where they went. She told me she had become embroiled in an argument with her husband that escalated until they started to hit each other. There were four other people at their house at the time, and they'd all witnessed it. As I was sitting there trying to keep her calm and get more information, those four other witnesses came out and started to give their perspective of what had occurred, talking over each other in their varied states of intoxication. I noticed that there was a 15 or 16-year-old kid who had some blood on the side of his shirt. It wasn't until I pointed this out that he checked and found he had three stab wounds on the right side of his rib cage.

My backup arrived, along with the rest of the cavalry, and we began to sort the scene out. The victim identified her assailant and told us he'd fled on foot. Our K-9 officer immediately began the process of tracking our bad guy as I started to sort out what happened until my boss showed up. My sergeant and I then searched the entire house, even though all the witnesses told us he'd fled, and the stabbing happened outside. After searching the house, my boss told me to keep at the file, but he would try to get CID to come out and take over. I began to take statements from the witnesses who hadn't been injured and learned that Bart, the victim's common law spouse, had indeed been responsible for both stabbings. It turns out that Bart and our female victim were in a domestic relationship and had been for many years. It had always been a tempestuous relationship, and each had been charged in times past with assaulting the other, but they just couldn't seem to move on. It was clearly true love. That is until our female victim thought she had fallen in love with someone else; the young 16-year-old boy who'd been stabbed in the side. (I've learned over the years that love is not only a "many-splendored thing," but it is also blind, and sometimes just plain stupid.)

Bart came home to find a party going on with his wife and five young people in the house, in varying states of intoxication, and his wife of eight or nine years in flagrante delicto with the 16-year-old. Bart became understandably angry but didn't get physical. He pulled the kid off his wife, and then started to yell and scream in rage at the lot of them. So much so, that they all decided to leave and go somewhere else where they could continue the party. It was fortuitous that Bart had come home, because now she had someone to take care of the child they shared, while she left with the child she was sleeping with.

The group of five left the residence and got into a half-ton truck belonging to one of the witnesses. Obviously with five people and one truck, there wasn't a lot of room, and so there were a few people sitting on other people's laps. Our female victim was sitting closest to the passenger door, window down, with her new beau sitting on her lap, when Bart came out of the house with a black handled 9-inch bread cutting knife. All the witnesses agreed that Bart didn't say a thing as he started swinging the knife. He shanked her young paramour in the right side of his chest and ribs, through the open passenger window. At that point, the kid dove across the seat toward the driver of the vehicle. The female victim didn't see her new love being stabbed but saw and felt him dive toward the driver and by instinct, looked toward the open window to see what he was trying to get away from. Bart then stabbed down with all of his strength and stabbed her squarely in the forehead. He hit so hard in fact, that the tip of the blade bent upon entry, causing little but superficial damage to our girl. (None of us knew that at the time. The doctor informed us the extent of the injuries, hours later.) Although appearing gruesome and bloody as all get out, the bent blade merely stopped as it went through the bone, thus saving any real damage to the frontal lobe of her brain.

She thought that she may have lost consciousness for a second, because when she looked up again, Bart was gone. The other witnesses gave us a direction and area he was last seen so our K-9 officer could do his magic. After we searched the house, we went to business, taking more statements. I was almost finished taking a statement from the soberest, most coherent person there (a relative term, I assure you,) when they said, "You know, there is a back door to the place, right?"

It was like one of those "Oops" moments that just struck me. We had to search the house again. I called my sergeant over and we went through the residence again. When we went to go down the stairs into the undeveloped basement, my boss and I both noticed at the same time that the light to the basement had been on when we checked it the first time, but now it was off. I looked at him as if to ask if he had turned it out when we left. He read my mind and shook his head in the negative. I knew I hadn't turned it out either. Going down those stairs was a hard thing to do, but we both took solace in the fact that we'd asked earlier if there were any guns in the house and been told there were not. If Bart was down here and tried to hurt one of us, at least he was probably bringing a knife to a gun fight.

I headed down the stairs first announcing that we were the police and to come out. When no one answered, I went down the stairs slowly. The problem with those stairs was the wall at the base of the stair formed a T intersection, opening into large undeveloped rooms on both sides. When you are clearing a room, you do what we call "cutting a piece of the pie," meaning gradually and from a distance, move to the side so that you can see into the room you are about to enter. My problem was that I had to do this to both the left and the right of the doorway. As I went down the stairway, I would stop on each stair and move slowly to the far side of that step to see inside the room that I was going to for anything concerning. I was almost at the bottom stair when I saw a white running shoe pointed away from me, looking like the person wearing it was on his tip toes. I came up on target and shouted out "City police, show me your hands!"

I went down to the next step and could see better and saw that the person standing there was un-able to show me his hands. They were fairly visible, as was the noose that he had tied around his neck with an electrical cord and hung himself from a floor brace on the undeveloped ceiling. He could have stopped his death at any time by just getting back all the way up on his tip toes. He would have probably been able to undo the knot. He was clearly committed, because he died there in the basement, hanging from an electrical cord, after thinking he'd stabbed and killed his cheating wife and her young lover.

The good news about this whole sordid tale was no loose ends. It wasn't a "who done it" and there would be no criminal charges laid. The stabber was dead, and the one stabee was old enough to consent to having sex with the other stabee. (Age of consent in those days was fourteen years old.) The young kid's stab wounds were relatively superficial and were sewed up by doctors who first ensured that there was no internal damage. Apparently, his diving across the seat away from Bart as he swung the knife probably saved his life. As for Bart's wife, the big thick bone in her forehead saved her. There was no permanent injury to her that a few stitches to her forehead wouldn't fix. There were a few funny things (at least funny in the eyes of a cop) that happened as a result of this sordid tale.

When I talked to the Ident guy, he told me that after the doctor was sure there would be no lasting injury to her, he tried to get the knife out of her head, but it took quite a bit of work. I am led to believe there might be a clandestine photo taken of the doctor with his knees braced at the head of the examination bed, both hands wrapped around the handle of the knife and tugging for all he was worth, trying to get the knife out of the head of our very intoxicated victim, moaning "ow" every time he tugged. The other is when they cut Bart down, I discovered that Chase, my former partner, and now full fledged investigator in his own right, had a weak stomach or struggled with offensive smells as bad as I do. Chase was asked by the Ident guy to hold Bart up so he could cut the electrical cord and get him down. As Chase lifted the man up, wrapping his arms around the body below the hips, the bowels of the deceased's body evacuated (or had already, and no one noticed until they went to move him.) As Chase was holding the body up so the Ident guy could cut him down, he was dry heaving as bad as I would've been, but it was him, not me. A passing of the torch, or changing of the guard, so to speak. It's always good to see the new generation stepping up and taking over duties that you would have been stuck with less than a decade earlier.

****

During any given day, a cop may be required to deal with, and hopefully solve a wide variety of problems. Each situation is different just like the person involved. What works to resolve one issue, might not for something similar because of the human factor. During a single call for service, a cop might have to become a social worker, a marriage counsellor, priest, psychiatrist, or any number of other vocations to get the job done. It's one of the reasons why the job is so difficult but at the same time, why most of us do it. It is a challenge, and never the same thing twice. One of the most difficult and potentially dangerous situations that we deal with concerns people that have mental health problems that are bent on killing themselves. Some can be talked out of it with the right words sprinkled with real compassion. Some even want you to do for them, what they can't do for themselves. For some, there is simply nothing you can say or do to prevent it. It is important to remember that sometimes people mean it when they say that they want to die, and for those few, you can't say or do anything to prevent their death. At that point, a cop is then stuck figuratively (and sometimes literally) cleaning up the mess.

Although there is nothing that could have been done to stop this next incident, and it had a very graphic ending, it was also one of the reasons why I started down the path to becoming a Crisis Negotiator. One of my buddies was the negotiator for this call, and it didn't end well, through no fault of his or his partner's actions. They tried to save a man for something like four hours, and continued trying, right up until the moment they witnessed him take his own life. There are some people that are "closure motivated" and no amount of talking is going to get them to see reason.

There is a train bridge here in Lethbridge that is still the longest, tallest train bridge of its kind in the world. The bridge spans the Old Man River and is 1.6 kilometers across and 93 meters in height. It is one of the landmarks of the city. If you spend any time here at all, you can't help but see it. Because it is so large, obvious, and in-your-face, it also has become a siren's call to those in the area who are thinking about ending it all. Get on that bridge, take one small step and there is very little doubt about the outcome. Over the years as a crisis negotiator, I've spoken with many people up there who wanted to kill themselves, some of which came to Lethbridge specifically to do so, using that bridge. Almost every member of our service has had to get dispatch to call and have the oncoming train stopped while they go out on to the bridge and try to talk some poor lost soul out of ending it all by jumping to his or her death. When it looks like it will take more than a few minutes, they call a negotiator to come and do the talking.

When you walk out there, you can see down between the railroad ties to the river valley below. There's one side of the tracks on the bridge that has a place that you can crouch down if a train happens along, giving you about a foot or so of clearance between the side of the bridge and the moving train. (I've never been up there when a train goes by, but apparently the bridge is supposed to sway side to side at least a few inches. That is a lot of metal moving by the force and weight of the train.) On the other side of the tracks, there's nothing to stand on. There is nothing between the ties and the chest high steel I-beam. When people jump, it is usually through this opening, so they don't even have to climb to the top of the I-beam. You just step out into space between the ties and down you go. Underneath the bridge deck itself, there are crossed beams of steel leading down to the ground. That brings us to the crux of our story.

My buddy Jim had been a negotiator for a couple of years when he was called to the bridge to talk someone down. If you spend any time in the Negotiator Unit in Lethbridge, you end up getting a lot of these calls, so they become sort of vanilla. This one was different. The way Jim described it to me made my skin crawl just to talk about it, let alone be out there, trying to convince the guy to accept our help. The suicidal man had climbed down from the bridge deck, to the crossed "I" beams underneath. He was only a few feet below the train tracks, but about 275 feet from the ground. He would hang there on the strength of his hand grip alone. When his hands and arms tired, he would pull himself back up on to the relative shelter of the beam, using his arm strength alone, resting on his forearms and elbows. What made it worse was the fact the guy refused to talk. He wouldn't even tell Jim his name. To bring a person in crisis to a point where he can see this, and then seek help to change the behaviour, requires some sort of communication. It can be a one sided conversation for a while, but eventually the other person has to participate, or it will be an exceptionally long (or short) negotiation, with a relatively predictable outcome.

This guy didn't say a word for just under four hours, in the baking sun. He would hang from the steel cross beams for as long as his hands would allow, nothing but air and river bottom beneath him, then climb back up to the cross beam and sit there, staring down at the valley below, not acknowledging that the police were even there, let alone talking to them. Even when the man would only hang on by his fingers, Jim would talk to him as calmly as he could, trying to convince him that life was still worth living.

Of course, the inevitable eventually happened. The man who still hadn't even given Jim his name, hung down from the beam one last time, using only his fingers to keep from falling. This time however, muscle fatigue had set in, and the man tried to climb back onto the beam but couldn't. His efforts to save himself became more and more laboured until he started to lose his hand grip. Jim told me that he wanted to reach down himself and give the guy a hand, but it was too dangerous. One of the tenets they teach you as a negotiator is that they may go, but you should never put yourself in a position, either mentally or physically where they can take you with them. It was this guy's choice to be in that situation. It's just foolhardy to try and do something where the probable outcome is *both* of you dying. The last four hours, Jim had put his life in jeopardy to save this guy. He could not have done anything else. Just before he fell, he looked my friend Jim in the eye and said, "I don't want to die." The only words he had uttered all afternoon. The drop is so long that the Forensic Ident copper at the scene took 9 photographs of him falling with an auto-wind camera before he hit the ground. (Count that out in your head! That is a long fall.)

When we say Constable so and so did something, it becomes "The Police" who did it. When I use the name of my friend Jim as the guy who tried to talk that troubled soul out of such a permanent solution, it helps you realize that we're human, just like you. Jim could live across the street from you, and his kids could be in the same classroom or play hockey with yours. Yet, when he went to work that day, he spent 3 or 4 hours in the hot sun, trying to talk a guy out of doing something horrible, then witnessed what happened when he couldn't. My friend and his partner put their lives in danger to try and save the life of a troubled stranger, without even knowing his name. They also took on the baggage that witnessing something so horrible and final brings. Some people say, "that's his job" or "that's what he gets paid to do." That is certainly true, but most of those people wouldn't be out on that bridge trying to help a troubled soul, right up until he utters his last words, and then screams out his last breath. They would be calling the police to do something about it.

DEFECATION MAGNETS

The next year I had a new partner. It was my third recruit, so they must have thought I wasn't an abject failure in training the first two. I think it had less to do with the trainer and more to do with the trainee anyways. My philosophy about training became about showing them the ropes, and what a good work ethic looked like, and let slip the dogs of war, or something like that. I thought I'd training all figured out. What did I know? Mack was an awesome guy and smart, especially about things like leadership. He was a former soldier who'd been deployed to a war zone and had been shot at and heard and felt artillery bombardments. We didn't have to deal with any of that, so in comparative terms, he needed very little warning about being aware of his surroundings and vigilant about our safety. I also didn't have to teach him about work ethic at all. He had that in spades. He only struggled with two things. He wasn't a very good technical writer and our team sergeant hated him. I was a pretty good writer so I could help with the first, but the second problem was something I could never figure out or fix. They were both military vets, and both had served overseas. It felt like the team sergeant was putting Mack through boot camp again. It was unfair as heck, but Mack did better at putting up with the sergeant's crap than I would have.

Together, Mack and I also became what one might call "defecation magnets" if there are such things. It was evident in almost everything we did, including our very first call together. A neighbour on the main floor of a residence was calling in to report that they believed the tenant beneath them in the basement suite was smoking marihuana. They wanted it to stop,

107

as they had small kids with asthma problems. It was our very first call together, so I knocked on the door and told Mack that I would do all of the talking. Unless there was a bail of weed on their living room floor, I had no intention of arresting or charging anyone. (Weed was the only drug we dealt with on a regular basis back then. Ahh the good old days.) This was going to be a conversation about living together in the same building as another family, and how to show some common sense and respect for other tenants. Until the door opened.

S o, there we were, standing in front of a door that'd been flung wide open by a local drug dealer I knew very well, and Mack would get to know over the coming years. His shocked face gave it all away to Mack, but I didn't need the look on his face to clue me in. Right there in plain view from the doorway, we saw every step in the process of making weed oil. There was even a five-gallon pail of isopropyl alcohol, open and sitting next to an open stove that was gas powered. They were stupid enough to have highly flammable liquid next to an open flame. There was a garbage bag full of shake. (Shake is the stems and pieces of the marihuana plant that have a lower THC content than the bud. The THC present in that part of the plant is leeched out by a process using isopropyl alcohol, heat, and some other ingredients, to make weed oil.) Four arrests on our first day, and it was only getting started. Unfortunately, the day had just become about this one file. We wrote a search warrant, and the exhibits alone took us hours to process and make safe before being put in our exhibit control room. Mack's first investigation was so complicated and lengthy that I thought at the time I was scaring him off, but he was good. He didn't understand the minutiae I'm sure, but that would come. What he saw right off the bat was that every call we go to, could turn in to something unexpected. Like the first traffic stop he did on his own.

****

S o, there we were, travelling on South Parkside Drive by the golf course when we got a speeder travelling westbound toward Mayor Magrath Dr. It was time, and I told Mack that it was all his, and to tell me if he needed a hand. We stopped the guy and Mack talked to him for a few minutes, then let him go. As he was walking back to our patrol vehicle, the offender was driving away. Mack told me when he got in the car that the driver said he'd just received a call at work from his wife saying their young kid was sick and in the hospital. He was in a hurry to get there and apologized for going too fast. Mack had decided to warn him. I told him that he'd made a good choice and didn't think anything else of it. I took him around to a couple of my "fishing holes" to find us a ticket or two, and

I soon forgot about the traffic stop.

The next day, Mack had a phone message from a Major Crimes detective. (We call it the Violent Crimes Unit now.) He was investigating the suspicious death of a small child and asked us to come see him. It turned out that the guy we stopped on South Parkside was on his way to the hospital to show concern to the child that he'd shaken so badly that the kid eventually died. His first traffic stop was a homicide suspect. If I'm not mistaken, the first time he ever testified in court was for that file. We were only together as partners for about four months. In that short time frame, we could tell that things were starting to shape up to being an exciting partnership.

****

Almost every call we went to together, turned in to a story to regale the team with when we were done. There was the usual good-natured ribbing about the two of us not being able to complete a single work day without some off-the-wall occurrence happening. We would also take turns blaming one another for attracting such weird incidents. I can clearly state now that it was obviously all Mack's fault. (I say that because I am writing this, so I get to decide whose fault it is.) Especially the call about the deaf lady who defecated in her pajamas when she met us.

So, there we were, responding to a sexual assault in progress on the west side of the city. The complainant lived in a duplex and had called police to report the tenant in the other side of the duplex was screaming at the top of her lungs, and they believed that she was being raped in her own apartment. To further complicate things, the complainant told dispatch that her neighbour the victim, was also deaf and mute. My first thought was the same one you're thinking right now, but I was training Mack, so we responded to the incident as if it were real, all the while discussing possible permutations or differing outcomes and how we would adapt to the possibilities when we got there.

When we rolled up the callers were outside of their house looking worriedly at the door of their neighbour. I let Mack do most of the talking, and he learned that the lady had started screaming, yelling, and banging on walls while in the second-floor bedroom. She wasn't answering her door, nor was she answering the telephone. We approached the door and knocked, then rang the bell with no answer. Of course, it was possible she wasn't answering because she couldn't hear us knocking or ringing. We then had dispatch call her telephone with the same result for the same possible reason. I went up to the bedroom in the caller's apartment to see if I could still hear her. Sure enough, even before I turned down the complainant's blaring stereo, you could hear someone yelling and screaming in the room, and things being knocked down. It didn't sound like something that would normally occur in someone's residence, and it also sounded like there was someone in the room taking a beating or at least being pushed around. There was no second voice, but that didn't mean the neighbour wasn't in trouble. I went back downstairs and told Mack we had to go into the residence, and he would need to breach the door.

Now at the time, I was about 6'1" and around 250lbs, and I considered Mack huge. He was about 6'4" and about 270 or so, and all of it muscle. We got laughed at once by a Mountie buddy I had because of our size. We once visited the Lethbridge RCMP Detachment to see one of the new issue Mountie cars, the Chev Impala. My buddy was standing to the rear of the vehicle when we both got in his car. When Mack got in, the springs on the passenger side groaned, and the vehicle sank decidedly to his side, until I got in the other, and the car evened out, but sat so low that the springs were probably of no use. When Mack and I looked at each other inside the car, our shoulder flashes were almost touching. There was definitely insufficient room for us extra large crime fighters in that car. So, you get the idea about what happened to the door of the apartment when I told Mack to take it out. I forgot to tell him to kick the door near the handle. Instead, he basically shouldered it, causing it to splinter into about 946 different pieces of wood. I mean that door exploded!

As we gained entry, we could still hear screaming coming from the second floor, so I led the way up the stairs, gun in hand to the sound of the assault. The stairway was about eight stairs up to a small landing, then a sharp 180 degree turn to the right where there were eight or nine more stairs. I got to the landing while Mack was still coming up the stairs behind me, so when I turned, I could clearly see up the stairs, as well as down the stairs where Mack was following me up. Just as I got ready to go up the second flight of stairs, a dark figure came at me from the top of the stairs, holding a baseball bat and screaming like a banshee. I came up on target, and then saw it was a woman in a dressing gown. She was screaming unintelligibly at us and waiving the bat. I put my gun back down, even as she started down the stairs, and hollered to Mack, "Baseball bat!"

The woman was fixated on me and was coming right at me, baseball bat in hand. She didn't see Mack to her left as she got to the lower stair landing, and he reached over the railing and ripped the bat from her hands. Now, *he* maintains that pointing my gun at her caused her to lose control of her bowels, but I had a front row seat and I *know* she had no problem charging little old me even with my gun pointed at her. It was when the behemoth she didn't see ripped the bat from her hands, her demeanor changed. My partner had clearly (and literally!) scared the crap out of her.

At that point, she almost seemed to be coming out of a trance. I think this was the first time she noticed it was the police in her house. We tried to talk for a minute, but she was fully deaf and could not read lips. I took out my notebook, and we began to communicate by writing to each other. The first thing she did was ask for time to clean herself up in the bathroom. I asked her if there was anyone in the house first and she said she was alone. She then went into the bathroom and cleaned up what Mack had caused. She came out a short time later and we began to write messages to each other.

It turns out that she had been having problems with these neighbours (the ones who called us) for some time. That night she'd been lying in bed and the neighbours started playing their stereo so loudly that, even though she was deaf and couldn't hear a thing, the bed was vibrating to the music. She'd been having numerous other problems with them, but this was the final straw, and she admitted that she snapped.

She got up from bed and started banging on the wall they shared, screaming and ranting. The neighbours, not being able to understand her, thought that she was being hurt, and called the police. I asked her why she hadn't been answering her door or the phone. (I learned that she had a light rigged up to turn on and off when the door bell or the telephone rang.) She told me that she was so angry that she sort of lost control and didn't even see the lights flashing. She also admitted that at first, she didn't notice we were the police, and had every intention of braining me with her bat until my partner had taken it away from her. We then apologized for breaking her door. She thanked us for coming and told us her son would be over in the morning to fix it. I asked her if she wanted us to speak to the neighbours about the noise problems. She was okay with that, and when I talked to them, they were mortified. They didn't even think for a moment that they were bothering her. They thought if she were deaf, she couldn't hear, and didn't even think of vibrations. They promised to do better and have a dialogue with her now that they knew more about how they had been causing her problems.

Mack and I have worked together many times over the years, first on patrol teams, then while he was in the training unit, and I was in recruiting. We were also in different sections of CID at the same time, and then partners on the same patrol team. He was eventually promoted to Staff Sergeant and was my boss for a couple of years. Although we have remained really good friends, we have continued to argue over who caused that poor deaf woman to lose control of her bowels so many years ago. Sure, I'd pointed my gun at her, but he had ripped that bat from her hands like she was a two-year-old. He may outrank me now, but I am writing this, so I win the argument again. It was all his fault.

****

There was only one thing Mack did when he was a young copper that drove me mental. He had the occasional collision with his patrol car. We never had a collision while we rode together, but he made me want to pull my hair out when I was his acting sergeant. I was the poor fella who had to go to all of his collisions and sort them out. Back in those days, we were supposed to write them tickets if they contravened a section of the Highway Traffic Act. At least Mack had an excellent sense of humour about it. He even asked me once if he could write the ticket to himself. He told me that he really needed the stat, as he hadn't quite made his quota for that month. I would like to say that I live without sin, but if you drive day in and day out for twelve hours a day, you'll inevitably have the occasional collision. I've had a few, but none of them have been my fault. Trust me, I'm the police! (My wife doesn't believe me when I say that either.)

So, there I was, driving around as the acting sergeant. Mack had completed his training and we were no longer causing mischief together. (He was now doing that on his own.) It was a day shift that had been relatively uneventful. That all changed when one of the guys on the road queried a random licence plate and it came back to a person who was wanted for a very serious and violent offence. I started heading toward the general area and tried to co-ordinate a high-risk vehicle stop. High risk stops require more planning and more coppers who are assigned specific roles in the stop. There are at least three vehicles involved and they are orchestrated so that the driver and any passengers of the offending vehicle can be controlled as much as possible to mitigate risk to the public, cops, and the offender you are trying to grab up. I was giving advice to the young cop who was following the bad guy, coordinating other coppers to get to the scene, and trying to figure out the best location to do the stop, all while driving on a busy street myself. Trying to control chaos - and I loved it!

We finally had the trap set, and it would happen at the corner of 3rd and Mayor South, one of the busiest intersections in the city, but with a twist. We would funnel the bad guy into the parking lot of the closed KFC restaurant right next to the Mazda dealership on that corner. This would be off the road, sheltered, and nowhere for the bad guy to run if done correctly.

All the moving parts were set, and I told the fellas to execute. It went like clockwork, except for one thing.

While I was talking on the radio and looking over my shoulder to see my guys do the stop, I made a turn on to the sidewalk in front of the Mazda dealership. I was only going about 3 kilometers per hour, and as I got to the curb, I applied my brakes, and the pedal went right to the floor. I collided with two brand new mini vans on the Mazda lot because the brakes of my ride had failed. I was just creeping along, so there shouldn't have been much damage to the three vehicles, but they were all new, including the PC I was driving. The cost added up quick! I called my boss who called the acting traffic sergeant to deal with the collision while I was still coordinating the stop. That was a touch embarrassing because that acting sergeant was Cal, one of my best friends from college. He was really smart and knew the job of a traffic cop better than any other member of the service at the time, (including his own boss). I'd just put him in a position where he'd probably have to write me a ticket. After the arrest of the driver of the high risk stop, he called me over.

Cal started giving me the gears about adding to his ticket numbers for the day, and then said something weird. "You were turning and hit the brakes at the same time, right?" I hadn't told him, so he met or exceeded my opinion of his investigative skills. I said I had, and I asked him how he knew. Instead, Cal took me in my car to the back-parking lot of the police station, and with me in the passenger seat, drove in a tight circle, then jammed on the brakes. It happened again! No braking at all. Then he explained that he'd just read a report, published by some traffic enforcement association or other in the US, that said there was a computer glitch in the first generation of the type of car I was driving. It turns out that if both steering and brake input were put in at the same time in a forceful enough manner the computer would default to the steering input, in essence turning the brakes off. When I stomped on the brake because of the excitement, I had triggered that flaw in the computer and the brakes failed. No ticket for me, and I was still able to give the gears to Mack. The next one, however, I was unable to remain blameless. There was no way that even Cal could change that. In fact policy was changed, and the driving instructors used the collision scene photos (and my name) as an example of why we abide by the new policy.

****

So, there I was, driving around aimlessly on the south side of the city when a priority call was broadcast for the cars working the north zone. A father had called in, saying that his adult son had a 52-ounce sledge hammer, and was trying to gain entry to their house by breaking the door down. In those days, not everyone was issued a taser, and we didn't even have holsters to carry them on our person. They were in a blue box in the car, and if you thought you might need it, you took it out of the box before getting out. Obviously not the best set of circumstances, but they were new, and we were still trying to figure things out. Anyway, I had one of the only tasers on the street that day, so I started heading to the call. I told the copper that had been sent to wait up the block, or around the corner until I could get there. He agreed, and I accelerated to the call, lights and sirens blaring. (I was a long way away.)

I was almost there, when I heard that the guy who I was going to back up had pulled his police vehicle up, right in front of the residence. This caused the guy with the sledge hammer to stop fixating on his dad's door and start fixating on getting my partner. Bryan was already out of his vehicle when the offender changed tactics and started coming toward him, sledge hammer in hand and over his shoulder, as if ready to use it on Bryan. When I got there, I could see that my partner had his pistol drawn, and was backing in circles around his stopped PC, giving commands to "drop the hammer," as the offender stalked him. Bryan used his vehicle as the only cover he could, until I arrived with another option. There were of course, huge dangers to this. Bryan was walking backward, and the offender was walking forward, and they were only about 10 feet apart. If Bryan fell, the guy might be on him before he could get a round off, depending on how he fell. Even if he did get rounds off, he could still be hurt or killed. Bullets aren't magic and don't drop a bad guy unless hit in exactly the right spot, movies to the contrary.

I pulled into a four-wheel skid, with my vehicle ending up perpendicular to the flow of the road as I stopped. When I got out, the front of my car was pointing right at the front door of the complainant's house. I got out, taser in hand, and rushed to the aid of my partner Bryan. I was in such a hurry that I left my driver's door open with the window down, engine still running, and the red and blue lights still turning. The guy saw me come, and he stopped chasing Bryan and came at me. That is until I brought my taser on target, with the laser sight on his chest, telling him to stop. He was about 25 feet away from me, and the weapon had a maximum effective range of about 21 feet (and that's being generous). When he saw the red dot on his chest, he stopped moving altogether, almost as if deciding what to do next. I lunged forward to hopefully put myself in range and deployed the taser.

The top prong deployed well and hit right where I aimed. The only problem is you need both prongs to hit, so the electricity can arc between the two. The second fell to his feet, meaning he was about a foot or two out of range. I went to reload, thinking he was going to come at me, sledge hammer swinging for my melon, but he did the opposite. He took off running up the street, weapon still in hand.

Bryan was in way better shape than me and was off in pursuit on foot. I began to run north up the road behind them both, still trying to reload my taser. The guy headed east across the road as I was catching up to them. As I got close, he turned directions, to start running back south, toward his dad's house, and our two police cars. When I looked in front of the offender, I had a sinking feeling and knew why he was running back. My car was in the middle of the road, running, with window down, and door wide open, pointed at his dad's house and silently screaming to the guy, "Steal Me!"

The guy got to my car, got in and closed the door just as Bryan got there. The bad guy was trying to put it in gear, but he hadn't put his foot on the brake to allow the shifter to engage. He kept pulling on the shifter as Bryan got there and emptied almost his entire container of pepper spray on the guy through the open driver's side window. The bad guy worked through it, as if it didn't happen. I ran up, reloaded taser in hand, just as the bad guy figured out why the vehicle transmission wasn't going into drive for him. He put his foot on the brake, threw it into drive, took his foot off the brake, and was about to mash it down onto the accelerator when my taser hit him. The 50,000 volts went through him, and immediately caused him to straighten out like a board. That would have been perfect, except for the one foot that was hovering above the accelerator. That one went down, and my PC took off like a shot, right across the sidewalk, up the front lawn, and finally right into the front of dad's house. Dad was standing on the sidewalk in front of his house, and the car missed him by about three feet.

Mack still gives me the gears about that one, as if trying to make up for all of those fences, cars, and pieces of concrete he used to back into when he was new. I remain unrepentant! Sure, I was involved in the creation of policy. "Thou shalt never leave thy car running." But I shudder to think what would have happened had I spent even one second longer in getting there for Bryan. Sure, he should have listened and waited around the corner like I asked, except for the very real possibility that the guy breaks in and kills his father or mother by the time we get there. It turned out that "God" told the guy to break the door of his dad's house down so when the police got there, he could force them to shoot and kill him. That way he could join his dead little sister in heaven. This 20-year-old was truly a mess and got the help he needed as a result of this incident. He could have been dead from a bullet from Bryan's gun in a totally justifiable officer involved shooting. This is the nature of policing. Micro-second human judgements made using limited information, often with life or death consequences. What if I hadn't saved the two or three seconds by leaving my door open and the engine running. Is it possible that as a result, I didn't get there in time with my taser and Bryan was killed, or more likely, was forced to shoot that poor guy? I know it's only a few seconds, but what if either one of them was your son?

MY NEXT TWO PARTNERS

The next year brought another two partners. First, Rachel and then about 4 months later, Marcus. Rachel was the second woman I had trained, and we got along great. She was smart, witty, and she was great at ethical decision making. After I'd trained her, she came to me once about a problem she had with another team member. She saw this senior member of the team arrest someone for public intoxication who, although under the influence, was not too drunk to take care of himself. (The main criteria for such an arrest.) He was just being a jerk to the older copper. The cherry on top was that he'd placed his arrest in her PC and told her to take him to jail. I talked to the "prisoner" and agreed with her and showed her what to do to fix the issue, both in the short term for the kid, who she drove home instead of to jail, and in the long term, backing me up when I went to our boss and explained what had happened. The kid apologized for his behaviour and thanked us for the ride. The guy that made the false arrest had been one of the acting sergeants on the team, and that was the last day he was ever given that responsibility. I was so proud of her for doing the right thing. She once even called me out for "old school" policing and told me in no uncertain terms that she expected better of me.

So, there we were, going to a call of a young man running into traffic. When vehicles stopped for him, he would jump on the hood of the car, sitting there until someone forced him to get off their car. The curve ball was that while doing all this, he was as naked as the day he was born. We got there just as he jumped on a min-van and was rubbing his naked butt on the hood right where the hood ornament might go. When

117

we got out, he started to run down the middle of the street. We gave chase and caught up to him a short distance later. He then put up a fight, causing us to "use open and closed hand strikes to try and obtain his compliance." In the old days we described it differently, but it amounted to the same thing. The problem was that while we were totally justified in using that level of force, Rachel was yelling out with every justified strike "Stop Resisting!" I was yelling out, timing every syllable with a close handed blow, "Don't you ever run from the police again!"

After the dust up and the bad guy was in custody, she told me in no uncertain terms that what I'd been saying was unacceptable, and she expected better of me. She was not only one hundred percent right, but she'd also proven that she was my kind of cop. Truth speaking, doing the right thing all the time, as best she could, and dragging her old, earlier generation FTO into the current decade, kicking and screaming if she had to.

****

Another call we went to gave me all kinds of ammunition to tease Rachel later in life, when she had a kid of her own. We'd been dispatched to assist Child Welfare to check on a little girl who'd possibly been the victim of neglect. I knew this family from a previous dealing the year before. I had stopped a car in the downtown core of the city for erratic driving, thinking that the driver might be impaired. It turned out I was right, but there was more to the story. When I got up to the car, I knew the driver as a person who frequented the downtown, looking to buy prescription pills. (This was before coke, crystal meth, fentanyl and carfentanyl were prevalent.) I arrested her for impaired driving and called someone to help me with the eighteen-month-old baby in the car seat in the back. When my backup arrived, and I had my subject in cuffs in my car, we went to the kid, and found her diaper soiled. This little girl had been wearing that soiled diaper so long that the acid in her feces had burned the back of both of her little thighs, right down to the backs of her knees. Welcome to the world little girl, and the consequences of having a drug addict for a mother.

So, there we were, at the door of the house of this same woman, with a child welfare worker, who admitted they were there to take the kids again. (I never asked why they'd given the kids back to her in the first place. It would've been wasted breath.) When we knocked on the door, a kid of about 5 or 6 answered the door and then with a smile at us, looked over his shoulder into the other room, said, "Mom, it's the f$%&ing cops!" In fairness, the little kid had no idea that the adjective describing the police at their door was inappropriate, rather it was something he'd learned from his environment. We walked into the apartment without being asked (the powers of child welfare workers are sometimes better than those the police have when it comes to entering a house), and there was the little kid I'd taken from the car seat six months prior, standing at the top of the stairs looking at us. I'm sure she didn't recognize me personally, but she immediately put her arms out as if she wanted to be picked up. A little kid putting their arms out to us, welcoming us to pick them up NEVER happens.

I got to the top of the stairs and picked her up. As I was lifting her, I noticed her hair was crawling with lice. I was committed now, and the kid didn't know what was wrong, except she wanted to feel loved. As soon as I got the kid near my face, she snuggled her face into the crook of my neck, and I could almost feel the kid let out a sigh of relief. I was heart broken for the environment these kids were growing up in, but we were doing everything we could to help fix it. The comical part about the story is that Rachel refused to touch the kid, and she was the one with the degree in Social Work. She'd previously worked for Child Welfare. (She later told me that situations like these were exactly why she'd changed careers. She hardly ever wanted to give kids back.) At the end of our shift, we had to go buy that special shampoo for lice treatment, and Rachel said she'd never forgive me. That is, until a few years later when she had a kid of her own. It is amazing how kids make your opinions change about so many things.

****

Another call we went to early on in her training helped her to realize that this job could go from counselling someone to the possibility of having to shoot them, in the space of a heartbeat. We'd been dispatched to a support service for the mentally handicapped, where a client had assaulted one of his workers. The worker wanted police to speak to the guy to let him know what he'd done was inappropriate. Something we wouldn't even go to nowadays, but it was a different time.

So, there we were, in the conference room of the support service company building. They had the client there, sitting quietly waiting for police to come and talk to him. He was a large guy, about 20 years old, 6'1" and just shy of 200 lbs, but mentally he was like a ten year old. He would lash out, and then apologize. He also didn't know his own strength. He'd slapped his worker, so they asked us to speak to him. I went up to where he was sitting and began to talk to him. He was a really nice kid but clearly had issues. I felt like I was talking to my five year old son, and that's what got me into trouble. I got too comfortable with him, got a bit too close, and sat on the edge of a table, with a leg on each side of the corner.

This, of course made it impossible to back up if the kid became violent.

At first our conversation was a really good one, and he told me he understood what I was telling him. Then halfway through the conversation, he suddenly stopped talking, put his head in his hands and started crying, saying "You don't like me anymore."

I'm pretty sure he was speaking about his worker, but I kept talking anyway, and put a comforting hand on one of his shoulders. He immediately changed, and I found myself in a bear hug with my feet almost off the ground. He was trying to lift me up off the ground at first but couldn't quite do that. The problem was that he'd pinned me to the corner of the table, and I couldn't disengage. As I was about to push him backwards, he grabbed my collapsible baton from my tool belt, and without extending it, began to repeatedly hit me in the back of the head with it. He was cranking me pretty hard with it and I was seeing stars. I remember thinking that if he knocks me out, my partner will probably have to shoot him. I didn't want that to happen, and besides him hitting me in the head was starting to hurt.

I pushed with the backs of my legs as hard as I could, but the table didn't budge. I did cause the kid to break his hold on me though and take a step back. He still had the baton in his hand and immediately came in for more. I grabbed the wrist that was holding the baton, twisted it behind him, and lifted while still twisting for all I was worth. I lifted him right off of the ground, and up against the wall, still twisting the arm that had the weapon in it. I suddenly heard this really loud crack, like an old oak tree limb had broken, and then his wrist went right to the top of his head, as he dropped my baton. I pivoted my body to my left, away from where he had dropped the weapon, still holding him in the air. I then threw him to the floor, and finally landing all 250lbs of my fat butt on top of him. At least I remembered to do what my partner had asked me. While I was rag dolling him all over the place, I was diligently hollering out "drop the weapon" and "stop resisting."

When he hit the ground, he stopped fighting. He was still conscious but had become very passive. As I got off him, Rachel was already at my side looking to handcuff him. She went to cuff the hand that I had twisted, and then stopped. He was laying flat on his back with his one hand palm down like you would normally do while laying face up. The other arm was still twisted at an odd angle. I was no longer twisting it, but there was a big bump up high on his humerus. His palm was facing out from his body, but the rest of his arm was positioned so that his hand should have been palm down. I guess he had it coming, but I still felt bad. Rachel went to handcuff him anyway, and I stopped her. He was entirely passive now, and I contacted dispatch to call paramedics. It turns out that the twisting motion while lifting him off the ground caused a huge amount of pressure to his upper arm, and it broke in what's called a spiral fracture. I felt awful about it, but he'd rushed me. I was worried that a few more shots to the melon and he might have knocked me out. I looked at Rachel, and I think it was at that point she saw that she'd really changed careers. She knew she would probably have had to shoot the kid if he kept hitting me in the head or if I went down. When I got my faculties back, it was also a great training moment, about complacency and putting yourself in a poor tactical position. It also taught her about fighting through tough spots. The alternative really isn't very attractive at all. She learned all these lessons and many more and was on her own in four short months.

****

Marcus was another guy who I got along with immediately, but for a different reason. He was four years older than me, and a retired member of the Canadian Armed Forces. He'd been deployed in the first Gulf War, and more importantly, he was from Quebec. Marcus has a French accent when he speaks English and was guilty of sometimes thinking in French. (Sometimes he would write "the car blue" instead of "the blue car" in his reports.) I could definitely relate, remembering how I tried to be as fluent in French as I could be when I lived there, and some of the mistakes I'd made. In fact, that's probably why they put us together. I could understand and help him with the struggles he was having writing reports. We had a lot of fun together and went to some pretty dicey calls. I even got to practice my French when we were driving around. I'd been home from my mission at this point for about sixteen or seventeen years and had forgotten most of what I knew. It was a good thing I'd been practicing because we went to a call after about a month together that I had to do most of the speaking, and it was all in French.

So, there we were, enroute to a call where the complainant said he could see people trying to steal his vehicle. We were close and went to the scene. When we got there, the vehicle the owner reported being stolen was gone. We looked around the area for a short period of time, and then went to take a statement from the victim, who spoke French, and barely spoke any English. (Or he could but wouldn't). Right away I got an odd vibe from the guy. He was excited about things that weren't that big of a deal and didn't care about things that were. I was trying to get him to tell me what happened, but his story was wandering, and all in French, where my skills had deteriorated greatly over the years. The guy's French was almost unintelligible (or at least I wasn't understanding him very well), so I cut out a few steps and asked him specifically about what he had seen just before he called us.

"I saw the guy getting into my car and driving off." He finally cut to the chase.

"Did you see where he went?" I asked.

"Ya, he is right there!" the man said, pointing at an empty rocking chair in his living room.

I looked at Marcus, with a questioning look like "did he just say what I think he did?" look on my face.

Marcus still teases me about that bewildered look on my face to this day. (I tease him back that at least I can spell "bewildered.") His response to my questioning look was classic, and in English.

"Ya, he said he was sitting in that chair." Then he added, as if I needed it pointed out to me like I was his simple cousin from down on the farm. "He is F%#&in crazy."

As we arrested him to take him to the hospital to be checked out, I was actually laughing so hard that Marcus had to cuff him and let him know what was going on. I felt bad laughing at a crazy guy, but it's okay, he thought I was crazy too. I think Marcus might have thought the same thing.

****

As I write this, I realize that we dealt with a lot of crazy people while we were together. One of the most committed suicidal people I've ever met was while I was with Marcus. His name was Keith, and he was really motivated to kill himself. Just a few months before we dealt with him, two other coppers had occasion to taser him in the shower. It seems that Keith took a long knife into the shower with him and started carving his chest up. (I don't know if it's the knife of choice or the easiest one to get, but the 9" bread cutting knife seems to be the knife used by those bent on hurting themselves, and sometimes others.) He was tased in the shower, in running water. The hospital patched him up, and determined that he was not suicidal, and released him back out into society. To say that Keith's father was frustrated with the healthcare system is an understatement. Marcus and I had occasion to deal with both Keith and his dad a few months later.

So, there we were, heading to a suicidal person call. The woman who called 911 told dispatch she'd been sitting in the living room of her apartment and was interrupted by her roommate Keith, who came up to her asking for a smoke. When his voice sounded funny, she looked up, and noticed that there was a black handled knife stuck into the middle of Keith's throat, just below his Adam's apple. The knife bobbed as he spoke to her and moved up and down like a diving board when he swallowed. She screamed and called 911. Keith walked back to his room.

Marcus and I rolled up, first on scene and went in to see if Keith was still alive and if he was willing to go to the hospital. I still had a taser - this was still before we had enough to issue them to everyone. It was actually a fairly stupid way of doing things. The policy for the use of the taser requires another member to be present with his pistol out covering the member with the less-lethal taser in case the deployment didn't work, and the subject turns from suicidal to homicidal. This meant that the senior guy had the taser, and the brand-new guy had his gun out. This policy didn't make sense to me. The roles should've been reversed. My concerns were solved a few years later when they got enough tasers for everyone on a patrol team. We were stuck with what we were stuck with at the time, but my one solace this time was at least the guy with the gun next to me, although new to policing, was a combat veteran who was old enough to at least be aware of the possible outcomes and to make the right choice.

We went to the apartment, and the caller told us she didn't think he had any weapons in his room, other than the knife that was already in his throat, so in we went to see if he was alright. It was a long, narrow room, with a bed on one side, and closets and clutter on the other. Keith stood at the back of the room, next to a small window. He now had an electrical cord wrapped around his throat, just above the knife handle that was still protruding out of the cleft of his throat below his Adam's apple. Keith had a hand on each end of the cord and was pulling out from his body as hard as he could in an attempt to strangle himself. I didn't say a word; I simply shot him with the taser as soon as I got within range. It worked like a charm. Keith went as stiff as a board and fell over sideways, landing on the bed. (Thankfully, he landed on his side, because the knife was sticking out of the front of his throat. Had he gone face down, he would most certainly have died.) We cuffed him up and held him so his neck would not be jostled and called in the paramedics. They carried him out of the room, and to the ambulance.

I went outside and saw Keith's dad, who'd come to the scene. Keith had apparently called his father to say goodbye before trying to kill himself (again). Upon seeing the knife in his son's throat when paramedics brought him out, dad was understandably emotional. I told him what we'd done, and he just came up to me and hugged me. He then spoke at length about how angry he was with the medical profession, and how proud he was of the police and paramedics for doing all they could for his son. Here was a man who was literally at his wit's end, relying on others to take care of his adult son who clearly could not take care of himself. We learned that Keith died about a year later from an overdose. Knowing Keith, it was probably a planned overdose. I don't really blame anyone. How are they supposed to stop a person that is absolutely committed to killing themself? Imagine having the willpower to stick a knife into your own throat. That takes some serious commitment. Or he was so disturbed he didn't know what he was doing. Either way, there is no safe place to house people like that in today's day and age. Keith needed long-term help, not a week or two in the Psych Ward.

****

I have one last story that occurred when I was training Marcus, and he wasn't even there to witness it. We were at the hospital as a result of the arrest of someone under the Mental Health Act - another person who was not well enough to care for themself. When we got to the hospital, and our subject was safely in a secure room, the doctor asked one of us to go up to the Intensive Care Unit and help the porter and hospital security. There was a fellow there who'd been admitted the evening before after taking a bunch of pills in hopes of killing himself. He was no longer in immediate danger and needed to be moved from the ICU to the Psychiatric wing of the hospital. I told Marcus to stay with our prisoner, and I went up to ICU to help move the patient they were talking about.

So, there I was, alone, in the ICU, speaking with a security guard (this was before they had Community Peace Officers working at hospitals), and an ICU nurse. They took me to the room where the patient was. When we went in, I didn't recognize the guy, but that didn't mean anything. They told me he'd been really good since he woke up and was alert and aware that he was on his way to the Psych ward. As I approached him to say hello, he pulled a stolen reflex hammer from under his covers and lunged at me with the pointed end. (They used to use little rubber hammers, but now they are a round rubber disk on top of what looks like a hard plastic straw. This plastic straw had been broken and the end was really sharp.) I slapped at the sharp end and then used enough force to get it away from him, but I had to close the distance between us to get it out of his hands. That is when the real problem started.

He dropped his weapon and grabbed the handle of my gun and started to try and pull it from my holster. I clamped down on it with my hand, but that was all I could do. He was lying on a bed, and I was off balance. My entire right side, holster included, was trapped next to the bed. This incident made me a true believer in all they say about crazy people having super human strength. I had my right hand on the gun to keep it in the holster and began to hit the guy as hard as I could with my left hand to get him to let go. This wasn't very effective, but it was all I could do. The nurse and the security guard just stood, slack jawed while I tried to keep my weapon. After I gave him about 15 or 20 shots to the head, I looked over at the security guard and shouted at him, "You can help out at any time!" The kid seemed to wake up and went to grab the hand that was closest to him. It was enough to allow me to break free of the loon's grip. They gave the patient a sedative that seemed to work pretty quickly. The security guard and I took him down to the psychiatric unit. I hoped that while we were in the elevator, the guy woke up and started pummeling the guard. I promised myself that if it happened, I would sit back and let the guy get in a few shots in before I intervened.

I was pretty frazzled and went out to the car to get myself together before I went back in to get my partner. I didn't realize how dangerous that situation had been until I got to the car and had to shift my belt to get around the seatbelt assembly. I found that my holster had almost been ripped from my belt. There was only about one and a half inches of the leather still attached. I was shocked that I hadn't noticed until that point. I pray almost every day before I start work, asking for protection for me, my teammates, and the people we deal with, but the prayer I offered in that police car was one of the most reverent and meaningful prayers I'd offered in a long time, thanking my Father in Heaven for sparing me. I had to get myself together before I went back in to get my partner. I used it as a teaching moment, so that he would not let what happened to me, happen to him.

****

After we were all done training, our sergeant and staff sergeant decided to experiment and double us up in two man cars for the rest of the year. We picked a partner and were then assigned a beat. The only time we were not together was when one partner was on holidays. This was a great idea, and would have worked too, had we only done it on nights. Most calls for service on day shift are one man jobs. (My neighbour made me angry this morning, but I will call the cops when I wake up.) The calls after midnight, two coppers are almost always required. (My neighbour has done something that I need the cops for, right now!) By doubling up all the time, we left way too many calls for service for the oncoming shift. It was an awesome idea except for that one flaw. I was partnered with Rachel, and we were a crime fighting machine.

One call that Rachel responded to while I was on holidays shows how callous and plain stupid some cops can be. She'd been dispatched to a domestic assault at the hospital where the subject might still be in the area. When she got there, she learned what had happened and was disgusted. The victim of the assault had been held against her will in her home by her common law spouse, where he continually beat her, among other things for many hours. The beatings got so bad that he thought she might die if he didn't take her to the hospital. She begged him to take her, promising she would tell no one, and would demand he stay with her the entire time. By the time this loser agreed, she already had a broken orbital and cheekbone, among many other, less visible injuries.

This "man" took her to the hospital, and she kept her word to him, mostly because he was standing or sitting next to her the entire time. She claimed she'd fallen off of her bicycle and that's how the head injuries happened. The triage nurse thought something was wrong but had them have a seat while she went for help. While the victim was sitting there, she saw two coppers from a different jurisdiction walk by. She made a break for it, and shouted out to them to help her, pointing at her boyfriend who was still sitting in the waiting room, saying "Please help me, he did this to me!"

The poor excuse for a police officer looked her in the eye (and therefore could not have missed the visible signs of assault on her face), pointed at a payphone in the lobby and said, "This is Lethbridge City Police jurisdiction. You should go dial 911." And then walked away without a backward glance.

Thankfully, the triage nurse who'd sensed that something wasn't right, had gone into the back where there were two burly firefighters, and asked them to come help her. They were there and heard what the cop said to her. They immediately grabbed this poor woman and took her to the ambulance bay. They got her in to their ambulance and locked the doors waiting for us to get there. The copper that so kindly pointed out that this was not her jurisdiction, watched as the perpetrator walked out to his car and drove away. I found out about it the next week when we went looking for the guy to execute the arrest warrant that Rachel had obtained.

This story is not to pick on that other police agency. (That is why I didn't identify them by their agency.) I know many fine members of that Service who would be appalled by what happened. I also know a couple of guys who are on our Service who would probably do the same thing if they thought they could get away with it. The reason I tell this story is to admit that we all have bad apples, but they are very few. More importantly, we are even angrier than you are when something like this happens. People tend to accuse us all of being equivalent to that one copper that did A, B, or C. It's frustrating for us because we want to smack them just as badly as you do. That poor excuse for a copper ended up being transferred to another area after we informed her boss of what had occurred. I don't know if she's still a cop, but I sure hope that she considered some changes, either in attitude, or employment, after reading the complaint we sent to her boss.

MURDER, HEART ATTACKS, AND A HELICOPTER

The summer after I trained my seventh or eighth recruit, there was a glut of property crimes. At the time, there was only one detective sergeant whose primary responsibility was to investigate property crimes. (i.e. break and enters and thefts). They decided to second a few guys from patrol teams to form a property crimes task force of sorts to get a handle on the situation. I was one of the guys lucky enough to be selected, and I was immediately sold. There were 6 of us and we were partnered up in twos. The unit was shut down a couple of months later, but my partner and I were able to stay a bit longer because we still had a file or two we were finishing. That summer was all it took to focus me on CID again. There were no constant radio calls. When you needed to write a search warrant, you sat down and did it, without the constant interruption of another call for service. Sure, the file load was large, but it was back on patrols as well, and you got to see your investigations through to their logical conclusion. I came back to teams after my secondment with a fire lit in me like no time before.

So, there I was, back on teams after my very short stint in CID when a murder suicide came in. A newspaper delivery person went to an address on the south side of the city to collect for the newspapers she delivered, when a little 5 year old girl answered the door. The delivery woman asked to speak to the little girl's mom and the little girl said she would go get her. The girl came back a few minutes later crying, saying that she couldn't wake her mommy up. The delivery woman went in to check and found the woman dead in her bed, having been bludgeoned with a baseball bat, and then smothered with a pillow. The blood spatter was everywhere, including the ceiling, indicating that the attack was very brutal and violent. It also looked like the woman had taken a long time to die. I was the acting sergeant that day and happened to be a long way from the dispatched location. I called Jordan, a younger, but really sharp guy on the team, and told him the scene was his until I got there. He said that he was on his way. A few minutes later he told me he'd arrived and moved the kids from the house to his car but couldn't go in. He told me he'd tell me why when I got there. I stepped it up and was there in about five minutes.

It turned out that this was Jordan's aunt's house, and the kids sitting around the breakfast table when the collection lady came to the door were his young cousins. They were in his car with him, so I told him to wait with them, and try to get information from them if he felt he could. He hadn't gone in but told me the husband and wife had been having marital problems of late. I went in and found the woman dead on her bed. There was blood spatter everywhere. It looked to me like the murderer had struck the back of her head with the bat while she was either asleep, or at least lying down, causing some very catastrophic and probably fatal injuries. The pillow over her face was probably to make sure she was dead, and most likely unnecessary. I didn't bother looking at her eyes for petechial hemorrhaging (an indication of suffocation), as it was obvious that she was dead, and I didn't want to contaminate the crime scene. We cleared the house to make sure there was no one else inside and found the husband hanging in the basement, also dead for some hours.

Detectives were called and took over the scene. I left a few guys there for scene security and left the experts to it. I learned later that the husband, a seasonal employee of the City, had been struggling with mental health issues. (I sort of knew him. We both played in the same city basketball league for a few years.) As his mental health deteriorated, his hours at work diminished, and to add the cherry on top, his wife (Jordan's aunt) told him she was leaving him and taking their children with her. That was obviously the last straw, and he beat her with a baseball bat, then smothered her with a pillow just to make sure she was dead. He then went to the basement and hung himself. It struck me how close those children probably came to death. There is not a doubt in my mind that the Lord protected them that night as their father walked by their bedroom door, on his way to the basement to kill himself after having killed their mother. It was already an horrific crime scene. Two more little bodies would have been exponentially worse. I'm also thankful that Jordan, the buddy that I sent there originally, stopped himself from going into the house other than to get the kids out. I can't imagine what he would have had to deal with if he saw his family member the way I had that day.

****

A few months later, I was part of a team that was sent to knock door to door looking for a missing five-year-old girl. Little Jessica was a hard one for me. I wanted to work in CID in the worst way but working this file had to be hard on the investigator. (One of those CID investigators was my friend Jake, who'd been with me at my first murder, and told me I might need my gun when we went in to the mall together to look for the murderer.)

There's nothing quite like going door-to-door and asking citizens if you can search their house for a missing little girl. It surprised me (and impressed me) that so many were willing to let us in and search. The few that didn't, were identified and sent up the chain. I know it sounds rather byzantine, but we are talking about a five-year-old girl. A few days later, her body was found by a woman out for a walk near the river, about fifty kilometres from Lethbridge. The guy who was eventually arrested was a family friend; he was caught in the act of trying to kill himself. I think our CID guys were doing surveillance on him when he was getting ready to kill himself so arrested him just before he did it. Anyway, he wrote a suicide note that was almost but not quite a confession. (It was a cris de coeur about how he could not change his pedophilic ways.)   Anyhow, he was remanded into custody, and sent to the psych ward first. The hospital wanted help from police to guard him until the doctors felt comfortable releasing him to go to the correctional centre to await trial. It was a pay duty (meaning extra duty that paid at overtime rates), so I volunteered for a night shift.

So, there I was, sitting on a chair at 2 o'clock in the morning in the psychiatric ward, in front of the door of the soon to be convicted murderer of little Jessica. He'd been causing them problems from time to time, but so far, hadn't even come out of his room while I was there. When a nurse or a doctor went in, they didn't want us in there with them, and promised that they would call us if he got out of hand. So, I was sitting there, reading a book, when he came to the door wanting to come out. I stood up and wouldn't let him by me. I mentioned earlier I am a pretty big guy, and he was a scrawny little man who barely came up to my shoulder. He tried to walk past me, and I stepped in front of him again, asking him to please go back into his room. I was very careful, because I didn't want to do anything that would give him ammunition against the police and sabotage his trial. He then started repeatedly poking me in the chest with his finger, and yammering on and on about something, emphasizing each syllable with a poke to my chest. That was about all I could take, so I caught his finger, bent it a bit, and told him to stop touching me. He may have ended up on his knees from the amount of pressure I was applying to his finger. Then he blurted out, "You just hate me because I killed that little girl!"

I was shocked that he'd said it in the first place, but there were about four hospital staff members watching this and heard him say it. I told him to go back in to his room, and if he needed anything to ring his buzzer and the staff would come to him. The next morning, I told detectives what he'd said and under what circumstances and thought no more of it. I was never subpoenaed for the trial, so I figured they didn't use the *res gestae* statement he said to me. (*Res gestae* is Latin for "things done" or words to that effect. It means words that are blurted out. Those statements are often admissible as evidence in Canadian courts, depending on the circumstances.) I checked the newspapers during the trial and saw a Globe and Mail piece from June 20th, 2002, by Dawn Walton quoting Alberta Court of Queens Bench Justice Peter Martens when he gave his reasonings for finding him guilty of first degree murder. One of the many reasons mentioned by Justice Martens was the "spontaneous utterances about being a killer and murderer to hospital security guards". I can take being mis-identified as a "hospital security guard" if it's for a reason like that. The down side to reading that article in June of 2002, was that I was doing it at home after having suffered a heart attack three weeks after my 38th birthday.

****

So, there I was, in May of 2002, working a set of seven nights in a row. (That was our shift rotation at the time.) On the second night, I went to a call of a drunk who'd passed out. I was backing up a new guy who was driving the van. When we got there, the subject of the call was a regular. I checked on him to make sure he was okay and then just sort of picked him up and helped him to the back of the van like I had done hundreds of times before. This time, I felt like I had pulled a chest muscle. I can still point to the exact place - it was on my right pectoral, very close to my sternum. It didn't hurt anywhere else, nor did I have any of the other signs of a heart attack, like jaw pain, radiating chest pain, or left arm pain. I'd worked through worse, so I worked for three more shifts. By the third night it was getting a bit hard to breath and every time I bent over, I got dizzy. My back was killing me, and that one place in my chest still hurt. It was my intention to work my seven nights and then go see a doctor on my six days off. I guess I was starting to look pretty grim at work because my teammates, especially our K-9 guy Sid, kept harassing me about going to the hospital. I finally gave in on the fifth nightshift, three days after I "pulled my chest muscle," but only after we cleared up the last call in pending. (By this time, we had computers in our cars and so I knew how many calls were waiting for a cop to become available.) Sid and I went to the last domestic on the screen, "fixed" a marriage that had taken ten years to fracture, and then went to the hospital.

They admitted me to Emerg, and I sat in one of the rooms waiting for the doctor to come see me. The doc happened to be a friend of mine, and I'd even taken him on a couple of ride alongs to experience what we do. They took my blood, and hooked me up to machines and monitors, and told me I would have to wait until the blood tests were back. Three or four of my buddies and I sat in my room and cracked wise about things until the doc came back into my room about 30 minutes later. He told everyone else to get out, and one of them to take my gun with them because I would be staying. He slammed a nitro patch on my arm and the chest and back pain went away in about ten seconds, and all of a sudden, I felt good enough to go back to work.

A plane trip to Calgary a day or two later, a quick angiogram, the next day a double angioplasty, and I was good to go. Well, not really, but you know what I mean. They put two titanium chicken wire stents in my heart to re-open two veins that were 100% blocked. The recovery time seemed to take forever. The really unfortunate thing was the specialist told me that I couldn't drive for the next 30 days, in front of my wife. She became my jail keeper who claimed she loved me enough to make me follow the rules. Oh, how the tables had turned from when I was the boss when she was sick. (I wasn't then either, but she lets me pretend from time to time.) Anyway, I had the heart attack in May and was ready to go back to work full duty, in the beginning of September. In all seriousness, it really was an eye opener, and I had to change the way I did some things and thought about some things. The one thing that my wife made me quit was my elected position to the Board of Directors of the Police Association (the police union.) I'd been elected to represent my brothers and sisters a couple of years earlier. I was beginning to be pulled in a bunch of different directions anyway. I'd been selected the year before to become a Crisis Negotiator and I was constantly getting called out on overtime, usually in the middle of the night, for that job. I needed to rest at some point. The old ticker got a workout that winter, proving I was able to work full duty. The doctor said I was ready, but I was a little concerned until I saw the guy walking up the street, covered in blood.

****

So, there I was, leaving an alarm call on 2nd Avenue South, near 13th Street. It was bitterly cold, about -30 Celsius and there were piles of snow everywhere. As I went to turn south on 13th Street, I looked to the north to make sure I could make the turn safely and I saw him. He was walking South on 13th on the west side of the street. The thing that immediately drew my attention was the fact that he was shirtless and covered in blood. I thought that he was either the victim of a pretty horrific assault or he had just committed one. I waited and let him walk in front of me until he got to the south side of the intersection, and as he walked in front of my car, I could see he had a knife in his right hand, holding onto the handle, but with the blade pointing up against the inside of his forearm, and toward his arm pit. He was still walking southbound, when I turned my vehicle to point the headlights to the curb, opened my door and got out. He was now standing in front of a two storey apartment building that had the dubious, but well known nickname of "Devil's Corner." The landlord rented his apartments, that were about the size of hotel rooms, to people from a lower socio-economic strata. Many of his renters suffered from mental health issues or other unnamed (often addiction related) issues.

I stood in the "Y" of the door of my PC, with my pistol out, and pointed it at his feet and shouting out to him to drop the knife. He looked over at me, as if seeing me for the first time. He got a creepy smile on his face that looked even scarier by the fact that his chest face and arms were covered in blood. He brought the knife up, looking like he was preparing to charge me. He took two steps toward me, and I stepped clear of the door of my car to gain more mobility and space, brought my pistol on target at his chest and said, "Three more steps and you are a dead man." I swear I didn't want to sound like Dirty Harry or anything like that, and there was no one else there to "impress." I just wanted him to understand the repercussions of his actions. In any event, when I said that, he stopped smiling, kind of shook his head, and stopped moving toward me. He looked around and saw an open door behind him, turned and ran toward it.

The door was not to any specific apartment, rather to the stairway that led to all the apartments on the second floor. I had to go after him, and quick. I left my car running (again, contrary to policy!) in the middle of 13th Street South in the 200 block, parked perpendicular to the sidewalk, facing west toward the apartment building. It was in the southbound lanes, door wide open, emergency lights turning, as I ran through the door and up the stairs after the guy. I didn't have time to call on the radio for help, and I *couldn't* while I was running. We didn't have shoulder mounted hand sets at that time. Instead we had to go to our waist, pull the radio from it's holder and key the mic on the side and talk. I was busy running with my gun in hand, up the stairs to the second floor of an apartment building, behind a guy with a knife who may have been leaving a murder scene, for all I knew.

So much adrenaline flushed into my system that I got to the top of the stairs at about the same time as the bad guy. I only had my left hand free, so I punched the guy between the shoulder blades so hard that he fell on his face on the top landing of the stairs, right next to the door of the first apartment on the second floor. I put my right foot on the hand that held the knife. I couldn't put my gun away because I was so close to him that if he turned over or got the knife hand free, he could stab me with it. As I knelt on his back with my left knee so he couldn't turn, the apartment door immediately to my left opened.

I guess we were making a lot of noise - him running up the stairs, and me doing the same, all the while shouting, "Stop police!" and "Drop the knife!" Even though it was the wee hours of the morning, clearly someone was awake, and it turned out to be the girlfriend of the guy I had pinned at the top of the stairs. I was standing on his wrist, but he was still trying to waive it around and try to get at me with it. I was shouting at him to drop the knife and avoiding the side of him that held the knife. She started screaming at me to leave her boyfriend alone. I grabbed the doorknob, and pulled it toward me to close it, trying to keep this girl off my back or worse, possibly trying to intervene.

So, there I was, in a hallway in a really poor tactical position with no-one to blame but myself. I was kneeling with my left knee in the back of someone who I thought was a crazed murderer, covered in the blood of his victim. My right foot was on top of his right hand that held a bloody knife. My right hand held my pistol, pointing at the guy, but tucked in close to me so he couldn't take it from me. My left hand was holding onto the door knob of the apartment right next to me to prevent a woman claiming to be his girlfriend from joining in the fight. You see my predicament? I had no more hands. I had no way to get on my radio and call for help. The same radio I should have used before getting out of my car. (All you young kids out there, remember. . . dispatch is our friend. Let them know where you are at all times!) My teammates didn't know where I was or that I needed help. I was contemplating holstering my weapon for a moment so I could get to my radio, when I heard a voice.

"Mike, you up there?"

You can probably imagine the flood of relief I felt when I heard Manny's voice. He was a K9 guy who had just cleared the alarm with me. He'd circled back around and found my car parked in the middle of the street, lights on and engine running with the door open. I hadn't been so thankful to hear someone's voice in a long time. I hollered out what I had. I heard him run up the stairs, and so did the guy under me, because he flipped the knife down the hallway even though I had a foot on his right wrist. When Manny got up the stairs and I'd holstered my weapon, we turned the guy over to handcuff him. That's when we saw where all the blood was from. He'd slit his wrist almost all the way up to his elbow and was still bleeding. He was clearly motivated when he started sawing on his arm, which made me think how close I'd come to a suicide by cop scenario. I knew, when I thought back to that smile he gave me when I had initiated my stop, this was his initial intention. I was a half trigger pressure away from shooting him, and I guess me sounding like Dirty Harry brought him out of his trance and changed his mind. Whatever the reason he had for changing his mind, I was thankful I didn't have to shoot him. (I would have but was thankful I didn't have to.) I was also thankful for the doctors and nurses who had taken care of me through my heart troubles. It turns out that I could still go through a very stressful, life and death experience without a twinge from the old ticker. It was the first time I was really sure that I would be okay.

****

Around that same time, one other thing happened you should hear about. A prank that was so brilliantly planned and masterfully executed, that I have to include it, even though I wasn't involved. There were so many moving parts and people involved or in the know, that it made this one almost unbeatable in the pantheon of practical jokes. It was so good that it managed to snare a second, unintended new guy in the web. I've confirmed it happened just the way I describe it by Carl, the mastermind, and Dale, the victim, whose locker is now right next to mine. Even though he was the "victim", Dale is the first to admit that this prank was first class.

Carl and a few of the older guys on their patrol team had decided to prank young Dale as a sort of "welcome to the team" kind of thing. They tossed it around for a while, and once they got to know him a bit better, came up with a plan. Dale is a big history buff and loves anything to do with flying. If he'd been a young man during World War II there is no doubt in my mind that Dale would've done whatever it took to fly a Spitfire or Hurricane fighter for the British Empire. To give you an idea of how knowledgeable Dale was about this stuff, I have a Great-Uncle who died flying a Hurricane fighter during the Battle of Britain. When I showed Dale the old black and white picture of my uncle standing next to the wing root of his fighter plane, I swear he probably knew the squadron my Uncle flew with, just from the markings on the aircraft. He loved anything that could fly. That was his weakness. He also had a special affinity for helicopters. One of his seasonal jobs prior to policing was as a fire jumper, where he and the team he worked with would be choppered close to a forest fire and dropped off to fight the flames.

Carl went to Drew, the acting sergeant for the night, and they hatched the plan. An ambitious and multi-faceted (some would say overly complicated) plan, that if successful, would go down in the history of the Lethbridge Police Service as one of the best of all time. (Maybe not as good as blowing up a stuffed bird with real explosives in a locker room with innocent bystanders/witnesses present, but perhaps a close second.) Ty was the set-up guy, and he took his task seriously. He was probably the best actor of the group and had fallen prey to pranks in the past. (His police car was the one I mentioned previously, that ended up with the soupy cow manure on the floor when he left it unlocked at the back of the station.) Ty had a healthy outlook regarding these sorts of things. He firmly believed that if *he* was fair game, so was *everyone else*. His task was the opening salvo, but also the lynch pin of the whole operation. He had to sell it on the radio for the rest of the pieces to fall into place. Dispatch was even given a heads up so they wouldn't joggle anyone's elbow, so to speak.

The opening act had Ty transporting a fictitious older lady to the hospital for some innocuous reason like arresting her under the Mental Health Act. When he got to the hospital, he called Drew, the acting sergeant on the radio, and informed him that his subject had taken a turn for the worse at the hospital. He went on to say that STARS air ambulance had been called to take her to Calgary but there was a problem. It seemed that the lights of the helicopter landing pad at the hospital were on the fritz and the pilot needed a secondary landing pad set up. Drew assigned the task to their primary target, Dale.

It was decided that the perfect location for this secondary landing pad would be a large parking lot to the south of the Lethbridge Lodge in the downtown area. The parking lot to the south of that building was huge and empty at that time of night, more than big enough to handle the chopper. (That lot is now home to a Tim Horton's restaurant, a bank, an investment firm, and a physical therapy clinic, each with their own building. Like I said, the lot was huge.) Drew assigned Dale to take as many road flares as he could find and set up a landing pad for the chopper. He needed Dale to set up a pad as close in dimensions as possible to the original, so Dale's first task was to go to the hospital and with his handy dandy measuring tape, ascertain the dimensions of the official landing pad, then recreate it in exact detail, in the downtown parking lot. Dale jumped at the chance. He is a details guy.

He hurried to the hospital and got his measuring tape for traffic collisions out of the trunk of his car and set to work in obtaining the dimensions of the landing pad. Ty was still at the hospital and had warned security and the nursing staff of Emerg about the reason why the crazy copper was out in the wind measuring their landing pad. All of them thought the cops had too much time on their hands, but to a man (figuratively speaking, as most of the nurses were women), were pleased with being "in the know" about such a masterful prank, and in awe of the planning and all of the moving parts involved. When Dale had his measurements, he adjourned to the parking lot downtown, where he would begin the plotting of a temporary landing pad.

A small but manageable problem arose soon after Dale left to set up the new landing pad. The problem (not really a problem, more of an added bonus) was that another young guy on the team volunteered to help. The mastermind and a few of his buddies were all sitting on the hoods of their cars, on the second floor of the Hudson's Bay parkade, which was conveniently across the street from the site of the soon to be created temporary helicopter landing pad. From this vantage point, they were in a great position to comment on the efficacy and diligence of Dale setting up the landing zone. (In fact if it hadn't been so windy, they would all have probably had popcorn and sodas to enjoy the show.) When Dean radioed the acting sergeant to ask if could help Dale prepare for this life saving flight, Acting Sergeant Drew didn't flinch. He encouraged it, with the caveat that Dale was to be in charge of the construction. After all, Dale had the dimensions of the needed landing pad and the experience of jumping in and out of the occasional helicopter. Soon the new kid was out in the wind with Dale, setting up the landing pad.

It is amazing the amount of noise a car engine accelerating sharply makes at three or four in the morning. The boys on the parkade heard Dean wind that old car up from miles away in his haste to come help Dale. Drew actually was a bit worried at this point that Dean, in his enthusiasm to help his teammate, might hurt himself or someone else in his haste to get to the parking lot. He felt compelled to get on the air and tell Dean that there was no rush, as the helicopter was not expected for some time yet. Dean was so excited that he didn't clue to the fact that Drew somehow knew he was rushing to help his teammate.

Dale had been thinking ahead and gone to the station to get a large box of flares... I mean a **large** box of flares. Now, with all the tools and knowledge they needed, our two heroes set out to diligently re-create the perfect landing zone to help save someone's life. They even checked it for any foreign objects loose on the ground that might be caught up by the blade of the chopper thus causing it damage. This was what they signed up for. They tried to set the zone up in a large circle, putting out unlit road flares. The plan required them to set up the area to exact specifications and then, when they heard from Drew that the chopper was close, they would go and light the flares. There is a spike on the bottom of each flare that you can stick in pavement, so they stand up, and more importantly, won't get moved around by the rotor wash of a helicopter or the hurricane force winds that are often present in Lethbridge in the spring and fall. While these two selfless servants of the city were working diligently to save a life, the boys were across the street on the second story of the parkade, speaking frankly amongst themselves about the work ethic, skillset, and gullibility of their two teammates.

Drew gave them a few minutes after they set it up to rest before the main event. When the time came, he called them and told them that it was time to light the flares. The chopper was about ten minutes out. The two victims pranced out in excitement, lighting the flares to ensure the safe landing of the chopper. They didn't even think to wonder how the boss knew they had constructed a circular landing zone when he got on the radio and told them they needed to ensure that the zone was in the shape of a box, not a circle. Our heroes were now in a time crunch, so they ran around, hurriedly moving lit flares from a circle shape to a square shape. When they were done and were waiting for the chopper, Drew and the older fellas on the team wanted to show their appreciation, so they turned on the red and blue lights of their PC's and drove them to the edge of the parkade to be in the line of sight of the newly created helicopter landing pad, to let the young fellas know they'd been hoodwinked.

A bit of a snag occurred when it became obvious that the two fellas standing by their burning flares still didn't get it. They later admitted that they thought their teammates across the street with their emergency lights on, were just trying to help the pilot see the landing zone better. Drew had to actually drive down to them and tell them they had been hoodwinked. The boys took the news with good natured grace. I hear that Dale even took a bow toward his teammates, who were still across the street, sitting on their cars with their red and blue lights illuminating the sky, helping to guide in the non-existent air ambulance pilot to a safe landing, but that is unconfirmed.

Sometimes, I really love this job!

So, There I was… 34 years wearing the badge

NEGOTIATOR SCHOOL AND MY FIRST CALL

In the fall of 2000, I applied to become a member of the Crisis Negotiation Team which is part of the Tactical Support Unit. Tactical Support encompasses the Tactical Unit, the Negotiator Unit, and the Explosive Disposal Unit. The staff sergeant I had at the time had been a negotiator until he was promoted to staff sergeant and told me he thought I would be good at it. At first, I didn't see it, as I can sometimes be impatient. (Everyone that knows me, just rolled their eyes at this point, and muttered to themselves "Sometimes?") If any job in policing requires patience, it's that of the negotiator. (In retrospect, I think that staff sergeant may have been trying to put me in a position where I would learn a skillset that would make me a better, more well rounded cop.) I was successful in my application and found myself at the Canadian Police College in the early part of 2001. This was not the first course I'd been sent on by the Service. I'd been to Edmonton a few times on Domestic Violence Courses, but this was the first one at CPC in Ottawa. The course instructor was an expert in his field. He also taught at Quantico Virginia for the FBI and Europol in the Hague. He was brilliant at his trade, and I was a sponge. I immediately saw the day to day applications of the concepts we were taught. Every statement obtained from a perpetrator was a form of negotiation. As I look back on the cause and effect of things throughout my career, I believe that going on this course, and applying the concepts it taught in the investigative side of policing, provided me with the skills to achieve my goal of working as a homicide detective. I didn't just learn patience, but I also learned to approach interviewing with a plan and as a psychological exercise.

The course itself was only two weeks long, and there were about 24 other coppers from across the country who'd been selected from their police services. There were classroom sessions, and smaller scenarios to work through, usually with one of the other coppers in the room playing the person in crisis. The basic concepts they taught us were so simple it is a wonder that they still work after being used for years. The reason those principles work is because they're based on human nature. The concept of reciprocity is so *simple* that it shouldn't work anymore. Bad guys should see it coming a mile away, and yet it still works. If someone does something for you, or helps you with something, you have an innate desire to pay them back. For example, when I gave Albert that breakfast sandwich years before, he would only talk to me about how he tried to kill someone. He felt like he owed me for something I had done for him months prior, and even though his lawyer told him to keep his trap shut, he talked to me.

Of course, you don't start off by trading a pizza for hostages. It starts with the "Behavioural Change Staircase." Most people negotiators deal with are in such "crisis mode," they're usually not thinking, and certainly not about the repercussions of their actions. A negotiator's job is to show that we're actively listening to what got that person to that point. When a certain amount of rapport is built, we show empathy for them. Not fake or manufactured empathy, but real, honest feeling for the poor schmo. This is often a subject who started his or her life behind the eight ball, lacking either life skills, cognitive ability, or both. Sometimes we even have a normal person who's made one bad decision after another (usually with the assistance of drugs or alcohol), and then wonders how he ended up so far off the rails that he finds himself on the phone with a negotiator and surrounded by a tactical unit.

When the person in crisis can tell that you genuinely give a damn about them and why they are there, you can start building rapport. Empathy is what **you** feel, rapport is when **they** feel it back. That is when they start to trust you and you can then start down the path of influencing their behaviour. When you can influence their behaviour, they are open to changing their behaviour. It is that simple.

1) Active Listening
2) Empathy
3) Rapport
4) Influence
5) Behaviour change.

The reason it's called a staircase is the elegant beauty of the concept. If you are going along and believe you are progressing, and you try to go to the next step, but you can tell the subject hasn't bought into what you're selling yet, there's a simple solution. Step down one step on the staircase until it works, and you can progress to the next step. If you are self aware and actively listening, you can tell if an attempt to go to the next step has succeeded or not.

Sounds easy, right? Well the hiccup in all of this is that cops by nature are problem solvers and for the most part, try to solve the problem in the quickest way possible so you can move on to the next problem waiting on the pending screen on our MDT. (Mobile Data Terminal; the in-car computer enslaving all modern cops.) From a cop's perspective, the toughest thing about negotiating is learning to slow down, be thorough and thoughtful. That difficulty is exacerbated by the fact that this course is one of the few at the Canadian Police College that has a "years of service" requirement for those coppers selected to go. Your service might think you're the best talker/negotiator since sliced bread, but if you haven't been a cop for at least five years, you are not eligible to attend the course. By the time you've been a copper that long, you obviously think like a cop, solve problems quickly, and move on to the next call in pending. Frustrating, right? It was the best thing that ever happened to my career.

The other thing to remember as a negotiator is the types of people that you will deal with. The vast majority (at least 95%) are what we call "Expressive" subjects. These are the folks who are having an existential crisis (usually fueled by an intoxicant, pre-existing mental health problems, or most often, a combination), and have acted rashly as a result. His reasons are often "My wife left me," "My boss fired me," "My house burnt down," "My dog died," or "God hates me." You get the drill. This is the guy who interrupts his wife and her lover in the act, and rather than punching the guy out, or his wife for that matter, he chooses to let them go, gets his gun, and decides whether to kill himself for the next ten or eleven hours. (Or goes to the bridge to jump or some other permanent, but poorly thought out solution to the problem.) Most of these types of people are not in a permanent state of crisis, but instead have had some life-crisis push them over the edge. They are usually seeking a way to get back their mental equilibrium and seldom want to hurt anyone else. They usually just need someone to listen to them until they get themselves back on track with the occasional nudge of a good negotiator.

Another type of subject is the "Instrumental" person. This is the guy whose goal of robbing a bank was interrupted by the police, and now he has hostages. The hostages are a means to an end, not the target of his ire. He

142

is a little more dangerous because he views his hostages as things instead of people, but usually the subjects in these circumstances are hardened criminals who know the system and can usually be worn down. They also know that the cops aren't leaving and won't actually get them a helicopter, no matter what they say or do. They also know that if the hostage is hurt, their sentence becomes considerably longer.

The third and by far most dangerous, is the "High Risk" subject, later euphemistically called "Closure Motivated." This is the guy who was interrupted while kidnapping his wife because he was going to kill her. This is the smallest subset that negotiators talk to, but clearly the most dangerous. These are the guys who might need to be convinced to walk to a window or to the back porch to pick up the cigarettes they asked for because the "robot just couldn't quite make it up the stairs." When they get to the point where they are visible, the negotiator's job is over, and the sniper's job begins. It is one of the things negotiators must be ready for. We are cops after all. Saving the life of the hostage or victim takes precedence over even our own lives.

It's easy, and I suppose necessary, to classify or type the different subjects that a negotiator will run into, but two things are very important to remember. The first is that every one of them is a small combination of all three types. (An expressive subject may have also planned to take his wife hostage just to reason with her, but there might be an "or else" planned as well.) The other thing is that **ALL** of them at least appear to be "Expressive" in the beginning of the incident. This, combined with the fact that the vast majority of subjects we talk to are more expressive, makes it very important to continually assess and reassess the subject's goals, objectives, and mental state. They may start out being one thing, and then turn into something else entirely.

That's a lot for just one person, so our policy (which reflects the national standard) is to call out three trained negotiators if available. One as the primary, one as his secondary or coach, and the third is the negotiator liaison, who is continually assessing the subject and then updating the incident commander. As a new negotiator, you spend some time as the secondary, then move up to the primary, then finally as your time in the unit winds down you go back to the secondary or the liaison. We have a term limit on specialty units in Lethbridge, and a negotiator's tenure in the unit is ten years. I was in the unit for eighteen years before they added that rule. I had a really good, eventful run.

So, there I was, on the final day of the course and about to take my final exam. It was scenario day! At the time, the Canadian Police College had an agreement with one of the local universities to have actors come in and play the subjects in crises. My scenario was a relatively simple one, but a very common one for my neck of the woods. I was to speak to a girl who was on a ledge of a large apartment building and was going to jump. To avoid some of the distractions of real life, I would not be able to see the jumper, rather this would be done over a "throw phone" because she had threatened to jump if a copper came within sight of her.

The young girl said her name was Caroline. She spoke English to me but had a French accent. She would occasionally mutter to herself in French, but still staying in character, saying things to herself someone in that situation might mumble. I was again appreciative of the fact that I'd just recently trained Marco. I'd been practicing my French but wasn't nearly good enough to negotiate in that language, so I kept it to myself. The moment I started talking to her, she began to cry. Sometimes it was just a gentle weeping, but every now and then, she would progress to uncontrollable wailing. It was very unnerving.

About five minutes into the conversation, I started talking like it was a conversation, rather than a test. I forgot she was an actor playing a role, and sort of forgot my role as a cop who was trying to solve her problems. Instead, I just listened to what she was telling me, letting her get it all out. I used the occasional verbal indicator that I was following along and understood what she was saying a simple thing like "uh huh," or re-phrasing what she was saying, or simply identifying her emotion, by saying things like "that must have made you angry." or "you sound frustrated." At one point she said something in French, and I responded, so she started to go down that path. Luckily by that point, the conversation was so natural and seemingly real that when I told her I was more comfortable in English, it wasn't a problem for her. I found the time went by way too quickly, and when I finally asked her to come down from the ledge, come in to the apartment and speak to me in person, she just said "okay" and hung up and came into the room.

Two things struck me immediately. The first was that the time allotment for the test was about forty minutes and we'd used all of that and then some. The other was that she was dry eyed and smiling. When she walked up to me and kissed both of my cheeks the way they do in Quebec, I blurted out incredulously to her in French that she'd been faking the tears. She smiled, patted my cheek, told me I was so sweet, and that she had simply been acting. That girl had serious acting skills. The debrief was even more amazing. She told the other members of the class and, more importantly my teachers, that I was a natural, and if I had asked her to come out ten or fifteen minutes earlier, she probably would have.

****

I passed the course and was soon on my way home. The things I learned on that two weeks were career changing for me, but the added bonus was I got to know some coppers from other agencies around the country. Some of those contacts have lasted over the last twenty years. One guy comes to mind right away. He works in a police service in the Greater Toronto Area. He was a guy who was just starting down the path of working in the undercover and intelligence side of policing when we were on that first course together. He was also a really gifted negotiator. He definitely had the gift of gab, and I have had the opportunity to see him a couple times over the years. The last time I saw him, he helped me out when I needed a hand with some ideas about undercover work for a homicide I was investigating. That is one of the best things about going away on course - you make contacts across the country and can exchange ideas. It also helps you realize the problems you might think you see at your agency, or your city aren't any different, or at least very similar to those that others might have, no matter where they work.

I had a few minor call outs as a negotiator when I got home, but I wasn't the primary. I spent my first few calls learning how we run things and being a coach or secondary for guys who have been doing it longer. It was an eye opener. Some things we did were actually executed better than the CPC "standard" and in some ways, we were woefully inadequate. Most of those inadequacies were as a result of lack of equipment. There was no budget at all for the unit at the time. As the police service grew, and as liability seemed to become something that we thought of more and more, we began to come into the 20th century. (I know we were technically now in the 21st century, but it was still progress.) My first call as the primary came that fall, a month or two after the attacks on the Twin Towers in New York. There was a second scare happening south of the border that had to do with some nut mailing active Anthrax to US congressmen and senators. Four or five people died, and numerous others were injured. Enter two drunken boneheads named Stan and Marvin.

S o, there I was, called out as the primary negotiator to speak to Marvin and Stan. They were two criminal masterminds who thought it would be funny to beat the crap out of a neighbour over something trivial.

145

They then fled into their rented house (that happened to be next door to the victim), thinking this might prevent their inevitable arrest. When the responding coppers knocked on the door, (it was not fresh pursuit so they couldn't kick the door in without a warrant), our two heroes claimed they had AK-47's and a large envelope of Anthrax and were willing to use it. They also said they had two hostages and refused to come out. Marvin was known to us as a person that had the occasional illegal handgun. (A few years later, he was shot to death in a drug deal gone bad in another jurisdiction, returning fire from his own pistol as he met his end.) The responding officers got warrants to enter the house and arrest of these two halfwits. The Tactical Support Unit was called to encourage them to surrender.

By the time I got involved, it was the afternoon of the next day. The incident had occurred overnight, and warrants had been obtained after that, Tac had been called out and we were deployed at the same time. When I say deployed, that might lead you to believe that we were sent to the scene and used a bullhorn to shout them into submission. The beauty about negotiating is they need to hear you voice, but you don't necessarily have to be right outside the door of the house when they come out. That's what Tac is for. This was in the days when very few people had cell phones and almost every house still had a land line. It was a five minute exercise to have the telephone service provider lock the telephone in question out. They couldn't receive any incoming calls except for those we made and every time they took the receiver off the hook, it automatically called my negotiator phone. If they wanted to use their telephone, the only person they could get was me on the other end.

The Incident Commander's plan was to talk them out, no matter how long it took, as long as they didn't hurt anyone or make any credible threats toward anyone. They'd given us no demands, other than to leave and that they wanted more booze. It seemed they had drunk the place dry while sitting in the comfort of their own living room. Because of Marvin's history, we had to assume he was being truthful when he said he had a gun or two in the residence. The threats he and Stan were uttering toward their two "hostages" were so weak that the two other drunks in the house were probably their friends who happened to be partying there when the altercation with the neighbour occurred. (That turned out to be exactly the case.) My job became easier as they sobered up. The problem was, as they sobered up, they also realized they had really stepped in it. It was time to get them to see reason, but they weren't stupid and knew jail was their next stop. It was pretty easy to have them release their two "hostages" at this point. Their friends wanted to leave anyway. We didn't even have to give them anything to get them to let the two guys out. The Incident Commander's plan had worked so far, so we would a talk a bit longer until Marvin and Stan agreed to come out as well.

That was a great plan from my perspective. I was sitting in the command centre of the second floor of the police station, with my feet on the table, agreeing to any kind of break Marvin or Stan wanted. If they wanted a break for a smoke, we agreed to it as long as they would agree to accept my call back in five minutes. I actually got the feeling like I was their grade school teacher agreeing to their potty breaks. From the perspective of the tactical unit, it wasn't an optimal plan. When this "siege" started, it was about 15 degrees with a bit of a breeze. Considering it was late autumn in Lethbridge, it was considered really nice out. While I was negotiating my little heart out over the next four or five hours, the temperature had dropped to -15 degrees, with rain, freezing rain and then snow mixed in. (I had no idea the weather had changed so drastically – I was inside.) The Tac boys were not impressed with me, the boss, and most definitely not the two halfwits in the house. Tac had deployed in their summer gear, but because of the 30 degree drop in temperature, they had to send someone back to the station to get their winter gear. "Not impressed" might be considered the understatement of the year.

Marvin and Stan were the only two left in the house and I was now talking almost entirely with Stan. Marvin was more of a hardcase than Stan, and now that both were sober, Marvin knew with his criminal record he wasn't going to help him much come sentencing time. He was also the main perpetrator from the original assault. When they decided to give it up, Marvin went out the door first, and followed every direction to a "T". When Stan exited the residence, I knew that he wasn't taking my directions, or the entire situation very seriously. I am told that when he went out of the residence, he refused to get on his knees because there was snow on the ground, and he didn't want to get wet. He made a poor choice and the Tac guy that was arrested him "showed him to the ground" for everyone's safety. Stan suddenly realized that this was no longer a joke.

It was my first call as a primary, and I learned a lot from it. Knowing what I know now, the entire episode would probably have been over within the first or second hour. The two knew they were caught and were no longer emotionally elevated or under the influence of anything. They also knew the inevitable outcome. I got teased a bit from my buddies on Tac, who claimed I did it to them on purpose to teach them to carry the winter gear with them. I told them I didn't even know what the temperature was because I hadn't been the guy controlling the thermostat in the command centre. I also added the subtle dig that this was the real reason why I became a negotiator instead of a "tac ninja". It was good that my first call as a primary was relatively easy. I was able to ease into it and learn things on a relatively unimportant call. I would one day use the tools learned in these less intense calls when I talked a murderer into surrendering to police, or a suicidal person into giving up after struggling to understand him for the first few hours due to the rifle in his mouth. Eighteen years of negotiating gave me the opportunity to participate in a lot of interesting calls.

****

One of the other things that happened around that time of my life was, of course, the terrorist attacks in New York and Washington DC on September 11th, 2001. Everyone old enough to be alive probably remembers where they were on that horrible day. I'm no different. My wife and I were taking my young son on vacation to Utah to visit my mother and other members of my family. Our son was only four years old and so we usually made the trip in smaller increments. We had stopped on the evening of September 10th in Great Falls, Montana to stay for the night. That is a city about three hours south of Lethbridge. We weren't sure whether we were going to take one or two more days to get to just outside of Ogden, Utah where my mother lived. We went out for dinner, did a bit of shopping, and went to bed, ready to hit the road again in the morning.

S o, there I was, waking up to this horribly loud alarm clock in the hotel room. I'd obviously forgotten to check the alarm before going to bed to ensure the last occupant of the room hadn't set for six in the morning. Then, of course, I couldn't get back to sleep. My wife and young son were still fast asleep, so I turned on the television, mostly out of boredom. The first thing I saw was a replay of the first plane flying into the World Trade Centre. I thought it was a heck of a movie, until the scene cut to a clip of the second plane hitting a building, and a news anchor, almost in tears, stating the obvious. I was in shock and was riveted to the TV to learn more.

It was about that time that I heard loud running footsteps in the hotel hallway. I looked through the peephole and saw two or three men run past my door, all dressed in their American military flight suits. There is an air force base just outside of Great Falls, and there must have been a course with some of the course attendees staying at the same hotel we were at, or a general recall and escalation of readiness was called, because these guys were running down the hallway, all appearing to be about to go to war. Then it struck me. They actually were running toward battle. It was sobering.

When my wife awoke a short time later, I told her what'd happened, and we discussed whether we should return home or continue on to my mother's house. If we decided to go home, I could only imagine what a mess the Sweetgrass point of entry would be, so we decided to continue on to my mom's place. We drove the rest of the way that day and arrived in Utah later that evening.

My mom lives a very short distance from the Hill Air Force Base in Utah. It turns out that Malmstrom AFB (the base in Montana), wasn't the only airbase put on alert. Fighter jets took off over my mom's house every 15 or 20 minutes for what felt like the next day or two. I saw very few land, and most of them appeared to be flying east. I realized after the first ten or twenty planes took off without coming back to land that they were going somewhere specific, and they would be in harm's way very soon. I also saw one news story while watching my mother's TV talking about American allies rallying and was proud to see that Canada would be fulfilling our NATO obligation. (Many of my fellow citizens have since forgotten that there were fellow Canadians in those towers as well, not to mention our pledge to help our partners when attacked. I was worried for my fellow citizens going to war but know that they felt the similar feelings that me and my brothers and sisters do when we go to a tac call or some other life threatening call. "I have been trained, and if I don't go, who will?")

It was especially encouraging to see what was happening in Gander, Newfoundland. Planes had been diverted there and the citizens of that small city took in every traveller they could into their own homes. It was a troubling time, but I was glad to see that people were rising to the occasion and remembering their humanity and helping their brothers and sisters any way they could.

Even though these attacks had a horrific cost, something that was truly refreshing was how the public was reacting to the first responders who ran toward danger to help rescue people from the Twin Towers. I was so proud of my NYPD and FDNY brothers and sisters who were running into those buildings to help people that they'd never met before, and literally saving lives at the expense of their own. Race, religion, sexual orientation, political affiliation, or any other thing that people use today to separate and quantify us meant exactly **NOTHING**. Seeing pictures of black cops helping white citizens or vice versa was not even commented on by the media. They just said, "Police Officer," or "citizen" instead of putting a descriptor in front of those words. One picture drove that home to me. A cop and a lady, covered in dust leaning on each other. It was so moving that I couldn't tell who'd saved who. Both were exhausted and grief stricken. Race could be discerned if you tried hard enough, but it didn't matter to those looking at it. All you saw was two human beings leaning on each other for support and safety. As I sit writing this, 19 years after that attack, I can't believe how far we've fallen. When did we start thinking that one's race, religion, orientation, politics, or profession mattered more than what a hero of mine, Martin Luther King described as the content of one's character? Why are any of those things more important now than they were twenty years ago, and who made that decision for us?

FINALLY, A "BIG CITY DETECTIVE"

I came back from my heart attack smarter, and more focused. It wasn't because I hadn't been that way before, it was the fact that having a potentially life ending illness tends to help you understand what's important in life. It was also the start of a change in my role on the team. I'd finished training my ninth recruit before I left and realized I would probably not train anymore. My boss had started to use me more often as the acting sergeant when he wasn't there. There was added pressure. It's one of the most difficult jobs in policing. One day, you are just a call taker on the team and just another one of the guys. The next, you are required to be the boss, hold the team together, and encourage them, but also take those that make the occasional boneheaded play to task. Then you are back to being one of the guys the day after. It is a difficult position to be in if you haven't laid the groundwork over the years of being a steady and hard working, earning the respect of the team. I don't know if I was any good at laying that ground work down, but I never had any problems working as the acting sergeant. Most of the guys on the team knew I had a desire to one day be promoted, but those that knew me understood why I wanted the promotion.

I returned to work in the fall of 2002, and by January of 2004 I was promoted and more importantly, transferred to the Organized Crime Section within the Criminal Investigation Division. I remember being called into the boardroom by the Chief so they could tell me the good news. The staff sergeant who convinced me to apply for the Negotiator Unit was now an Inspector and in the room. The Chief shook my hand and then pointed to a whiteboard that had the command tree where every sergeant and staff

151

sergeant was assigned. I saw my name next to my friend Alec, and the unit that we had both been assigned to was ECU. I was happy my partner would be Alec, but I didn't even know what ECU meant until someone told me that we had changed the name of the Fraud Unit to Economic Crimes Unit. And the penny dropped. It was a good thing the Chief had moved on to congratulate the next guy and tell him where he would be going because I was so disappointed, and just stupid enough to let the boss know. That is where my ex-staff sergeant, the newly promoted Inspector came in. He took me aside and explained a few things to me.

It turns out, they knew that all the investigative courses I had applied for were related to Domestic Violence. That was the unit I really wanted. The inspector told me all the jobs in CID were investigative in nature, and even though this might not have been my first choice, it got me back there. I would now be on the call out list. These calls are almost always serious, you usually got to keep the file, as long as you had the capacity to investigate it. I soon found out this was a bit of a blessing in disguise. In almost every ECU file, the money is already gone, and it is usually not an "in progress" type of investigation that has to be acted on immediately. Almost all could be put on the back burner, while you worked a more serious or violent crime. (The first call out I got in that four year period was a stabbing, and the last was an attempted murder. A detective is hardly ever called out to that fast breaking fraud.)

One of the added benefits of going to the Criminal Investigation Division was working with a great group of guys in both the Organized Crime Section and the Major Crimes Section. Organized Crime included the Special Operations Unit (Drug Unit), Intelligence Unit, Property Crimes Unit, and the Economic Crimes. They had also started putting constables in CID. A couple of my friends were in the Property Crimes Unit, and we were able to work files together without having to respond to radio calls. One of the changes I noticed right away was the fact that I could actually plan my day, usually without outside forces intervening. I was no longer a slave to the radio or MDT. If I needed to write a search warrant, I sat down and wrote a search warrant, sometimes in one sitting. There was no requirement to listen and constantly respond to a radio! (Only the cops reading this will really understand how counterintuitive that is, but it's the first and biggest change you notice when you work in CID.) The added bonus was when I was tasked with something I hadn't planned on, it was usually something I had wanted to do for years. It didn't break my heart to have an aggravated assault, a triple stabbing or an attempted murder get in the way of my plans to write a search warrant on a fraud file.

Another bonus of going to CID, was they trained you to death. I got all the regular investigative courses like Major Crimes (a two week, "how-to investigate a homicide" course), and Forensic Interviewing (a two week, "how-to interview homicide suspects" course). Then they sent me on job specific courses like Fraud level I and II. Almost every regular patrol copper is scared of investigating frauds. (They're somewhat technical, and detail oriented, some of the details needed are in areas cops are unfamiliar, like the banking world.) In fact, most cops spend at least some time during every fraud investigation deciding whether they are civil or criminal matters. If they're civil, we tell the victim to sue the person and conclude our investigation without charge. I was just like every other copper until they sent me on a course, and I learned that they were easier than I had previously thought. Amazing what a little training will do. Another beauty was that I gained a ton of interviewing experience. Fraud interviews are relatively easy because you can generally point to a bank statement or something like that and say to the bad guy words to the affect "I know you did it, I have the proof here. I just need to know why." I had a lot of success during my time there, and that translated to success later on.

Speaking of training and courses they send you on, a funny thing happened when I got home from the Major Crimes course. So, it turns out my wife is a bit of a TV cop show junky. She doesn't care as much for the "Hill Street Blues" kind of cop shows that concentrate on patrol work and how weird people are. She loves detective shows like "CSI" or "NYPD Blue." She was almost as excited as I was when she learned that I was going to the Canadian Police College for two weeks on a course to learn how to investigate Homicides and other violent crimes. She was right - it was one of the coolest courses I have ever attended.

Major Crimes was two weeks at the Canadian Police College in Ottawa, concentrating on teaching concepts like how to read blood spatter evidence and how to interview. (A little bit at least. There's another two week course called Forensic Interviewing where all you do is learn how to interview bad guys for major files. They sent me to that one later the same year.) There was even a day set aside to discuss case law and other tricky things with a Crown Prosecutor. Ours was from Saskatoon, Saskatchewan, and she used the LPS investigation into the death of little Jessica Koopmans from a few years prior as an examples on how to do things the right way.

The final exam was a two day affair. The class of 25 was divided up into 5 "syndicates", and each syndicate was tasked with solving a real homicide. They brought a couple of detectives to the class from the Greater Toronto Area who presented the beginnings of one of their older, solved homicide investigations. They provided pictures of the scene that an ident guy had obtained. They also gave us copies of the statements of witnesses, obtained by patrol coppers, prior to our arrival. They even included some of the real pictures from the autopsy. (This was necessary because they show the stab wounds to the head of the subject and the angle of the wounds, which we later learned became important in finding and interviewing the bad guy.) The test started when the instructors said, "This is the information we had when we got there. You are now the detectives that were called out to the scene. What do you do next?" For the next two days, one of the representatives from each syndicate would go up to the instructors and give them the next two or three steps we would take if it was our investigation. If we decided to do a neighbourhood canvass, they gave us a statement or piece of evidence they'd obtained by doing that task in real life. If we missed, forgot, or chose not to do a necessary task, we missed out on the evidence or statement. It was one of the coolest final exams I have ever taken, and when you solve the crime, you feel like you could slay a giant. After that adrenaline high, we were taken to the airport. After promising to keep in touch with the other 25 or so coppers from across the country (and other countries as well), we headed home.

The one problem with a course in Ottawa is the flight there and back. I am not a big fan of flying in the first place and feel really dirty after sitting in a plane, so close to people I don't know for an extended period of time. To make matters worse, the return trip always gets you to Lethbridge around midnight. When I got home, I told my wife I was beat and needed to have a shower. While I was showering, my lovely wife was putting my clothes away or in the laundry. That is when she came across the 4 inch course binder with all of the material. Unfortunately, it also had the photos of the crime scene. I hadn't even thought about it until I came out of the shower.

When I finished my shower, I found my wife was sitting on our bed, engrossed in the contents of the course material. She had the scene photos spread around, and she was actually looking at the "head shot" of the deceased. It was the picture showing pieces of dowelling inserted into the stab wounds by the ME, to show the depth and entry angle of the knife wounds. (This is sometimes done to help determine where the bad guy was with respect to the victim when he was killed and can sometimes tell you things like if the perpetrator was left or right handed.) She said, "I can't believe how detailed these photos are. If I didn't know any better, I would think that this was a real dead person." Mortified, I apologized to her and told her that it was an actual murder victim, and that was one of the steps the Medical Examiner had done to help solve the crime. It didn't gross her out too badly, but I think at that moment, she came to the realization I would be investigating real murders and other violent crimes and that they were not as antiseptic and sterile as what she watched on TV. I know that she understood from an intellectual perspective but having the picture of an actual murder victim in her hand, and knowing that I might be investigating something similar, made it all too real for her.

S o, there I was, working my first large fraud file. The bad guy had been convicted of a $300,000 fraud about four or five years prior. At that time, he'd been a bookkeeper who worked at two different businesses, one of which was an organization that ran many of the facilities and apartments for older, retired citizens. Some were also extended care facilities. So, in essence, our hero had stolen from the grandparents and great grandparents of people in our community. He got a three year sentence for it, and his wife was found guilty of helping him, and did just under two years. I knew her in passing. We were members of the same church and had been in the same ward (our word for parish) at one point. I didn't recognize her husband's name.

When he got out of jail for these previous convictions, he lived in British Columbia for a year or so, and then moved back to Lethbridge. While he was in jail, his wife had divorced him, so he came back to Lethbridge to be closer to his kids. (At least that is the excuse he told me when I later talked to him, although I also found out that he was running from something in BC.) When he came back to Lethbridge, he approached one of his previous fraud victims who also happened to be one of his former church leaders. Our boy told this faithful Christian man that he'd paid his debt to society and was back in Lethbridge to be near his children and to be a better father. He claimed he was a changed man who was in the repentance process, and just needed someone to give him a chance. The victim gave him a second chance and offered him a job as a bookkeeper for his business. I know some of you just said to yourselves, "Well the victim deserved it if he let him have access to his money again." That is the definition of what a good fraud artist can do. They can talk you into things that you would never think you would do. You don't believe it would happen to you, right up until it does.

The problem with this bad guy, was he was unusually good at streamlining businesses, and found money that they didn't know they had, or helped them save money they didn't know they could, and then stole it from them. He was usually able to hide the theft for a year or so, and then the wheels would fall off. In a period of ten months, the man embezzled in the neighbourhood of $70,000. That's when we got the call, and I was assigned the investigation. It was a relatively easy one that I could've done when on patrols, but it would have taken ten times longer because of the time it takes to write warrants and interview people while still going to other calls or working nights when witnesses are asleep.

The first thing I did was contact the RCMP detachment in BC where he'd lived when released on parole. I spoke with a Mountie who was less than enthusiastic about helping me. He told me he had our boy as a suspect in a fraud of over $120,000 in their jurisdiction, but that he was only a part time detective. In the winter months he did CID work, but for the summer he was back on patrols. I asked him for the information he had on his investigation so I could add it to my information to obtain a search warrant, and then share the results. He said, and I quote, "Nah, this is way too complicated for you to understand. If you arrest him and he starts talking, call me and I'll come to Lethbridge and interview him on my stuff."

It would appear that he was much better at this than I was, so I decided I would just let him get to it on his own. I wouldn't be calling him for any reason at all. I felt comfortable in the knowledge that this extremely competent Mountie would have matters well in hand without my paltry assistance.

I wrote the warrant on his bank accounts and found my missing money right away. (For all you Canadian coppers out there, this was before 2005, and Production Orders weren't a thing yet.)   When I got the warrant results back, I was surprised. For an accountant, he wasn't very good at covering his tracks. In fact, it was so easy that for a day or two, I thought I was missing something. No one was this stupid. He would print off cheques in his employer's name, and put himself as the payee, and then use a stamp of the business owner's signature. He would deposit the money in to his only account, and then every transaction he made was by the use of a bank card. I found every single cent that I was missing, and the money that was missing from the business in BC as well. (There was nothing I could do about that. It was a different jurisdiction, in another Province. I had called the investigator and he'd informed me that I was too stupid to help him out.) One transaction on his account bothered me more than most. It was a transaction that happened in Cardston, Alberta. He cashed one of his employer's cheques, and then the next transaction on his account was a purchase made at an LDS book store in Cardston. He stole money from his boss, then bought church books with it.

I finally got the bad guy into the office after a song and dance with his lawyer. I got him in the box, and he was very well coached by his lawyer, so wouldn't provide me with any sort of statement. The thing that shocked me (and disappointed me more than the book purchase in Cardston) was one of the first things he said to me. When he came in, I read him his Charter rights to counsel and all the rigamarole that goes with that. Then as an ice breaker, I said to him that I grew up around here and we were of a similar age, but I only knew his wife from church, and didn't know him. He immediately said to me, "Yah, you know me." I was stumped and asked him how I knew him, and he told me. Right after I had arrested him and informed him of his Charter rights, he told me we served in the same LDS mission in Quebec and were there at the same time. I'd never met him in the mission field, but to say I was disappointed would be an understatement. It threw me off so much, that when he said he didn't want to give me a statement, I didn't even try to change his mind. I just gave him his court documents and released him.

Our boy decided to hire and then fire the next three or four lawyers, until the judge made his next appearance (two years later) a requirement that trial would start, whether he was ready, and represented by counsel, or not. That next appearance came, and he pled guilty. He got three years in jail. About a year later, I received a call from that brilliant Mountie in BC who said I wasn't smart enough to understand his file. He asked for the information I had obtained in my warrant. I told him that I wasn't sure if I could without a court order. He assured me it would be alright. I told him I'd get back to him after talking to our Crown's office. The Crown Prosecutor that I spoke with told me that he didn't get anything obtained *by* a court order, *without* a court order - especially when she learned I had offered to include him, but he wouldn't provide me the information about his file. I called him back and told him the bad news. In a panicked voice he asked if we had at least obtained a signature or a handwriting sample that they could use. I helped him out as best I could and told him in a veiled sort of way that a warrant on the guy's account would probably be helpful for him. He thanked me and hung up. They later tried to charge him with fraud over with less than six months remaining on the sentence he was serving. When the judge found out that they'd started their investigation before mine, had an opportunity to piggy back on mine and chose not to, and *then* waited until he was just about to be released from custody before they laid their charges, he dismissed the new charges outright. The Judge cited the fact that it looked like the investigator was abusing the system to keep the subject in jail longer, when they could have done it at the same time as mine. If they had done that, he could have imposed a global sentence. In essence, that copper's arrogance made it possible for a judge to find the bad guy not guilty of a $120,000 fraud – a fraud that I'd obtained evidence of about three weeks into my investigation. At least they always get their man.

****

One file that stuck with me that first year was the assault of a six-month-old child. We received a call from patrols to assume an investigation that they'd been called to at the hospital. The attending pediatrician contacted police when they started to treat this young child with a serious fracture to both the radius and ulna of one of the child's arms. The majority of broken bones of children are commonly known as "greenstick" breaks. If you break a dry old piece of wood, it does just that, breaks right in half, depending on the force applied. When you apply the same force to a live, green branch or tree limb, it doesn't break and separate cleanly. Instead, it stays together but has portions of the bone fray outward, usually in the direction opposite from the point where the force was applied. This fracture was different. It looked like the bone had exploded into pieces. That sort of injury usually happens as a result of a huge amount of force, possibly with a twisting motion or something similar; it very seldom happens to young children because their bones are so soft and pliant.

S o, there I was, going to the hospital to investigate this possible assault while the parents were still there. The mother was sixteen years old, and the father was seventeen. When I spoke to the doctor, I was shocked. Doctors are usually reluctant to give a definitive answer when asked if the injury was as a result of an assault, but this doc was awesome. She said that in her professional opinion, there was no other way to break the radius and ulna of a child in that manner without applying a manual snapping and twisting pressure. Now I just had to figure out *who* had applied that pressure.

When I spoke to the mother, I discovered that she was a meek person who appeared to be a push over, or at least easily led. I had to be careful interviewing her because I might have been able to get her to admit to killing Jimmy Hoffa, and she most likely had no idea who that was. Her father was in the interview room with her and did really well letting her answer the questions without interjecting. One thing he added that the girl really didn't want to tell me, was that the birth father had the child the day the injury occurred while she did some homework. (She was taking grade 10 classes at home.) When they got the child back that evening, he wouldn't stop crying. At first they thought colic, until the arm started to swell. This little mouse of a girl could no more sneeze on that child than apply enough force on the arm to shatter it the way the doctor described. Having seen my fair share of Domestic Violence victims over the years, I thought it was very possible she was having similar "pressure" applied to her as well.

When I interviewed the father of the baby, I knew I had my guy almost from the beginning. He was evasive, and blamed the mother of the kid, or her parents. The one problem was he claimed that he was never alone with the child and his parents could back him up. I spoke next with *his* father who made sure I knew that he was a paid minister for one of the churches in town. He came across as believable and claimed that his son would never do such a thing because his boy didn't have a violent bone in his body. When pressed, the grandfather admitted that his son had been alone for at least part of the day with the baby. The father of the baby admitted his child rolled while on the changing table and he had to grab him really quickly to prevent the child from hitting the floor. He claimed however, that he'd caught the child around the waist, not by the arm. It was starting to shape up, but there was still no proof I could take to court about how the injury occurred.

My next step was to learn a bit about the history and background of everyone who had access to the child. I quickly discovered that the victim's paternal grandfather had lied to me about his son not having a violent bone in his body. I contacted the RCMP in the jurisdiction the father of the child lived prior to moving to Lethbridge and learned a great deal. It turns out that the kid had "played a prank" on his older, mentally challenged sister that got him in some trouble before the family moved to Lethbridge. The young boy took the family dog, a favorite pet of his autistic sister, and put it in the dishwasher, closed the door and started it up. This of course, killed the animal. When the grandfather came home from work that day, he found his son burying the evidence (the dead dog) in the back yard, so no one would find out. This was apparently the last straw for that grandfather, who promptly called child welfare about his own child, and they placed the kid in a secure facility in that jurisdiction. While in that facility, he assaulted his worker, and then tried to burn the building down. So to sum up, we had an animal torturing, assaultive person who also liked to start fires. In one fell swoop, the young man hit every rung on the ladder to one day becoming a serial killer.

I went back and interviewed the young father, and eventually got him to admit he'd actually grabbed the child by the arm when it fell, and this he admitted, caused the injury. This combined with the testimony of the doctor who told me that there would have had to have been a lot more pressure put on that bone than just catching a falling child, gave me enough evidence to charge the boy. He pled guilty to the offence, and then he and his girlfriend moved to another province, leaving their child with her family. It gave me great pleasure in contacting and sending a copy of the case file to the Violent Crimes Section of the jurisdiction where they moved, to give them the heads up about "Future Ted Bundy" moving into their fair city.

Another small joy was going with the child welfare worker when he told the grandfather of the victim he would only be allowed supervised visits to his grandson because he had lied to us about his son, putting his grandchild at further risk.

****

I loved the environment of the Criminal Investigation Division. We all went for breakfast almost every morning together, and sometimes the Lethbridge RCMP Major Crimes detectives would join us as well. I earned another short lived, but somewhat embarrassing nickname at a coffee shop during one of those mornings. I put on "a few" pounds when I was in CID, and we were sitting around a large table talking and laughing when one of the waitresses came over with some hot plates of eggs and bacon. She looked like she was one of Marge Simpson's sisters, and her voice was just as gravelly. She said "Move your elbows, Tiny. The plate's hot." And it stuck. (Thankfully only for a while. I really didn't like being called Tiny. Blue Eyes was way better.) We would talk about our files and run ideas past each other. It was a really fun environment to work in. There were many times that one or two of the old, retired coppers would come in the same restaurant and tell us lies about when they were "big city detectives" and all the crime they'd solved. We would roundly call them liars and tease them mercilessly about working without Mr. Marconi's wonderful invention called the radio. The exact same sort of thing that now happens to me when I try to shed pearls of wisdom on some of the young coppers who work for me.

Our Organized Crime Section Staff Sergeant was an old drug cop from when I was young. Josh spent the majority of his time talking to (some would say micromanaging) the Special Operations Unit, and generally left us alone. For example, policy required that all search warrants needed to be read and approved by one of the two CID staff sergeants. (Organized Crime or Major Crimes). That's a lot of warrants, so what Josh did was predictable. He read the first two or three of mine and **eviscerated** them with red ink. I was pretty sure I'd never made it past 5th grade English class after Josh was done with my first. After I got the hang of it and got one back from him without needing any correction, he told me he didn't want to read anymore of mine. I felt like I was seen by someone who I'd respected as a young copper for his ability, now saw me as almost an equal. (I think the real reason was the fact that Josh wasn't interested in fraud files. Once he knew I could write to his standard, he wasn't interested so he didn't want to take the time to read the details.)

There were a lot of funny moments as well. There was the time one of the

PCU detectives wrote a memo to the Crown's office that didn't meet Josh's standard. He ordered him to re-write it with some amendments. Thirteen times! On the thirteenth attempt Carter, the young PCU copper, took the original back in, told Josh that if it was not good enough they would have to meet in the parking lot to sort matters out. Josh signed off on the memo without comment, but with a bit of a sly grin on his face.

The only thing that Josh really took us to task over was our cell phone bill. Each of us had a flip phone (I know, I am really old) and we had to justify the bill at the end of the month if it was too high, or there was an unexplained expense. Carter was constantly getting jacked up for his bill. His boss would constantly have to defend him, saying that the majority of his calls were to confidential informants. This usually mollified Josh, but there was this one time. . .

S o, there I was, getting called in for a run of the mill stabbing on a weekend. I'd agreed to take the on call weekend for Carter because he had a great opportunity to go to Chicago and see the Cubs play with some friends. I had pity on the young man and agreed to roll the dice and take the weekend on call for him, hoping I didn't get called out. Of course, that never works, and there I was on a Saturday morning, working a stabbing. I was only happy with the fact that patrols had waited until the bad guy, who they located the night before in an intoxicated state, was sober before calling me. It wasn't going to be one of those marathon events, rather a five or six hour deal, and I would hopefully be done and have the rest of the weekend with my family.

About an hour in, I got a call on my company cell phone. I answered and it was Carter, who sounded like he was drunk, and in a bar. He was shouting over the background noise, telling me to turn on my TV and watch the Fox Sports baseball game of the week. He was only a couple of beers in, and currently in the left field bleachers of Wrigley Field, explaining all the noise. Carter was bragging (shouting) that he had just missed catching a home run ball and was sure he was on TV as a result. I told him that I'd been called in to a stabbing, and more importantly, it should've been him. He laughed, saying words to the affect that it sucked to be me. We talked for a minute or two longer, and then the penny dropped. I asked him if he was on his company cell phone.

I heard him laugh and then he shouted, "yah, don't tell Josh!" and he hung up. Working in CID was a good time.

LESSONS ON INTERVIEWING

I may have already mentioned that I'm not a patient man. It's something I've been working to overcome my entire life. Some success comes from learning from mistakes but getting older helps as well. Being impatient is a road block to success in the interview room. Things have changed over the years and the bad guy admitting to what he's done in a "warned statement" is becoming less likely. When they do admit to the offence, it's less likely now than ever that the courts will accept the statement as voluntary. This can be displayed by the simple fact of how many times the Supreme Court of Canada has ruled that we need to add more to the Charter right to counsel warning when we interview bad guys.

When I started, you simply stated, **"You are under arrest for _____. You have the right to retain and instruct counsel without delay. Do you understand that? Do you want to call a lawyer?"** That's it. There were no further charter issues if you said that, he claimed he understood and told you whether he wanted a lawyer or not. Now we go just a bit further. Those four lines have morphed into paragraphs of legalese that the bad guy has to have us explain in normal English. **"You are under arrest for _____. You have the right to retain and instruct a lawyer without delay. This means that before we proceed with our investigation, you can call any lawyer you wish or a lawyer from a free legal advice service immediately. If you want to call your own lawyer from a free legal advice service, we will provide you with a telephone and you can call a toll free number for immediate** legal advice.   If you wish to contact any other lawyer, a telephone book will be provided to you. If you are charged with an offence, you may apply to Legal Aid for assistance. Do you understand? Do you want to call a free lawyer or any other lawyer you choose?"

You would think that this would be enough of an encouragement for those in custody to call a lawyer, but it goes on.

All persons detained in police custody have a right to immediate legal advice regardless of their financial status. Detained persons also have a right to choice of counsel. You may choose to use the legal advice numbers, or a telephone book will be provided to you. The free legal advice number is 1-800-***-****.

You have a right to a reasonable opportunity to contact a lawyer. I am obliged not to take a statement from you or ask you to participate in any process that might provide evidence against you until you are certain about whether you want to exercise this right.   Do you understand? Do you want to waive your right to contact a lawyer?

Do you wish to say anything? You are not obliged to say anything, but whatever you say may be given in evidence. Do you understand?

Then there's an additional warning (called the secondary caution) given to the suspect if you weren't the one that arrested him. (For example, you would have to add this if you were the detective that got called out to interview the guy that the patrol coppers scooped up for the stabbing you were called out to investigate.) We were required to give this back in the 80's when I started as well.

Regardless of anything that anybody has said to you, or you have said to any other person in authority, you are not obliged to say anything unless you wish to do so, but whatever you say may be given in evidence. Do you understand?

Combined with the police caution changing over the years, comes the added "benefit" that coppers are trusted less by society each day. I was taught that there were three criteria that the court looks at to determine whether our "tricking" the offender into giving us the truth about his involvement in a crime should be admissible as evidence. They are, the severity of the offence, the sophistication of the accused, and what the public would find acceptable. In essence, if you have arrested a 12-year-old for shop lifting a candy bar, don't bother taking a statement. If on the other hand you have arrested an outlaw biker who has a twenty page criminal record, and you are investigating him for the murder of three people, then the public would expect you to do what you could, short of torture, to get the bad guy to admit to his crime. The sticky part there is that that public's view of police has changed since I started, and so what we are allowed to do has changed over the years.

Statements of bad guys admitting to their guilt nowadays, are often thrown out because they appear to be oppressive toward the offender. It is hard enough to get a bad guy to admit to what he's done, let alone have a court agree that the inculpatory warned statement was voluntary. A good friend of mine a short time ago convinced an offender to admit to a murder, and in so doing, provide information that only the investigator, offender, and the victim (who was dead) would know. The judge ruled the statement inadmissible because she felt that my friend had "seduced" him into admitting to the offence. All my friend did wrong was to be a decent human being to the offender, treating him with respect and dignity. The judge viewed that as seduction. (Not in the sexual sense of the word, but in the "you were too nice of a guy, and he should have felt more threatened by you" sense of the word.) We used to be closet psychologists in the box, trying to get the guy to admit what he did. ("The box" is copper slang for the interview room.) Now we are more likely to use the term "provable lies," whereby the accused is allowed to provide any story he wants, *then* we go and prove that everything he said was a lie, making him a liar in front of a jury. So now you can see why having patience is an important characteristic for a detective in the interview room.

When I was a young copper, and even by the time I got in to CID the first time, the way cops judged other cops on whether they were competent or not, had a lot to do with how good they were in the box. You could be the best search warrant writer, or the best tactical or strategic planner of your investigation and you would only be deemed "adequate" by your peers, unless you were good in the box. When I was young, I was a terrible interviewer. My interviews usually went something like this.

"Did you do it?"

"Nope."

"I have all this evidence to prove you did it."

"Maybe, but you are wrong, I didn't do it."

"Fine I am gonna charge you anyway."

Not a very productive interview, and not particularly successful if you aren't being entirely honest about actually having evidence. I was at about five or six years service when I was taught a few things by an old detective who'd come back to patrol teams before he retired. He showed me what I was doing by a small scenario. He told me to be the bad guy in the interview room, and he would be me. He then locked me in the room, and I sat there for about five minutes. (It felt like an hour.) Then he came in and we went through the "you did it" - "no I didn't," argument for a minute or so, then he stood up and said, "Fine, I don't care if you admit it or not. I have enough to charge you, so that's what's going to happen." (His language might have been a bit saltier, but you get the general idea.) He then walked out of the room, slammed the door, and left me locked in for good measure.

He waited for a few minutes and then came back in and took me to his office. He asked me what the first thing that went through my mind when he left. I thought, "Where the heck are you going, we aren't done talking yet." His response was "Exactly!" It was like an epiphany. I realized most humans have an innate desire to talk, and often times, confess. I wasn't a priest, but sometimes my job was to be their confessor.

As I got better at the words I needed to say, I had a lot more success, but would still have difficulties from time to time, oblivious to what I was doing wrong. I kept at it but seemed to have run into a brick wall. The easy interviews were still easy, the medium ones were easier, but the tough ones still didn't work. (Tough interviews are things like sex crimes, especially familial, anything to do with a child, and murder. It is harder to admit to having breached a societal taboo like sexually assaulting a child, than admit to a murder. Not even normal criminals like those folks.) One day, by happenstance, I saw a master at work, and more importantly, he saw me, and took the time to teach me a thing or two.

So, there I was, investigating an assault of a ten-month-old child. I only had about four or five years on the job, but I'd already been given my first interview lessons by my sergeant. (When he locked me in the interview room to prove a point.) In this case, the bad guy had driven his girlfriend and their sleeping child to her place of business, where she was picking up her paycheque. (You see boys and girls, years ago, people actually got a cheque instead of direct deposit. . . oh, never mind.) He was driving, she was sitting in the middle of the bench seat of his truck, and their son was in the car seat against the passenger door, sleeping the afternoon away. Our hero pulled over and let her out so she could go get her paycheque.

When she left, their child was sleeping, when she came out five minutes later, he was screaming like a banshee. She looked at him in the car seat and noticed a red mark on the side of his face that went from the jaw line to hair line, and from the ear to the nose. In essence, one entire side of the kids face was red. She thought it must be an allergic reaction or something like that and told her boyfriend to drive to the hospital.

Of course, when the doctor examined the child, after eliminating everything else, he realized that the child had been hit in the face. We were called and I was dispatched. I spoke to the mother first, and she was an emotional wreck. She told me her story, and I later checked with her business and found that everything she told me was true. When I spoke to the father, he was less than forthcoming, and wouldn't really say anything to me. They both agreed the child was fine before she got out of the truck, and the injury occurred while she was gone because he was screaming when she got back. I arrested the guy for assaulting his kid and took him to the station. I read him his rights. He said he understood and didn't want to talk to a lawyer, because he'd done nothing wrong.

When I got back to the station with the bad guy, the interview rooms on the main floor were occupied, so I took him up to the third floor to use the CID interview room. It was an afternoon shift and there was only one detective on duty. I asked him if he would let me use his interview room and he said it was all mine. This guy was a legend in the service that only got bigger each time he spoke to a bad guy. His name was Milton, and he could have been paid well as either a psychologist, or a stand-up comedian. He was that guy. I have been a copper for a long time, and I have never seen anyone better in the box than Milton, and I don't mean just Lethbridge either.

So, I took the bad guy into the room and asked him what had happened. The goal is to minimize the offence and then reel him in. For example, if he sexually assaulted someone, then "at least he didn't kill them". If he killed them, then "at least he was respectful toward the remains of the person and felt remorse." If he did all of those things, you have a psychotic serial killer on your hands, and there is an entirely different book written on how to interview them. So, I started to minimize the offence. I went with the corporal punishment route. . . "The kid was making lots of noise, you tried your best, but had to smack him to let him know what he was doing was wrong and went a bit too far." The guy was having none of it. In fact none of the themes or ideas I was using made any difference. I finally let my impatience show and blurted out, "So you are telling me that Captain Kirk from the Star Ship Enterprise, beamed into the cab of your truck, roughed your son up, and then beamed back out again?!" He said, "yup". At this point, I gave up. I told him I was charging him anyway and hoped that his relationship survived the assaulting of their child and walked out in a huff.

I saw that Milton walking away from the door, and thought he might've been watching and listening, but wasn't sure. I wasn't particularly proud of the interview but getting someone to admit to assaulting a child is a tough hill to climb. Lots of cultural taboos there and, admitting that secret to someone you don't know is a lot to ask of anyone, let alone someone who knows he has done something like that. I asked Milton if he would watch my prisoner while I went to get my notebook. I would only be gone about three or four minutes. He readily agreed and asked me if he could speak to the guy. I said he was welcome to give it a shot.

I was gone less than three minutes, I swear! Out of habit, I looked into the room peep hole before I went in. In that three minutes, Milton had the guy re-arrange the chairs in the interview room as if they were the bench seat of his truck and the bad guy was in the process of showing Milton how he'd reached across the bench and back fisted his child. I didn't go into the room, letting Milton finish what he was doing, and sat at his desk, looking at the interview room door in shock. Milton came out about three minutes later, waved me in, and then told me that this fine young gentleman wanted to apologize to me for lying. The guy admitted what he'd done and told me he was sorry for wasting my time. After I accepted his apology, I went to get some release documents to charge him. Milton was waiting in the CID bullpen, as if he wasn't a sorcerer and I wasn't the small town yokel who'd seen him perform magic.

"Teach me, oh wise one! I beg of you, impart your wisdom or magic upon a lowly and unworthy soul such as myself." I said, while bowing to his infinite wisdom and knowledge. Well not really, but that was how I felt. I asked him what I'd done wrong. He told me the secret - that there was no secret! He'd said many of the same things that I had. He then grabbed the desktop between us so hard that his knuckles showed white, and he got this evil stare going and his voice got tougher than I ever heard him speak, sort of like Batman, and he said, "You just said all of those things like this."

Epiphany! The bad guy didn't tell me because my body language showed him exactly how I felt about people who hit little kids. He was probably thinking that if he admitted it, I would jump across the table and pummel him. That's the way I felt, but I thought I had my emotions under control. Patience and control - who would have thought it would be that easy. . . and that hard. Fast forward about 11 years or so, Milton was retired by this time, and I was the detective tasked with getting a murderer to give it up in the box.

****

S o, there I was, working tasks for the homicide of Lyle. I'd dealt with Lyle and his family for many years. I'd known his sister since she was thirteen when I caught her driving her mom's car without permission - right into a fence. She later became a person who would call me and give me information, right up until she died in a car accident, when the driver (who'd recently stolen the car) wrapped it around a parked car. I'd also been the guy who investigated their mother's sudden death. This was different though. Lyle had been involved in some sort of fight in his own house where he was stabbed numerous times. The blood spatter evidence in the home was in the top five most graphic I'd ever seen. There were blood patterns from where the bad guy swung his knife up and down, spraying blood from the blade onto the walls and ceiling, and arterial blood spray from at least one of the victim's injuries.

Lyle ran out of the house, already dying as the blood sprayed from his neck wound, while he chased (or ran from) his murderer down the street. He got across the street, and then fell over backwards, into the garbage box of the neighbour's house. No bad guy to be seen, and just a blood trail leading from Lyle's open door to his body, lying peacefully face up, in someone else's trash bin. If anything funny can be gleaned about this set of circumstances, cops will find it, and we did. The Major Crimes detective, Ty arrived on scene before Ident did. He looked at the three stab wounds to Lyle's neck, and thought they looked self inflicted, with two of them looking like hesitation marks, before he did the one that caused him to bleed out. It was close to a long weekend, and many of us had plans, so my friend Martin called him and asked if he needed help. Ty demurred, admitting that he thought it was a suicide and thanked us. About twenty minutes later, Ident checked the rest of the body, and when they rolled Lyle over, they found a knife sticking out of his back, almost perfectly between his shoulder blades. When we got there, Martin mentioned it was the worst case of suicide he'd ever seen, which of course stuck through the rest of the investigation, and many years thereafter.

Anyway, through Ty's excellent work, as well as some interesting information obtained during a neighbourhood canvass, we identified a suspect. Two or three weeks passed before we had all of our ducks in a row and were ready to make an arrest. We were looking for a guy named Paul, and he wasn't that hard to find. He was serving weekends at the jail on an unrelated crime. Martin and I were tasked with going out to the jail and executing the search warrant, to obtain all of his clothing (in hopes he had been wearing them when he committed the murder), and to arrest and interview him. I assumed that I'd be given the task of executing the warrant and Martin would interview the bad guy. I was the newest guy in CID at the time, and Martin was the most senior. Like I mentioned before, interviewing is the task that all detectives were judged by in those days; meaning if you were a good at that one thing, you were a good detective, and if you weren't, then you just weren't quite as good as "the rest of us." So I was really surprised with what Martin said to me on the way to arrest and interview Paul. "Hey, I'm better with warrants and file flow, and you're a better interviewer. Would you be okay doing the interview?"

I was shocked at first but then I realized that he was right. I learned a lot of stuff from Martin over the years, but the concept he taught me by that simple statement was one of the most important. The file is more important than anyone's ego. He was simply assigning the right task to the right person. No wonder he was soon promoted to staff sergeant. He knew that he was going to take a verbal beating from the boys in CID when we got back. That didn't matter to him. He did the right thing for the file, no matter what others thought. I remembered this simple, but important lesson later in my career when I was the primary investigator of a homicide and assigning tasks. Know your investigators and assign the right task to the right copper. Martin was a stand up guy and a great mentor who was ahead of his time. I almost let him down right out of the chute.

We got to the jail and showed the corrections officer the Judge's order required to get Paul out of the jail and into our custody. When he was brought down to the admit and discharge area, I told him he was under arrest for first-degree murder and explained his rights. His eyes got really big when I said first-degree murder, and then he got quiet. When I asked him if he wanted to call a lawyer, he said he did. I told him my partner was just getting all of his stuff, including his clothing, and then we would go to the station where he could call his lawyer. While Martin was getting the clothes, I looked over at Paul, and saw that his lower lip was quivering. He was on the verge of tears, and it slipped out, I swear. It wasn't part of the plan; in fact I threw a wrench in the works that took quite a bit of work to repair.

"Oh man, this is freakin' killing you. You gotta get this off your chest." I said. And then he did.

He told me everything including his motive. It was awesome! Except for the fact that he'd said he wanted to talk to counsel first. In Canada, the bad guy can't be questioned before talking to counsel unless he waives that right. After he is satisfied with counsel, we can question him until the cows come home, but only after his lawyer says to him "Don't say anything to police, and don't sign anything." I tried to put the genie back in the bottle, but it was too late. I finally stopped him from telling me about every crime he'd ever committed, and then told him we'd talk more when we got to the station. I kept it inside but thought I might have just destroyed this whole investigation because of something I'd blurted out in a moment of impatience combined with empathy for Paul. I could tell it was eating him up inside, but I should have shut my mouth.

When I got back to the station, there were guys in the bullpen who were trying to high five me, and ecstatic that I got him to give it up. Most of them didn't think what happened was that big of a deal. After speaking with the Crown Prosecutor, it was decided that I needed to get a confession from him, without even mentioning any of the information that he'd previously admitted, as if it had never been said. I was with him in the box for seven and a half hours with a few breaks. We even ate pizza and drank Coke together, and I put up with his cigarette smoke while I ate. (I sometimes think that was the hardest part of the whole interview.) We started with getting to know each other, and I found out that he was adopted and grew up in Cardston and was not a big fan of members of my faith. He was a First Nations man and was a believer in Native Spiritualism. We talked about the similarities of our beliefs and then we started talking about spirits and where they went after the death of the body. I told him what I believed, and then asked him what he would say to his friend Lyle if his spirit was sitting in the third chair next to us. (As I said this, I started putting out large, printed photos of all the blood evidence at the scene of the crime, and the picture of his friend, dead with six stab wounds and a knife sticking out of his back.) He finally caved and apologized to Lyle for what had happened.

He went on to admit that the argument happened because they both used crack cocaine, and it was an expensive habit. Lyle was happy to sit around and use his welfare cheques to pay for his crack, augmenting his cash flow with the occasional petty crime. Paul talked Lyle into working for the same company he did, pouring concrete (or something equally exhausting). Paul warned him that it was hard work, but the money was good. Lyle agreed and Paul went to his boss and got him a job. Lyle worked for three days before he quit. They argued and then fought over Lyly making Paul look bad to his boss. Their fight eventually turned into a knife fight. Paul pointed to his throat when he told me that he stabbed Lyle three times in self defence. This was the exact same place where the three stab wounds were on Lyle's throat. I had the right guy. The location of the injuries had been "hold back" information that only the investigators and the perpetrator knew. Paul wouldn't admit to stabbing Lyle in the back at all, because that went against his story of self defence, but it was enough.

I was teased a bit about the interview and how I got to that point. My partner came out and gave me the gears because at the end, Paul cried like a little boy who got caught stealing ice cream. He'd also hugged me while crying, and I was wearing a white shirt and tie. My shirt was getting soaked by his tears and snot, and I was looking right at the camera with one of those "tell anyone and I will kill you!" looks, knowing that my partner Ray was scribing the interview (making notes for me) and was laughing as it happened. When I got out of the room, Ray told me he was going to take the tape and send it to my instructor of the Forensic Interviewing course at the police college. They have a video to show an example of every concept they teach, including when it's appropriate to touch a shoulder, or to let the person cry on yours. I really didn't want that to happen, and he finally acquiesced.

A conversation with the Crown Prosecutor later confirmed that what I'd done was a screw up, but not fatal. She also confirmed, after the fact, that what we did was the only route, unless we wanted to go to trial without any form of admission from the accused. We had enough to convict anyway, but when he admits it even after his lawyer told him not to, and the judge accepts the statement into evidence, it is more likely to cause a change of plea from not guilty to guilty. That's what happened in this case. He pled to manslaughter and got 16 years in jail. I learned a lot from that investigation and also had a bit of an inside laugh. Paul really, (and I mean REALLY!) hated members of my faith. In convincing him to tell the truth about the murder, I'd used a part of the lessons each missionary learns to teach others about church doctrine. It was about our beliefs concerning where we were before we were born, why we are here, and where we go after we die that convinced him to apologize to his dead friend for killing him. I'm sure Paul would've been that much more disappointed if he knew that a conversation about church doctrine was what got him over the hump to admit to killing his friend. I won't tell him if you don't.

FRAUD, INCEST AND ATTEMPTED MURDER, OH MY!

Working in the Organized Crime Section of CID was exactly what I'd been striving toward my whole career. The files were all too large, complicated, or convoluted to be done while still responding to 911 calls or dealing with drunks and crack heads. I felt like I was even busier than when I was in Patrol Division because, although there was down time in CID, there was always that one file sitting on your desk that you had to get ready for prosecution. I didn't even mind that I hadn't been assigned to the Major Crimes Section when I was promoted any more. If there was a homicide, we all chipped in. I never thought I would say it, but even some of the frauds were interesting, and not nearly as intimidating after I'd been trained to investigate them. For instance, the four million dollar fraud that took me 18 months to finish.

S o, there I was, investigating a file that'd been taken over the front desk. The sterling work of the desk constable who took the original complaint provided me with a three line statement. It said, "John took $650,000 from my family. He also took some from my mom. I want him charged." That obviously isn't a real quote, but you get the general idea. I'm sure the desk constable was busy that day and didn't know the right questions to ask. Grumping about young coppers that you wish were better is a waste of time if you don't teach them what you need, and then encourage them with the fact that they'll one day be in your place. I probably did that to a detective or two when I was young.

Anyhow, John was a financial advisor. He worked for a brokerage firm, before being sanctioned by the Alberta Securities Commission and fired by his employer. He decided he'd go out on his own and try and "generate wealth for those that he knew and cared about." He began to approach people at his church and offer them a great investment deal. All they had to do was give him a minimum investment of $10,000. He would guarantee them 10% interest per month for thirteen months, then the original investment back after 13 months. This is of course, a classic Ponzi scheme, in that he wasn't investing the money in anything, (other than himself), and had to come up with new investors to pay those he owed a thousand a month after they "invested" in the scheme. At it's zenith, he had defrauded 72 victims of about 4.2 million dollars.

Almost all of the victims were from his church, and he played the angle that he was a man of God, sent to this earth to help them make enough money to take care of their families. The majority of the victims were first generation Canadians, mostly from the Philippines, where the trust in banks and police is considerably different than it is in Canada. He had older people giving him their retirement nest egg, in hopes of retiring sooner, or wealthier. He convinced some young people to obtain numerous credit cards, max them out, and give him the cash. The interest rate he gave them appeared higher than the interest charged by the credit card company. (In what world does that make sense?) Eventually the whole scheme collapsed under it's own weight, and he started missing "interest payments" to his "investors." He had run out of new "investors" that gave him money to pay the older victims. Even then it took months for people to start coming to the police, and then more months for the cops (me) to sort out what was going on and find out how many people got taken. Imagine taking 72 witness statements from people as far away as Vancouver and Toronto, and then putting that file together for a prosecutor, and eventually a judge.

I contacted our Crown Prosecutor's office and told them what I had, looking for some assistance. They told me they didn't have the time or expertise to prosecute the file and would request Special Prosecutions to contact me. Ironically, I knew exactly how they felt, but there was no one that I could hand it to. The good news was that the prosecutor assigned was awesome. She was originally from Montreal, and one of the smartest prosecutors I'd ever met. She'd done these sorts of files before and walked me through the rough spots and warned me of the pitfalls. I'd contacted our Crown's office and been referred to "Special" right at the point where I was starting to write search warrants for the Securities Commission as well as the Investment Dealers Association. Neither of those two agencies were culpable in any way, but I needed to get the documents they had about John, the reason why he'd been sanctioned and eventually fired as well as anything they might know about what I was investigating. The beauty of the Special Prosecutions office is that they are involved earlier in the investigative process. For example, they require you to submit a search warrant to them for "approval" before it is sent to a judge to sign. (You can still do it your way, but if they are not happy with what you've done, they can always tell you they won't take the file, forcing you to go back to your own Crown's office, who are over worked, and referred you to Special Prosecutions in the first place.)

My partner and I executed the warrants on the two agencies in Calgary, and instantly hit pay dirt. The reason John had been punished by the Securities Commission, and eventually fired by his employer, was for doing the same thing on a smaller scale a year or two prior. He had received a $100,000 fine, among other things. He paid the fine and was back at it with different victims and higher dollar amounts a year or two later. That tells you how lucrative it was for him in the front end. (Right up until he got caught.)

When I had all the information I could gather, I called John in to give me his side of the story. When he came in, he'd come from his lawyer's office and told me that he would not be providing a statement. I may have mentioned it before, but this is one of the great things about the Canadian system compared to the US system. In Canada, we just say, "Are you happy with your lawyer's advice?" When they say yes, then I just say, "Excellent, you may not want to talk yet, but listen to me for a bit." I then told him everything I had, and how bad it looked for him. That is the beauty of fraud investigations. There was a paper trail of everything John had done. He couldn't deny it, he could only justify it, which was pretty hard when the year before he had been given a huge fine for the exact same thing. He cut his losses, and told me that he knew it was wrong, but he hoped to turn something wrong into a money maker for the people that invested into the scheme. A Court of Queen's Bench Justice later gave him thirteen years in prison. The sentence was eventually varied on appeal to ten years.

****

These types of investigations are a lot of work and are in area that I wasn't comfortable with. I'm not an accountant and didn't get into policing to showcase my math skills, such as they are. I was very thankful at the time for a couple of guys in the bullpen that seemed to keep everyone laughing. Steve was a guy who got promoted at the same time as me and was put in the Domestic Violence Unit. He was quite a prankster and was always there to lighten the mood. By that time, my staff sergeant had changed, and

Darwin didn't take jokes quite as well as Josh, who could dish it out as well as take it. They were bound to clash, like the immovable object and the unstoppable force. One of my favourites was when Steve went on YouTube and found a lengthy video of a phone ringing or something just as obnoxious. He then set his volume to high, turned the video on and walked away from the bullpen. Darwin, the new boss, heard the phone ring incessantly and loudly, with no one to answer. In a fit, he'd get up and look for the ringing phone and start to pick up individual phones on guys desks, hoping to answer it. It should've been a give away that it kept ringing, instead of going to voicemail after the fourth ring, but Steve figured he was an easy mark for that sort of thing, and I guess he was right. There was also the time my new partner Manny had purchased a new motor bike and was proudly bragging about the amount of money he'd be saving on gas, and the enjoyment he would get on his days off. Steve went and got some dirty motor oil and poured a small amount down the side of the crank case of the bike, and then a small pool of oil under the bike, to make it appear as though Manny's brand new machine was leaking oil. Steve only admitted to it when Manny started to call a tow truck to take the bike back where he had purchased it. Good times, unless you were Manny, I suppose.

Often times, members of the Criminal Investigation Division get called out to finish off an investigation that was started by patrol teams. It might be the severity or complexity of the investigation, it's potential length, or just because they don't have the manpower to give the file the attention that it deserves. No matter the reason, if we're called in, we take it over. Sometimes, however, we get called in to unravel a severe "goat rope" that was started badly by patrol teams, (by bad luck, or a screw-up) and then went down hill before we got there. We are then expected to salvage what we can, and make it all better, or something like that. I got called out to one like that in about 2006. The acting patrol sergeant at the scene had made a few bad calls that cascaded into a real mess. It came in as a triple stabbing, with six people involved. (All members of the same family). The patrol team had kept the file for almost ten hours before calling the staff sergeant in charge of the Major Crimes Section. When he learned what patrols had done, he turned them down cold, telling the acting duty staff sergeant that they would not come in to clean up their mess. (He didn't say it that way, but enough to get the message across.)

The next call was to my boss, the staff sergeant in charge of the Organized Crime Section. He felt the same way about how messed up it was, but he also learned that one of the six people involved in the case was a well-known drug dealer in town that our Special Operations Unit was investigating. There were also whispers that this bad guy might be cozying up to more "formal" organized crime entities, to grow his little empire. Although my boss didn't want to take it either, he agreed to call someone out to see what we could do. He called me and told me to go in and fix it if I could. He gave me permission to call out one of the Property Crime constables to help me if I needed it, and we were off to the races.

S o, there I was, called out to an investigation of a triple stabbing that the patrol team has been holding onto for too long. The acting team sergeant had left a probationary constable to write a search warrant for the house to get the knife, but they'd already given up the scene, losing continuity of the scene. (There was no way to say that someone hadn't gone back in after we left and cleaned and/or altered the crime scene. We couldn't even say that the knife was still there.) The poor young kid sitting at the computer when we got there knew that the warrant was going nowhere but thought that it was his fault. The first thing he did was apologize to us for "wrecking the file." I try not to throw other guys under the bus, but this was too much. I told the guy he wasn't to blame. The moment his boss told them all to drive away, they lost all hope of getting a search warrant. When my partner and I were done talking to him, he looked like the weight of the world had been lifted from his shoulders. This investigation would rest entirely on witness and culprit statements.

My partner and I interviewed all six people in this mess, with the primary task of trying to figure out who'd stabbed who. The fight revolved around two sisters, who each had a son and daughter of similar ages. The two sisters were in their late 50's or early 60's and their children, a boy and a girl each, were all in mid to late 20's, including the aspiring crime boss. The sisters had gone out together and come home to find their four children drunk and arguing. Seeing as how the two older women were even more intoxicated than their children, they were no help solving the argument. In fact the sisters soon took sides, and the fight was on. One of the older women was slashed across the cheek with a steak knife, wielded by her nephew, the aspiring crime boss. The two female cousins then got into it. Petra was stabbed in the thigh by Charity. When Charity couldn't pull the knife out of her cousin's leg, she grabbed another kitchen knife from the drawer, and grabbed Petra from behind by her hair and pulled her head back. Petra tucked her chin to her chest just in time to avoid having her neck slit, obtaining a rather nasty Jokeresque slashed cheek and mouth instead. Charges were meted out and eventual guilty pleas abounded.

Two good things happened as a result of this tale. The first is that the young probationary copper went on to become really good, and eventually worked for me when I was the Community Engagement Sergeant, and again when

I was a Patrol Team Sergeant years later. The other heartening piece of news involved the wanna be crime kingpin who'd stabbed his aunt in the face. He later fell in love and had two children with his cousin Petra, the one with the joker smile. They're still together weathering his intermittent absences whilst in and out of prison. Love is indomitable my friends! It wins out in the end, no matter what.

****

Speaking of love, there was a great prank pulled on one of our tactical team members by my buddy Carter around that time. Carter, the detective who called me from Wrigley Field in Chicago with his company cellphone (and paid the company back I might add), was also on the tactical team. He'd just gotten a sniper scope with an illuminating sight reticle. Ron, another tac team member, was an avid gun collector and a pretty conservative dude. This makes him an easy target from time to time for guys like Carter. So they were in the Tac Team locker room and Carter was showing Ron this really cool sight that sort of glows in the dark, or at least the sight reticle does. To show this cool effect, Ron and Carter were at the far end of the locker room and around a corner with the lights out. They heard the door to the locker room buzz open from someone using the key card. Ron didn't think anything of it. He just kept looking over this really cool development in technology. Carter on the other hand, saw an opportunity that he couldn't pass up. He immediately pulled his pants and underwear down to his ankles while Ron was looking at the rifle, in the dark. Sure enough about a minute later Syd, the team leader, walked into the change room area, and turned on the lights. He saw Ron standing there with a rifle in his hand and a smile on his face, standing right next to Carter with his pants and underwear pooled at his ankles and a bigger smile on his face,. Ron only noticed when Carter shouted out, "Can't a couple of fellas get a little privacy around here?" Ron started pointing at the sight of the gun and repeated the words "No, no, no!" and, "Illuminating sight reticle" over and over. Syd's laughter made Carter laugh with him, and Ron storm off in a huff.

I didn't know it yet but my time in CID was drawing to a close. I was coming to the end of my fourth year, and that's about how long these stints go. In the bigger agencies, like the RCMP, once a copper gets into an investigative role like this, they can potentially stay for the rest of their career. In the small and medium sized services, they need to spread the wealth around so that when that copper retires, he doesn't leave a hole that takes years to replace. The bad thing about that is, just as you are getting good at your assignment, you are moved out so someone else can have a turn. The good thing is, if you are ever stuck in a job that you don't care for, you are sure to be moved in a few years. Another bonus about our system is that you become pretty knowledgeable about the entire service, not just one or two niches. I've had the opportunity to work in CID twice. Patrols and Traffic as a constable and Patrols again as a sergeant. I also spent time in Recruiting, Special Projects, and Community Engagement as a sergeant. I've become more of a generalist than a specialist, because I've seen a lot about how the company works. (It also allows for great stories from a bunch of different places.) My last investigation during that first stint as a detective was an attempted murder, and the "victim" had it coming. (I know I am not supposed to say that but hold judgement on me until you hear the story.)

S o, there I was, called out for what would be the last time before I was transferred. The copper that I took the file over from was the first recruit I trained. Chase had turned into a good investigator in his own right but didn't have the time to keep this file. Patrols had come upon a man wandering the streets of a northside cul-de-sac with a huge knife sticking out of his back, between his shoulder blades. He was knocking on doors at five in the morning asking for help. People felt too scared to let him in but when he turned from their door to go to the next house, the home owner could then see the blade sticking out of his back. Numerous 911 calls later, and there I was, with a victim in the hospital, and his common law wife Kathy, under arrest and awaiting my arrival. By the time I got there, they'd given her a phone, but not spoken with her about what'd happened. It sounded like the guy was going to make it, but that was always an iffy proposition. The doctor's report later showed the knife had bisected his lung and missed his aorta by about 3 millimetres. Just a touch to the left, and she would have done what she intended.

Kathy was the poster girl for how a battered spouse would look and act. I went in to check on her to see if she needed anything and introduce myself before I started down the path of a formal interview. I immediately noticed scratch marks on her neck and both of her eyes were starting to purple up from bruising. I could tell that there was more to this story. Before I even asked her about why she was there, I asked her if she was doing alright, and if it was okay for us to take photographs of her obviously fresh injuries. I'd a feeling where this might be going and had to gather the evidence before it disappeared. It also gave me some credibility with her, to show that I was able to see more than just the fact that she had knifed someone. I was interested in the "why" of it as well. When we were done in Ident, I asked her if she'd talked to her lawyer, and if she was happy with his advice. She said her lawyer told her not to talk, so I asked her how her injuries happened. And she told me.

Kathy was only 22 or 23 years old, and she had three kids with the man she stabbed. They were 15-years-old when they got together, and she was 16 when she gave birth to their first child. Kathy loved him, but he was an abusive drunk. They were currently living in her sister's basement, sharing one room with the two of them and their three children under the age of six, because he'd burnt almost every other family bridge due to his alcoholism and abuse. On the night in question, he had some of his friends over and told her that he expected her to stay in their room and keep the kids quiet. Even though the guys turned into loud drunks, she did an admirable job of getting the kids to sleep and got a bit of sleep as well. At about four or five in the morning, he stumbled into the room looking for his work boots and clothing so that he could go to work. He stepped on the head of his oldest child, who understandably woke up and started crying. This was unacceptable, so our hero started beating Kathy with his hard hat, hitting her mostly in the face while also trying to choke her. At one point she thought she lost consciousness, because when she woke up, the beating had stopped. She told me she got up, went in to the kitchen and got the biggest knife she could find. She stopped talking after that, citing her lawyer's advice not to tell me anything.

I didn't need her to tell me what happened after that. Chase and his partner had done an excellent neighbourhood canvass and located two witnesses, both of whom saw the same thing. They both saw her leave the residence in stocking feet and run down the street in her night clothes, knife in hand and hollering to the top of her lungs, "I hope you die, you f#$&^$% bastard." Neither saw the act, but both then saw her walk back to the residence, no longer holding the knife.

I'm a bit of a perfectionist about my investigations. I have my name associated to them, so I work very hard to give the best product I can. I'm also fiercely proud of the Police Service. One of the things a detective does is dig a bit deeper and find out causes of incidents, rather than just highlighting the facts on the surface. When I dug deeper and discovered how many times, and under what circumstances we'd dealt with the victim and the accused, I saw where we'd failed Kathy. In fact, a book could be written on how we failed Kathy and her children over the past two years at least. I found that we had been to no less than 18 domestic disputes at their residence over the last two years. Not one charge was laid, and a few times, I could tell from the way the report was written that there would've been enough evidence to proceed if the copper in question had just dug a bit deeper, or cared a bit more (or in fairness, had a bit more time.) There were also two obvious breaches of our domestic violence policy. That wasn't just the copper at fault, but also his partner if there was one, and his boss who approved the report. It's easy to sit back in my detective chair and judge others' actions when I wasn't there, but this girl had obviously taken a beating for the two years she lived in our jurisdiction, and probably during the entire six-year relationship. I was also stuck. She had stabbed him and said the magic words, "I hope you die" as she jammed the blade in his back. I couldn't let it go and would have to let the judge know all the circumstances and trust that the right thing would be done at trial. I made sure that my case report had all of the information that I had learned about, not just the incident, but the history leading up to it as well. I saw a couple good things happen as a result.

The first happened when I went to the hospital to take a statement from the "victim" after he was out of surgery. He wasn't overly cooperative because I had to read him his rights for assault with a weapon and choking to overcome resistance before I got his side of the story. This was after he told me that he had fallen on the knife and didn't want to give me a statement at all. I charged him for both offences, ensuring that his first court appearance on the charges was a bit further down the road so he would be out of the hospital, and able to attend. The second was not only cool, but a good cautionary tale to those young minds who I taught in later years. This turned into a story about more than just how to investigate, but also about the reputation you gain by doing things the right way. I didn't see that value in what I'd done until my next transfer the following January to Special Projects and Recruiting.

My new responsibilities were varied, and for the most part, decidedly non-police related. (That same job, save the recruiting portion, is now done very well by a civilian, rather than a copper.) I was responsible for writing the Yearly Report of the Service and checking carpet wear in the building, as well as recruiting. (I swear I am not exaggerating. I actually had to keep track of wear and tear of the carpet in the building as one of my job functions!) One of my police related tasks was conducting background investigations for new recruits. I was also tasked with co-teaching the recruit class with a civilian English teacher from the college. She taught grammar and spelling, and I taught them how to take notes, statements and write case reports. (A case report is the document used by the Crown Prosecutor to provide enough information to hopefully convict the accused.) I'd never met the lady I taught the course with before, but we got along well. I brought in examples of various different case reports to show the students, including Kathy's file. I gave my co-teacher a copy of all of them.

While I taught my portion of the five day course, my teaching partner was reading the case reports. I teased her later about the fear I had that she would whip out a big red pen and start eviscerating my case reports in front of the entire class. I said it in jest, expecting a similar response, but instead she thanked me for being so meticulous and honest, especially with Kathy's file. I asked her what drew her to that one in particular, and she told me that Kathy was her goddaughter, and that she knew many of the incidents that I spoke of in the history of the file. She was impressed that the police would go to such trouble and detail, in pointing out their own failures. There is also an added dynamic to this and many other stories that I haven't shared on purpose.

Race means nothing to me. I grew up thinking that Kathy is one of Heavenly Father's children just like me. That made us brother and sister, so I've tried my best over the years to treat others just like that. Kathy is an Indigenous woman and had been consistently victimized by the man she loved, and then we failed her when we were called. She fell through the cracks of the system that was supposed to help her. We as a Police Service had let her down. I honestly believe that at least part of the reason she stabbed her spouse was because she felt no one else could help her, including us. Because I'd done my homework, and put down the truth in my case report, I'd serendipitously shown her family member that we'd at least tried to show that we cared enough to admit our failings and tried to make it right as best we could. It was a great teaching moment for the class, and for the young coppers I would lead and teach over the next twelve years. For those of you that need to know, the Prosecutor and the Judge did the right thing as well. Kathy got less jailtime than the "victim" did. It was a beautiful thing to see.

THE TRYPTOPHAN AFFAIR

The transfer out of CID was a difficult one for me. I didn't want to go, even though it was probably time to move. They usually leave you in those spots between three and five years, I had been there four. It wasn't the transfer that bothered me as much as where I got sent. As I mentioned earlier, I was transferred to the Recruiting/Training/Special Projects Unit. It was in the administrative side of the chain of command, a side of the job that I'd never worked before. This was my 20th year on the job, all of which had been working on the operational side. I was no longer required to do any investigations, other than background checks for new recruits. I hated it. Although necessary, most of what I did could have been done by a civilian. (In fact only a few years later, they shunted all the duties but the recruiting and training portion to a civilian.) Some of my duties included compiling the yearly report for the Police Service, ensuring all the door locks in the station were changed out that year, and as I mentioned previously, checking the wear of the carpets to make note of when they needed changing out. (I am not kidding.) I can't imagine why I wouldn't feel like a cop doing important but non-police duties like that, can you? The only saving grace of that short and difficult time in my career, was the recruiting side of the house. Doing background checks are investigations of a sort. I met some really good kids and their families when I did the home visits. I even got a blatant bribe from one guy. His wife made me cookies. (It worked, we hired him.) This was the class that I taught reports, statements, and notebooks during their training. In May of that same year (only five months in purgatory) I was sprung. . . Set free. . . Emancipated. . .You get the idea.

It turned out that one of the sergeants in Patrol Division had injured his back and needed a day shift job where he didn't have to get in and out of a car. I felt really bad for him, and especially when he found out that the injury would keep him off the road for the rest of his career. He's a great guy who'd been on my first patrol team. He was the new guy driving the van when I got hired and was pleased as heck when I showed up those many years before, if only for the fact that his days driving the van were numbered the moment I finished with my FTO. Jim was quite a character, and a hard act to follow. He was funny and bright, a pretty good negotiator as well. We were in the Negotiator Unit together for quite a few years until he got out. In fact, he was the negotiator on top of the bridge trying to talk to the guy that kept climbing up and down, and finally jumped. Jim was also very "colourful".

I heard of an incident when he was the acting staff sergeant one night shift. He was booking a prisoner into the cell block who'd been difficult to deal with. I wasn't there when this happened, but I heard that the bad guy had assaulted one of our coppers. The bad guy calmed down during the booking in process when he realized that we outnumbered him. After all the ruckus he'd caused, he started begging for a cigarette before he got put in his cell. Jim looked him in the eye, slowly fished out his own pack of smokes, even slower, took one out and put it in his mouth. Then, with excruciating slowness (you get where I am going with this) he lit the cigarette, calmly blue the smoke in the offender's face and said, "There's your F*%$#ing smoke," and had the arresting officer take the guy off to his cell.

On a more serious note that shows you what kind of guy he is, when I had my heart attack, and was lying on my back in recovery, after the double angioplasty, a nurse came over to me and asked me if I could take a call. I said, "I don't know, can I?" They had me in a bed where I was not allowed to elevate my head by more than 12 degrees, for fear I would re-open the incision in my femoral artery and bleed out before they could help me. I took the call and Jim had all of the guys from CID there on the phone, and he started telling me joke after joke. I honestly tried not to laugh, but a nurse had to come over and take the phone away. She more than half heartedly accused Jim of trying to kill me. He's a great guy and was a hard act to follow.

By the end of May, I was back on patrol teams, and happy as a bug in a rug. I'd been on teams for 16 years before I went to CID, so there was no real learning curve when I got back. There were a few pieces of equipment that were new, and some of the processes were different, but overall, things were good, and I was soon comfortable. I got along well with my boss. She was a former Domestic Violence detective when I was young, and I'd been on a few courses with her. She treated the team well, and we worked well together. An old sergeant once told me that his job was to make me be able to replace him. I now knew what that meant. There is a constant changing of the guard in policing. You notice it more in the small and medium size Police Services because you get to know almost everyone in the Service. I'd known and worked with her for a lot of years, but she would end up retiring a couple of years later. I was already in my twentieth year, and even though I planned to stay fifteen more, most of the guys and girls on the team considered me ancient. I'd seen a lot of change over the years.

One of the things I enjoyed most about being back on teams was the opportunity to teach young coppers. We had a couple of new guys every year, and I enjoyed helping to prepare them to replace me one day. The reason we had a couple new guys every year was due to the fact that the Service was growing, as was the city. When I started, Lethbridge had about 65,000 citizens or so, and had about 89 coppers. It was over 100,000 now and the authorized strength was getting close to 170 cops. Those teaching moments arrived by the bucketload, and often.

We were pretty tight as a team, always playing pranks on each other, and having a good time together. There was even an old friend, "The Brown Nose Award." It was an award that started being handed out to one deserving candidate after another for obvious reasons (the name describes it best), since 1983. It had skipped from team to team over the years and it found a home on the same team I had. I even had a couple of honourable mentions in it from when I was a new guy. The award had sort of morphed in to a "biggest screw up of the month" kind of award, and the winner (or loser, depending on your point of view) handed it out to it's rightful owner the next month. As I write this in 2021, it is still going strong, 38 years later. It's helped us collectively deal with some of the bad things we see. The city was getting more violent, and there was much more drug use. Street level drug use was predominantly weed and hash when I started, with a very small amount of cocaine. Cocaine and crack cocaine were going strong when I got back to the street from CID the first time. When you are a detective, you only deal in the big stuff, so you start to forget that there was a lot of bigger stuff that just never got transferred to CID, and you certainly didn't see the day-to-day effects of the drug trade. It was starting to tear the city apart. Then there were the regular, run of the mill calls, most involving some sort of mental health issue. We needed things to help us stick together and retain some semblance of sanity. The Brown Nose Award was one way we accomplished that.

So, there I was, going to a suicide on the south side of the city. The call had become sort of run of the mill, but the new kid assigned to it was learning so I went there with every intention of trying to help her get better. The subject decided to end it all and left a note for his wife telling her to call 911 and not go into the back yard. Of course, the first thing she did was go into the back yard, where she found the body of her husband who'd shot himself in the head. It was a bit worse than that though. The house they lived in was in a more affluent area of the city, and they had a door in the basement that led to some outside concrete stairs leading up to the backyard. He'd loaded a shotgun with a deer slug, put the butt of the weapon on the fourth step up, put the barrel in his mouth and pulled the trigger. He'd been standing at the bottom landing with the door closed behind him. When he shot himself, he fell backwards so his head (what was left of it) fell flush against the closed door. When his wife later came to the other side of that door and opened it, she could see the graphic and permanent results. The top of his head was missing so she had a clear view inside of his head, almost to his tonsils.

It happened to be a windy day, and when I say windy, I mean windy for Lethbridge, which is **REAL** windy compared to other places. The eastern foot of the Rocky Mountains causes some pretty brisk winds, especially in the spring and fall. That day the wind was a steady 50 to 60 kilometer per hour, with gusts of over 100. The neighbour to the east of the dead guy's house had a really nice white stucco siding, that is until his neighbour shot himself. The siding was now no longer white.

I went for a walk in the grass of the backyard, thinking I was far enough away from his body that I wouldn't track anything. It turns out I was wrong because when I went to put my boots in my locker at the end of the day, I found brain matter in my boot tread. It was a good teaching moment for the young copper assigned to the case. (I'd become too old and stupid to learn new things, I guess.) The young copper had to tell the neighbours they couldn't wash their siding until the Forensic Ident Unit came and took pictures. She also learned to wait for Ident before walking the crime scene, unlike her stupid sergeant who knew better.

Another thing that young copper learned the following week was "If the wind will pick up blood and gore and deposit it one door down, you should probably check two doors down." She learned that important axiom when the neighbour two doors down from the deceased came in to the front counter to see her. When she got to the front counter, the neighbour told her who he was, where he lived and presented her with a sandwich baggie containing a chunk of bone about 3" by 2". It had some scrape marks on the sides. He said "I think this is part of my neighbour. I'm sorry, but my dog found it in the back yard and was gnawing on it." Sure enough, the Medical Examiner told us a couple of weeks later it was the frontal bone (forehead) of our dead guy. He didn't tell us the size of the dog. We guessed it was pretty small though; the gnaw marks sure were.

****

Some of the young kids (who now aren't so young) were a lot of fun to have around. One of them wasn't young at all though. He was closer to my age when we hired him. He came from another police agency before us, and before that he'd been in the military and served in the first Gulf War. He was an acquired taste, but an excellent addition to the team. He had a few quirks though. He'd been known to enter into the occasional bet with his co-workers as to whether he would eat something that was relatively unpalatable, like say, a bologna sandwich in the back pocket of a homeless person. I wasn't there for it, but imagine it was a sight to see. Shane searched the guy he'd arrested for public intoxication, having consumed his share of hand sanitizer prior to arrest. (I purposefully left that ambiguous as to who'd consumed the hand sanitizer, as you shall soon see.) Upon searching the amiable drunk, Shane found a bologna sandwich in the back pocket of the fellow in a small baggie. He asked the drunk if he could have it, and the amiable but intoxicated gentleman said "Sure." At which point, Shane took the sandwich out of the baggie, made eye contact with his fellow copper who he'd bet, and took a huge bite, chewed, and swallowed with gusto. He then put it back in the baggie and told the owner how much he appreciated the bite, but he preferred a sandwich with more mustard.

Shane later bragged about an incident while he was still working at his former police service. He and a couple of other coppers were walking out the back door of the station when he saw an old tooth brush on the ground. He asked the other two fellas how much money they had. When they came up with about $1.45 or so, Shane offered to brush his teeth with the brush if they would pony up the coins. (No one carries cash anymore!) They agreed, so Shane gamely started brushing, and then took his hard earned money. I also once saw him have a lengthy and detailed discussion about the works of Lucy Maud Montgomery (Anne of Green Gables) with a drunk college student at a noisy party. He'd clearly read the books, more than once. He was a nuanced guy, but also a half-wit who talked another half-wit on my team into participating in the chocolate milk challenge one night shift. Shane puked all over the parking lot, but the other guy held it down, and in so doing, was sick for a week. So, I guess the other guy won?

Then there was Taylor. It wasn't all his fault, because some of the guys on the team made it easy. Like one night when Taylor was teasing another fella on the team he knew from high school. (They were both from the same hometown.) When the other guy asked Taylor something like "How would you know what my mother likes?" or something equally asinine, Taylor was waiting and obviously prepared. He said that he talked to her all the time. Terry called him on it, so Taylor went to his cell phone, ostentatiously speed dialed the lovely lady who wanted to talk to all her son Terry's teammates around the briefing table before start of shift. Terry's mom and I talked quite a bit, and she made me promise that I would take care of her little boy, as well as Taylor. Taylor is the same guy who, while still on probation, came to me with an application form, entirely filled out for what I thought was CSIS. (The Canadian CIA for you American readers.) He wanted me to give him a reference for the application. I spent a lot of time trying to talk him out of it, trying to give him all the reasons why this was a bad idea at such an early point in his policing career. He asked me to just read the application, and I kept talking, trying to make sense. He finally asked me a third time to just read the application, "Starting with the date". April 1st... This guy was pranking his sergeant while still on probation and had to hint at the joke because his sergeant was too thick to pick it up on his own! You gotta give the kid props but there must also be a comeuppance. Steve, the team staff sergeant got more than even for all of us. (At least I am fairly sure it was Steve. Even though it was brilliant, he still hasn't admitted to this, and retired about three years ago.)

S o, there we were, end of the first night shift, and we were all headed down to our lockers to change and go home after a long and busy night. I hadn't been as busy because I'd been the acting staff sergeant all night. My friend Steve had taken the nights off, so I had to bump up a rank to replace him while he was gone. There was a feeling in the air though, a sense of retribution, a recalibration of the scales of justice that had slowly become unbalanced. Taylor had had his way for far too long, and it was time. None of us knew it, but that time was now. You see, young Taylor committed the cardinal sin of admitting to a weakness a few weeks prior. He did this only to his FTO and she was sworn to secrecy. She would have kept her mouth shut too, if it hadn't been for Taylor teasing her about not being able to drive as well as he did, because he claimed she (a woman) was genetically disposed toward poor driving. As he was expounding on his theory, she was backing up their police vehicle down a road that was blocked. Just as Leah said that she was a much better driver than Taylor, she backed into a parked car, proving Taylor's point. (Yes that actually happened.) She claimed he'd distracted her, (true, but no excuse) and, as a result, deserved a lesson in humility.

She told us his kryptonite the next night, proving that one should ever anger a woman, especially a woman who is armed with either information or a gun. She had both and wisely chose to use the information. (Only because she believed it would hurt more.) Taylor was apparently scared of turkeys! That's right, turkeys. You know, the bird we eat during Thanksgiving and Christmas?! It seems that when Taylor was young, his aunt took him to a farm and went inside the farmhouse, leaving 8-year-old Taylor outside to play. He approached a few turkeys on the farmer's property thinking they might be friendly, because after all, who doesn't love Taylor, right? So when he got close to the birds, they came at him, and he ran. Realizing that the game was afoot, the birds pursued, wanting to get even for the slaying all of their relatives and then compounding that sin by cruelly eating them on holidays past. They gave chase right to the door of the farmer's ranch house. When he tried the door, Taylor found it locked. (He was unclear as to why his aunt had locked him out, whether she was having a romantic tryst with the elderly farmer, or more likely, tired of caring for her sibling's "know it all" child.) As he screamed and tried to open the door, the turkeys enthusiastically exacted their revenge for relatives lost, by pecking poor young Taylor into a permanent phobia.

The stage is therefore set, as we all unknowingly walked down the stairs to the locker rooms, tired, but with a sense of accomplishment for a job well done and hoping that the second night shift would go as fast as the first. When we got into the locker room, there was a foul stench in the air, almost as if Shane had left his gym strip out on the bench in front of his locker instead of secured inside with the rest of the toxic waste. No, this was far worse. When Taylor got to his locker, he saw why. There was what appeared to be a live turkey sitting at the bottom of his unlocked locker where his stuff used to be. Of course his locker was open! Need you ask why, dear reader? This is a police station and who would steal from a brother. (In reality your equipment is fair game, but you could leave a cool million in non-sequential bills, with no way to trace it, and the money would be safe. Your flashlight or boot lace might be gone if someone needed it, but that's another story.) Just down the room a bit, there was another "turkey" in another guy's locker. They were actually two very much alive Guineafowl, and we knew they were alive because they had defecated in the bottom of each locker.

There was general pandemonium, and of course, some of the guys brought their phones out to video Taylor's reaction. One of the better videographers even had the sound on so that when he (the videographer, not Taylor) started to dry heave because of the smell, it was there as part of the video soundtrack for all to hear. It became somewhat chaotic, when the birds escaped their cages (that should read lockers) and began to fly around the locker room, occasionally buzzing an unsuspecting victim like Doug, the big game hunter who was cowering in the corner like he was praying for delivery. (In the video, Shane is even asking guys how much they will give him to kiss the bird!) Taylor went upstairs, still in full uniform, telling the oncoming shift that he would rather work another 12 hours than go back to the locker room.

A funny thing happened as I was leaving. It was about 7:30 a.m. and my cell phone rang as I was getting into my car to go home to sleep. It was Steve who, although off for the night, chose that time of the morning, on a weekend he wasn't working, to call me and ask, "how the night was." I have known Steve since College, and I just blurted out, "Where did you get those birds?" He just said, "Whatever do you mean." He told me to have a good last night and we would talk the next week. We had a lot of fun on that team.

(As a post script to this story, it should be noted that no animals were injured in this well planned and executed escapade, other than poor Taylor's ego. The birds were safely relocated to a farm east of town, and as far as I know, lived long and happy lives together.)

****

I was also getting called out a lot during this time as a negotiator. I was now the most senior negotiator in the unit, and for a while the team commander, but it became too difficult to organize training days and courses while on shift work. One of the other negotiators working in the Forensic Identification Unit took over those duties. I only had to show up for training days and go on a recertification course when told to go, as long as the dates didn't clash with my regular job. One negotiator call from that time stood out as somewhat different. By different, it wasn't a suicidal person, but rather a guy holed up in his house with an outstanding warrant for his arrest for murder.

So, there I was, on my way to a house on the south side of the city. One of the less experienced negotiators in the unit had already arrived and was waiting for me. When I got there, I learned that the bad guy we were talking to was named Ross and he was wanted for the murder of his best friend, who he'd stabbed about 30 times a couple of weeks prior. The Violent Crimes Unit had been working on the file for a while, and they finally had enough to charge him. They had him under surveillance while awaiting the warrant, and when he left his house, they had a warrant to enter the residence to make sure that there was no one else there, look for weapons (among other things) and leave. When Ross was followed back to his residence, we knew he was alone and there were no weapons in the residence that he could use to hurt us or his neighbours. There were knives but throwing them at a Tactical member who had the residence cordoned off was relatively inefficient, and terminally stupid.

The scenario we found ourselves in, from a tactical perspective, had no real downside. Ross only had two choices, to come out or to kill himself. There was no one else he could hurt, and we wouldn't be "pushing the fight" with him. We would let him sit in there "until the cows came home." I took the bullhorn and went to the side of the house that the Incident Commander directed me and began to talk to him. Actually – it was more like talking to his house, saying the same things over and over again, because he wasn't answering at all. Bullhorn or loud speaker negotiations are always difficult to do at the best of times, and if they aren't talking to us, or even acknowledging our presence, it isn't much of a conversation.

The Tactical Team threw a few flash bangs (a hand held distraction device, that you throw like a grenade, and goes off like an artillery simulator.) No one came to the door. Then they decided to insert our throw phone by using the Explosives Disposal Unit robot to lift the phone (in a big, fairly heavy yellow box that also has a few covert cameras in the case etc.) through the front window. As the robot got to the front of the house, the operators couldn't get the arm to extend far enough to get it to the height of the window, let alone through it. I was across the street, with a Tactical Unit guy covering me, watching this comedy of errors unfold. I was in blue jeans and a "raid jacket," with my gun and badge on, but no cuffs or other less lethal options. (I was with a Tac guy that had a plethora of both.) While we watched, we were both surprised to see Ross wander out onto his front porch with a bottle of beer in his hand, and just sort of stare at the bomb robot, continually trying to lift the big yellow case with the phone in it up to his front window. I tried to get him to speak to me, but he just hollered out that he hated the loud speaker, and to come speak to me like a man, or something like that.

I got permission to cross the street with the tac member as my human shield, and I began to talk to him from about 15 feet away. He was surprisingly calm, considering my human shield had a Heckler and Koch MP5 pointed at his melon. He started off with, "I suppose you are gonna breach me for having the beer?" (He was currently bound by a court order from something unrelated requiring him to abstain from drinking alcohol).

"Probably", I said, but continued with, "but in the big scheme of things that won't mean anything, you and I both know it. We are here to arrest you for murder." He went on for a bit about how he was high at the time, and barely remembered stabbing his best friend about 30 times. He finished his point by saying that he didn't belong in jail for the rest of his life for that.

"You live in Canada, man. Even life in prison here isn't really life in prison, and you know it." I retorted. I'd decided to take a bit more of a hard line. Although he was an "expressive" subject, he'd also been in and out of jail his entire adult life. He knew exactly what was going on, and what he was looking at for a sentence. "And besides," I went on, "You beat the last murder charge, and walked away, free and clear." This was true. He'd been involved in an altercation a few years before with a gang banger with a gun. He'd been shot in the arm (I think), but I know he stabbed the shooter to death. The Judge deemed that to be self defence.

We talked for about three more minutes and then, after finishing his beer, he said, "How'd ya wanna do this?" This went so fast that I hadn't been briefed on a surrender plan. I made it up on the spot. I told him to turn around so his face was to the house and to get on his knees and we would handcuff him. He immediately did what I asked. I went to my waist where my cuffs usually were and found nothing but belt. Oops. I looked down to the waist of the tac member with me, saw his cuffs were where they were supposed to be, and took his. I then braceleted Ross up. As soon as I did, he started to cry, telling me how sorry he was. I introduced him to the Violent Crimes detective on scene and told him they would treat him well and said good luck to him. I think he got 6 years. It doesn't seem like enough jail time to compensate for the murder of another human being. I am glad it's not my job to decide.

SELLING A MOTORBIKE, AND OTHER NEGOTIATIONS

I was the sergeant of that patrol team for the next eight years. I saw people come and go, new coppers hired, and helped others off to their next assignment. In that eight years, I worked under four staff sergeants, two of which I went to college with and consider great friends to this day. I had some great experiences with that team and learned a lot along the way. In 2010 the Service changed the leadership structure on the patrol teams. When I got back to teams as a sergeant in 2008, there were as many as 19 constables on the team with one sergeant and one staff sergeant. The sergeant was required to deal with all the supervisory headaches of 19 employees, their days off, their illnesses and injuries, their evaluations and career counselling, as well as teaching them how to investigate the simple to more complex files. I thought I was doing pretty good at it, and I was, but there were things that I had learned to prioritize. For example, if I was writing a performance evaluation, and a gun call came in, I went to the call. There were a lot of evaluations that went unfinished those first two years. In 2010 the powers that be added a second sergeant to the team structure. I was insulted and felt that I was doing just fine, thank you very much. I was terribly wrong.

In the beginning of that year, I got a partner, who also happened to be the first young copper I ever trained. We got along very well, and it was a revelation! I'd always professed how important it was to have a team sergeant who'd been to many parts of the Service and gained experience and knowledge in different aspects of police work. That way, no matter what problem arose, he would have the answer. I thought I was such a good teacher. I was utterly fooling myself. Don't misunderstand, I am a good teacher. It is one of my greatest strengths. I just thought I was doing a lot of teaching over those first two years, and it turned out that I was barely keeping my head above water. With a partner, I could plainly see that I had *not* been doing all I could to help my people get better. Now that we had the time, our young coppers flourished. I remember the moment when I became "converted" to the two Sergeant system.

S o, there I was, working a night shift when one of my young coppers came to me asking for help. He was one of the guys from the recruit class that we hired when I'd been in recruiting. Miles was a good kid who wanted so much to succeed and was diligently striving to get better. You could tell he was a bit frustrated with the way things were. One of my first conversations with every young copper starts with the words "Where do you want to be in five years?" Miles wanted to be a detective. We had so many similarities. He'd been on a mission for the Church as well, also learning French. He had a lot of the same career and life goals I had, and I realized that I'd been failing him prior to this incident. The system was the same one we had when I was young, when our teams had ten members or less. They were now twice the size, and the call load had increased at least ten fold! A single sergeant could no longer keep up with both the administrative tasks and the operational ones. The system (and I) had been failing Miles, and I didn't know until that very moment.

Miles had approached me for help in interviewing a suspect in a very serious offence. He was investigating a sexual assault. That's hard enough for a young guy, but this one was an historic, incestuous, pedophilic sexual assault; one of the hardest types of interviews there are. The number of cultural taboos to get the bad guy to admit to, especially to a complete stranger, make it a real challenge for the investigator. Miles knew the law and rules around interviewing, but the nuance is where every young copper falls down. (I know I had struggled for years, and slowly learned how to get my style to work for me.) Teaching "nuance" is where experience helps more than anything. I asked my partner if he would take care of the street while I helped Miles out, and for the first time as a team sergeant, I was able to spend my entire effort on just one thing; helping someone else to get better

I walked Miles through the entire process, from where the chairs in the room should be, and who should sit where, right up to tactics to use in the actual conversation, and the themes to touch on, depending on the direction of the conversation. I was then able to sit and scribe for his interview. (The scribe is the guy in the video room who watches the interview, makes notes for the interviewer, all the while catching body language or tactics or themes that might work, and identify what isn't working.)

The bad guy came in for his scheduled appointment, and Miles went through the lawyer stuff with him, and then started the conversation. He was doing really well, and over the course of the next hour or so, started building to the crescendo with some pretty good skill. When he got to the tipping point, the guy would hesitate, and you could tell Miles didn't know what to do to get him over the hump. This happened a couple of times, and when Miles realized he was spinning his wheels, he took a break, and came to ask my advice.

One of the benefits the scribe has is a lack of pressure. He or she is able to see everything, without the pressure of coming up with the next thing to say. It is much easier from that chair to clearly see where the conversation has been, what parts worked, as well as those that didn't. Most importantly, interviewing a culprit is like playing chess. To get good at "the game" you don't just think what move you will make next. You have to think and plan numerous moves ahead, all while listening to what the bad guy is saying to the question you just asked him, and then change your plan on the fly, depending on his answers. Used correctly, a scribe can be an effective tool in getting the truth from the bad guy. When Miles came to me in frustration, I was prepared. I gave him three questions to ask, in order. If he got the truthful answer to the first, go to the second. If not, chat for a bit and then go there again. If he gave the truthful answer for question one and two, go to three. (Miles thought I was a magician, because I already had the three questions written out and in the order he needed to ask them. Like I said, it is way easier as a scribe to see what needs to be said without the pressure of being the interviewer.)

Miles went back in and just five or ten minutes later, had the guy admitting to the offence, and showing legitimate remorse, as well as providing information and details that only the offender and the victim would've known. The coolest thing about the entire experience for me was when Miles came out and thanked me. The look on his face gave me one of the best feelings I've ever had as a copper. It was better than if I'd done it myself! Not only had we solved a very serious crime together, but this kid would also remember this experience and how it worked for the rest of his career. He might even pass that information forward to the next young copper who needed his help when he became the team sergeant one day. I had helped him get one step closer to achieving his goals. I also knew I would've never had the time to help him if myself was the only sergeant on the team. I had been converted to the new system of having two sergeants.

****

From that point on, I got to spend just as much time teaching young coppers as I did the minutiae of running a team. My partner and I worked well together, making sure that evaluations were completed, and teaching moments were not lost because we were too busy. The unexpected bonus was, I saw that the young guys were having fun and I had been missing out on some of it. I still heard about some of the team members blowing off steam and playing pranks on each other when we awarded the vaunted brown nose award, but now I got to see them first hand, even if I was no longer taking part in planning them. I had to shut the occasional idea down, but overall, it was a good time. Sometimes I even became the victim, or at least collateral damage. For example there was the time my staff sergeant went on Christmas holidays and left me to act in his stead.

So, there I was, Christmas morning, working in "the bubble" as the acting duty staff sergeant. (The duty staff's office at the time, had five windows facing out into the atrium and the hallway. The office was in a central location in the building, where people walked by and looked in at the poor staff sergeant in the "bubble"). My boss had taken the set off, so I was stuck inside, doing staff sergeant things, watching real coppers work. My job was to approve reports, give advice when needed, and be responsible if the wheels of the city fell off. Not an enviable job, but there I was, being the very glue that held the Service together. (Obviously dripping with sarcasm). At about 7:30 that fine Christmas morning, I received a call from the Inspector in charge of Patrol Division. He sounded like he'd just woken up and began the conversation with an odd remark. "So, apparently we're selling the motorbike."

I was silent for a second, then said, "Which bike, sir?" Then before he answered, I knew what'd happened. There was an old Harley Davidson motorbike that was decommissioned and in the atrium of the station, still with all the police markings and lights. It was from well before my time, and in the atrium as more of a conversation piece or to show a piece of history. It turns out that Jay, my current staff sergeant, had been having a bit of a one-sided prank war with another staff sergeant. (Jay is the guy that had the magpie in his locker, and the guy who had shooed the janitor away by practicing drawing his pistol while naked in front of the mirror. He was entertaining, but sometimes, like now, more trouble than he was worth.) He'd taken about four or five very classy photos of the motorbike in question, without actually getting a picture of the Service logo on the side of it, and uploaded it onto an internet sales site, listing it for sale. The kicker was, he had listed the price so low that it was almost too good to be true, ensuring lots of interest. The seller's number he put on the advertisement was the cellphone of the staff sergeant he was picking on. It was Christmas Day, and the other staff had received over fifty calls from interested buyers. It was obvious that the inspector knew exactly what had happened and who had done it, and just asked me to clean up the mess without any comment.

I called Jay at home, and he answered on the second ring, as if he were waiting for the call. I told him what a success his little plot had been, and then asked him to take the advertisement down so I wouldn't get any more calls from the inspector. He cackled like a little kid, and then agreed to take it down. When I called the inspector back, the first thing he asked me was "How'd he take it?" It was obvious he knew exactly what was going on and who was responsible. So much for people working on the second floor being out of touch. Then again, this inspector was Chris who, as a constable, had helped me write my first search warrant for young Sally's sexual assault. He was a good guy and knew when to put an end to things by jumping on them with both feet, and when to softly suggest change. I've been lucky over the years, having the right people at the right time helping me to learn and grow.

****

Speaking of learning and growing, I was now the senior negotiator in the unit and had more calls under my belt than all of the other guys combined. That was through no fault of their own, but rather a lucky set of circumstances when I was in CID. The staff sergeant in the Organized Crime Section was not only responsible for the Economic Crimes Unit that I worked in, but among others, he was also in charge of the Special Operations Unit. (aka, the drug unit.) Whenever they executed a search warrant, or made a high profile arrest, I was the negotiator that Josh called to do the job, mostly due to my availability. I worked straight day shift at the time, and Josh would often have that unit plan ahead, so I was aware of the warrant and the needs of the Tactical Support Unit. I made sure that I was available whenever I could. I got a lot of reps and once, even ended up negotiating with the same guy twice, within a seven-month span. The first was about forty degrees below zero, and lasted six hours, and the second was about 35 degrees above zero and lasted a lot longer. Neither conversation went particularly well.

So, there I was, called out to negotiate with a suicidal man who'd barricaded himself inside his mother's house in the small town of Coaldale, 11 kilometres east of Lethbridge. It was bitterly cold outside, but I didn't really feel the effects of the cold for the first couple of hours. I was with the Incident Commander in the Command Center on the second floor of the police station. This was before everyone and their dog had a cellphone, and so we were talking to him on the landline. We had, with the assistance of the telephone company, seized the line so that he could only talk to me. Clyde was obviously under the influence of something and was very talkative at first. He was angry at one of the members of our Service for charging him with a domestic-related assault. He felt that no one had asked him his side of the story, so I did. He went on, ad nauseam, about how he didn't mean to break her arm, and that she drove him to it. As he got more worked up about the assault, he began to look to me more as someone with whom he could confide, not as a copper. As a result, he started playing music tracks on his stereo as loud as he could and dedicating the song to me. That was where the Incident Commander had reached his limit.

When the power to the house was cut the Tactical Unit began a "breach and hold" operation, whereby they gained entry to the house, but did not push further into the residence, fearing they would cause him to become more aggressive or act upon his suicidal threats. (This is called "pushing the fight, and we avoid it whenever possible.)

Clyde stopped talking to me at that point, and I learned a short time later that he'd exited the house. He'd broken out the bedroom window by punching it and cutting his hand up pretty good, then climbing out onto the covered hot-tub in the back yard. He was bleeding all over himself and the .22 calibre rifle he was holding to the base of his chin. He could go no farther because the team had him surrounded. He couldn't go back into the house either, because he couldn't climb up the way he'd come out without putting the rifle down, giving the team the chance to grab him up. Then the bad news came. The Commander directed me and my secondary negotiator to go to the scene and continue talking to him, in person from the inner perimeter. In forty below, for who knows how long. It turned out to be four very cold and uncomfortable hours.

When I got there with my partner, I was sent to the lane behind the backyard of the residence. I found my friend Mack, the guy who I trained earlier, when we kicked the door in to the deaf lady's house. He was now on the Tactical team and was on the inner perimeter. I used him as my cover as I began to talk to Clyde again. I could see that his right hand was bleeding, and he'd bled all over his right side, as well as the gun he was holding. (We didn't know it at the time, but his blood had leaked into the trigger mechanism and frozen the inside workings of the gun. I could've saved for hours standing in the cold if I'd known that.) It was a much harder talk, because he blamed me for the loss of power at his house, and I wasn't concentrating enough because I was freezing my butt off. At one point during a lull in the conversation, I said sotto voce, "Mack, just shoot this guy, I am freezing to death." Then my secondary negotiator cleared his throat and held up the digital recorder that was recording my every word. Ya, I was having a great night.

It all ended when Clyde had endured enough or decided that he would push the fight himself. He rushed the Tactical Team perimeter. He was still holding the gun, but it was not pointed at anyone. He soon dropped it when he was hit with every less lethal option the team had at their disposal, ranging from punches and kicks, a taser, sock rounds from a shotgun, a K-9 and my personal favourite, a .37 mm Arwen loaded with pepper rounds. He may not have been feeling much pain that night due to his intoxicated state, but the next morning, when he woke up in jail, my guess is that he was feeling it. He obviously didn't learn much from that incident because he was back at it that next summer, at a house in Lethbridge.

In the summer of that year, more substance abuse problems, combined with more domestic troubles, and we found ourselves with Clyde, barricaded in a house on the north side of Lethbridge, after the woman residing in the house got out and called the police. We surrounded the place and tried to talk him out again. This time, it was in the middle of a hot summer day, and I was outside of the house, at the window the entire time, because there wasn't a working telephone in the residence. I tried to get him to talk to me for twelve hours without a word from him. He actually went up into the attic of the house, so he didn't have to hear me. When the Tactical Team finally entered the residence, he was in the attic, and he began to throw bricks at them. We were pretty sure that he didn't have a firearm this time, but we didn't want to go into the attic to get him because of the increased chance of someone getting hurt. We thought that the heat in the attic would soon drive him out.

Twelve hours later, he was still in the attic, and I'd been replaced by a second negotiator. He had no more success than I had, but we had to keep trying. Clyde eventually caved, and instead of giving up, he punched the skylight out of the roof of the house while he was in the attic. I think the heat got to him, and he began to stick his head up through the hole. I saw the video played on the local evening news. He looked like a wack-a-mole, especially when he turned to one side, and saw my friend Mack, the same tactical guy that I had used as cover seven months before, also on the roof, with a shotgun loaded with a muzzle blast round of pepper spray granules. (It isn't like a mist, but rather like getting hit with granules of pepper in your face. You could tell by the look on Clyde's face that it hurt.) The stand-off was over shortly thereafter. He surrendered so that he could get some water and help for the burning sensation on his face.

I didn't really do a whole bunch as a negotiator on the second call and made more mistakes than wins on the first one. The reason I tell this story is because it isn't the first time I've spoken about it. I actually have a PowerPoint presentation of the two incidents. When you are a negotiator, you are required to re-certify every three or four years at the Canadian Police College in Ottawa. Part of that recertification process is the requirement to give a presentation to the class of one of your past calls. The goal is to share some of the successes and lessons learned from the call. I always play the audio of me telling Mack, "Just shoot this guy! I am freezing!" as an example of what not to say, especially when the call ends as a result of the use of every less lethal option available to us. More importantly, had the idiot pointed his frozen gun at one of the team members, he would've been shot and probably killed. How do you explain to the Fatality Inquiry that you were telling a team member to shoot the guy twenty minutes before they did? The audio recording has almost as great an affect on the class as the video I obtained from the media showing how the second call ended. Clyde taking a muzzle blast of OC granules has a certain entertainment value for those viewing the presentation. Surprisingly, after dealing with him twice in seven months, we haven't had a single problem with young Clyde since. Maybe he moved.

TEAM BUILDING AND VIOLENT CRIMES

As I got back into the swing of shiftwork, I forgot how much I loved it. I was in my late 40's and still enjoyed working nightshifts. I've always struggled with waking up to an alarm clock and found I got more sleep working nights. Just as importantly, I loved the type of calls we get on those shifts. When you get called to a disturbance at two in the afternoon, it's usually between two people who got into a dust-up the night before, or their neighbour pissed them off, but it wasn't important enough for them to lose sleep over, so they call the next day. When you get called at three in the morning, it's because they need the police there right now! This job can become addictive if you are not careful, and the calls you get on nights are the type that "feed the habit." The added benefit for me at this point in my career, was the chance I had to help young guys get better and at the same time be involved in some really cool investigations.

So, there I was, working a nightshift, when a stabbing call came in. The dispatcher told us a woman had been stabbed right in front of the main doors of a night club down town. Another copper and I were only a block or two away when the call came in. We got there before the dispatch could obtain any information other than where the victim was and the direction the assailant had gone. I spoke to a bouncer from the bar, and he pointed to a lady sitting on the sidewalk. He told me a woman had stabbed her, and then he pointed up the street at three women walking away. He told me the shortest of the three of them had done it. He mentioned that the other two were involved but had only punched and kicked the victim after the little one stabbed her. He also said the whole thing should be on tape because they did it right in front of the front doors of the club. I contacted the next closest unit and told them the location of the bad guys. The second unit was close enough that they got the three women who were walking north, only a block away from me. The bouncer was standing next to me, and we could both see the three people in question get arrested by my teammates, verifying that we had the right three in custody.

I turned my attention back to the victim and saw that she'd been stabbed in the neck area and the blade of the knife had broken off inside her body. The blade was still in her neck, going downward into her chest cavity so I had her stay seated without moving until paramedics got there. I spoke with her and asked her if she knew who'd attacked her. She told me she was approached from behind and it felt like she had been punched in the throat and then down her body at least eight or nine more times. The black handle of an old steak knife was on the ground and off to the side of the victim. The witnesses confirmed that they all thought she had been stabbed eight or nine times, because her assailant kept hitting her, then dropped the handle of the knife and walked away while her two friends punched and kicked the victim a few times for good measure. It was obvious the accused didn't know the blade had broken from the handle after the first blow. It's pretty difficult to tell a person with a knife blade embedded in their neck that they were lucky, but it would appear she was. If that knife had held together, she would most likely have been stabbed eight or nine times and killed as a result. I left one of my guys with her and told him to go to the hospital in the ambulance. My next stop was up the street where two of my younger coppers had scooped up the bad guy and her two friends.

When I got there, I found that two of the newer people on my team had detained the woman and her two friends. I went up to the woman and recognized her from many previous incidents. She recognized me too, and immediately went with the "you got the wrong people" defence. Her two friends backed her story up, claiming that they were all just in the wrong place at the wrong time, and they had done nothing wrong.

"So this his how you are gonna play this?" I began. "You sure you want to look like the hardened criminal in front of the judge?"

"I got nothing else to say to you." she said, looking at her friends when she said it. I had the two thick-witted friends taken over to the side of the road for a minute, and then spoke quietly to the girl I knew well. "You know, there is video in front of that bar, right? You really shouldn't try to stab someone where the deed can be shown to the jury in technicolour. And then there is the knife handle that you left at the scene will have you fingerprints and DNA on it." She tried to interrupt me, but I stopped her and went on. "Not to mention the fact that the person you meant to kill only got one stab wound because your knife was so old it broke off after the first hit. And finally, do you honestly think those two halfwits over there talking to my partners are going to want to go to jail for attempted murder with you, after this stellar display of planning and tactics?"

I could see her deflate. "The knife really broke?" she asked, seeming to give up before she started.

"Ya, the knife broke. You left the blade in her with the first hit, and then just punched her with the handle a bunch of times after that."

"Well, I hope that B*^%& dies anyway." She told me she didn't want to talk any more. A confession in about two minutes. I've left out the parts about explaining her constitutional rights and all the other things we have to do, so it was actually about fifteen minutes, but you know what I mean. We flipped the two girls she was with (got them to give statements against their knife-wielding friend). They claimed they didn't know what she was going to do. I don't believe for a minute that they didn't know the plan, but they gave us witness statements, and the doer took the wrap. She claimed it was over a man. The two young coppers who were present when I got her to confess thought I was better at this than I really am - getting a confession in ten minutes and all - but it really wasn't that difficult. Criminals who plan to commit their offences in front of witnesses, and video, with substandard equipment, are what we call "low-hanging fruit." If we didn't have stupid criminals, mediocre coppers like me wouldn't be able to write books about our exploits.

****

It takes courage and opportunity to successfully prank your inspector so well that it's remembered and spoken of for years to come, while at the same time ensuring that the action is light-hearted and funny enough that the inspector doesn't demote you to being the constable in charge of the coffee fund. It also doesn't hurt to be the first recruit that inspector ever trained when you stick it to him. All of those stars came into alignment for Ira, my patrol team staff sergeant a few years after I came back to patrols. I want to make this clear, I had nothing to do with this. I have no desire to be the constable in charge of the coffee fund!

Jerry was a new guy, just freshly on his own after having finished his field training. He was eager and willing, but still relied on the advice of others.

So, when he got dispatched that day to the sudden death, he was understandably a little nervous. Thankfully, the investigation turned out to be easier than most. He was sent to an extended care facility where an elderly person had died of natural causes. The deceased even had a DNR order (Do Not Resuscitate) on file with the staff of the facility. The family, patient, and doctor had already discussed his options, and decided not to use any "heroic" life saving measures when that time came. Our function going to these types of deaths is to first, determine as best we can that there is nothing suspicious involved. (A knife in the back is not covered by the DNR.) When that is done, we become an investigator for the Medical Examiner's office, and with their guidance, determine if the death was expected and natural. Finally, we help facilitate things like calling a funeral home and having them come to take the body. Overall, a fairly easy first sudden death for Jerry.

To make matters even easier, our policy requires a supervisor attend with the investigator for all sudden deaths. It's easier for a young copper to do this type of investigation knowing that the sergeant is coming to help him and will actually notice the knife in the back of the deceased if he doesn't. Jerry went to this call with the belief that all would be well, and he would have a robust safety net to catch him if he fell. If he didn't know what to do, his sergeant would know, and walk him step by step through the process.

It started out easy enough. Jerry was helped a great deal by the staff who'd been through these types of things often enough. He took statements and gathered information, all the while, waiting for the sergeant to show up. When he was almost done everything he knew to do, he received a call on his radio to speak to the sergeant in the parking lot of the building. He went out, and got a bit of a pep talk, asked what he'd done, and got directions on how to finish up, and then watched as his sergeant drove away, without even getting out of the car. Jerry went back inside to finish up, then headed back to the station to finish the paperwork.

Now, it's unclear whether he forgot the last step, or his sergeant didn't tell him the last step. After diligently taking statements and setting up family members with our Victim Services Unit, Jerry left the scene without calling the funeral home, leaving the body lying on the bed where he died. Jerry spent the remaining hours of his shift completing the paperwork, blissfully unaware of the missed last step.

That next morning, the director of the extended care facility contacted the dayshift staff sergeant to ascertain the expected arrival time of the funeral home to remove the deceased from their facility. The dayshift staff sergeant was just starting his first dayshift and had no idea what the caller was talking about. Having sat in that chair myself, I can imagine how I would have felt if placed in that situation. No one would want to sound so uninformed. More importantly, imagine the questions you would have to ask to gain enough information to answer that question. (It would probably start with something like "What dead body?")

There was a certain amount of fallout from the third floor, including some informative emails about the correct process in the investigation and procedure of sudden deaths. I'm sure there were some admonishments made to poor Jerry and more importantly, to his sergeant who, in my opinion, left Jerry in a terrible spot. If this were just a "one off", Ira would not have been given the golden opportunity I mentioned earlier.

Fast forward a few short weeks later, to a senior constable attending another sudden death, and another "what were you thinking" moment. An elderly man had died at home. It was another expected death, and many of his family were there when he passed. This copper was sent near the end of his dayshift and was not happy about it. (They take a long time and require a certain amount of empathy. Our hero didn't want the overtime, and his empathy tank was near empty that day.) While taking a statement from a family member, he learned they wanted to wait until another member of the family could get off work before the body was taken by the funeral home. They wanted to have an incense ceremony. This copper could have said no, but he didn't, even though he didn't want to wait for the missing family member. Instead, he told them he would leave the body with them and arrange for a nightshift member to facilitate the funeral home attendance when they were done. To say this was not acceptable would be an understatement, especially concerning what had occurred two weeks prior. Another round of memos and emails from on high ensued.

Chris, the Inspector in charge of Patrol Division had obviously had a bad month with these two incidents occurring withing weeks of each other. Some would argue that picking on him at this point would be cruel. Ira argued that he was having such a bad month that he needed a good laugh. All he needed was the ammunition to lift Chris's spirit. Shane and I provided that for him a few weeks later, in spades.

So there I was, dispatched with Shane, the bologna sandwich eating, chocolate milk challenge making, stranger toothbrush using, member of my team, to a sudden death on our second dayshift of the set. An elderly lady had passed away after suffering from cancer for some time. She'd been in and out of the hospital for months and when they could do no more for her, she asked to be discharged so she could go home and die in the comfort of her home. Heart-breaking by itself, but compound that with the fact that her husband of 60+ years, had been diagnosed with the exact same cancer, and was expecting to die only months later, the same way his lovely wife had. Shane and I were briming with compassion for this poor man and tried to make our time in his home as easy as possible. When he asked us if we could wait until his daughter arrived before we contacted the funeral home, I just about acquiesced immediately, but for what had occurred over the last month. I asked him where his daughter would be coming from and if we could help with transportation arrangements (thinking she was in another part of the city). He stated that she would be flying out from Hong Kong the following day. Of course we couldn't do that, and he understood. We finished our time with this very nice man and went back to the station for the paperwork.

When I told Ira what'd happened, he immediately went to the internet and started searching for a one page document describing assorted Chinese burial traditions. He then cut and pasted the information to a document that he could edit and went to work. He changed some of the content to speak on how important it was for a body to lie in state for at least 48 hours prior to burial. Ira then saved it and attached it to an email that he then sent to his friend Chris, the inspector who'd been sending all the emails out over the last month about proper procedure for sudden death investigations. Ira added in the email that we were going on nights the following day and would "zip over" to the residence first thing that evening and arrange for the funeral home to pick up the body of the deceased. It was obvious that Chris was at his desk with his email open because Ira's phone rang less than two minutes after he sent the email. Thankfully, Ira didn't lead poor Chris on too long before he informed him that the email was a joke. I don't think Ira wanted to take care of the coffee fund either.

****

The Service had just received our first new Dodge Charger to the fleet and Macie was driving it with her FTO Carter. It was very fast, and looked sexy as heck, but also had a keyless system, where you just had to have the fob in your pocket, and you could start the car by pushing a button on the dash. So Carter (the same Tactical Team member who pulled his pants down in the dark to embarrass a teammate, and the same guy who called me from Wrigley Field on his company cellphone) decided he would put one over on this new copper.

So, there they were, working a night shift, chatting outside after having just finished a call in an older residential area on the north side of the city. Carter had Macie driving and brought up a concern he had about their new piece of equipment (the car) that he thought needed experimenting with. He wondered how far their patrol car would go without the key fob still in the car. Would it shut down, or keep going, and did the emergency equipment work when the fob wasn't in the car? Well, Carter is a problem solver and was in teaching mode with young Macie. (She should have known better, she has three older brothers, and they are probably scared of her.) Carter had Macie sit in the car by herself and decided to make a great game out of how far she could drive from him with the fob in his pocket before the car would stop running. He got Macie to drive up the street very slowly to see if it would shut off at a certain distance away from Carter, who had the fob in his pocket. She went the entire city block at two kilometres per hour and it stayed running. He had her then turn the red and blue lights on and drive even farther, to see if that would shut the car down. No dice. It still ran like a top. So then he told her to drive with both lights and sirens on and see if that did it.

So there poor Macie was, driving on a sleepy residential neighbourhood at about two in the morning, up the street at about two kilometres per hour with her red and blue lights on, and sirens blowing for all they were worth. You could tell the moment she realized that she'd been had. The lights and sirens were turned off about a second after they turned on, and she came back to pick him up, finding him laughing hysterically in the middle of the road. If I were her, I'd have kept driving and made him walk back to the station, but she's a much nicer person than I am.

✳✳✳✳

I've heard that some guys have even involved folks that are "in conflict with the law" in their little shenanigans. I know of one where the arrestee got the better of the two guys messing with each other in the cellblock and all three of them had a good laugh as a result. I wasn't there but I heard it from both of the officers as well as the guy who was being booked in. He got them good.

One of our coppers arrested a guy for being drunk in public and decided to transport him to the station to give him a place to sleep for the night. The drunk wasn't a bad guy, just a homeless dude with an alcohol problem. He was also blessed with a great sense of humor. So he was in the cellblock with his arresting officer and the duty staff sergeant was asking him questions about his health to make sure he would be safe during his stay in the cell block. What I mean to say is that the duty staff sergeant was pretending to ask him questions, but really screaming at him in nonsensical words, trying to emulate German. The funny part is the arresting officer immediately picked up on it without a hitch and started acting as the translator, pretending like he could understand the questions screamed in ridiculously and obviously ersatz German. After the staff would scream, the constable would speak to the person under arrest in overly soft and obsequious English, with a German accent.

"Vatt he means to ask is do you zuffer from ze epilepsy or de zeizures, yah?"

The drunk smiled and was game and slurred, "no, I am good."

This went on for the majority of the pre-admission questions to determine if the subject was or might be in medical distress. All the while, the arresting officer was acting like the translator, and the drunk was following along and jokingly answering the questions, with a smile on his face. Then the duty staff sergeant threw him a curve ball (or at least the "translator" did, because clearly the duty staff was not speaking any recognizable language other than fake German while shouting.) The arresting officer "translated the screaming diatribe of the duty staff by asking the person under arrest, "He vants to know if you zink dis is funny?"

The drunk looked solemnly at the translator officer who arrested him, and said in a clear but drunken slur, "Nein!"

That was it. The pretext was over, and the drunken homeless dude had taken the day. He was kept until it was warm enough for him and released without charge. (There was no room at the shelter that night, and the hero of our story might have frozen to death had he not stayed with us.) I'm told that there is a great video of that somewhere, but I haven't seen it, nor do I know anyone who has it. It would have been funny to see though. That homeless guy is still my hero.

As we headed into 2015, the street started to become quite a bit more violent. There was more gang violence than ever before, and the introduction of fentanyl and then crystal meth were just starting to become so virulent that it would turn the system basically on its ear in the next year or two. That year, Lethbridge had six murders. (We have averaged one a year for the previous 27 years). Of the six murders, my patrol team was working during four. One was a triple homicide that was so messed up that I realized when I was on the stand for the preliminary hearing that there was something wrong with me. I wasn't ready to admit it or get help for it yet but knew something was going on. I will tell that whole story later. The other one we worked that year was the murder of Kiley.

Kiley was a woman with a substance abuse problem, hanging out in a house with others with the same issue. She'd made another girl, we will call her Marlo, angry for some unknown reason. In the argument, Marlo produced a knife, and promptly stabbed Kiley in the thigh, hitting the artery and watched her bleed out. She also got her own boyfriend in the forearm, but didn't mean to, as we shall soon learn. After the stabbing they got in a car and headed for the hospital, leaving Kiley and the home owner, (their dealer) to their own devices. We got the call as they were leaving, and there happened to be a few coppers in the area. We picked up Marlo in a car coming through the cordon point while they were on their way to the hospital. She hadn't even been identified yet as the murderer. The young copper on the cordon recognized that if there was one person stabbed in the car heading to the hospital from the general area of the murder, then those people might be related to the homicide. He detained them, got medical help for the boyfriend, and detectives were called out.

The detective interviewing her was brilliant and soon got Marlo to admit to the offence, but the usual weak claims of self defence and other nonsense were provided. So as a tactic, the investigator put her in a cell with her boyfriend whom she'd inadvertently stabbed earlier. He'd been treated and released from the hospital and was under arrest as well because at the time we thought he might have assisted Marlo. The investigator put them together to see if they would talk about the case and see what his involvement was. In essence, they were sure about her, but not sure how he fit in.

So, there these two boneheads were, sitting in the same cell, talking about their undying love for each other. Marlo even said at one point that if he waits for her release on parole, she will be a much more appreciative bed partner, and the physiological changes she would undergo for not having sex for years might make the act more pleasurable for him as well. She then asked him how his arm was doing. He started to whine a bit, about how it hurt, and he didn't expect her to do that to him.

She said, "Well, the next time I go to stab a b^*&%, get the F&%$ out of the way!" and then she laughed.

I'm not sure if they ever even found out the real reason why Marlo stabbed Kiley. She admitted to the offence, so I'm sure she probably gave a self-serving one, but I never heard whether they got the real reason out of her.

Seeing as how I was being transferred to the Violent Crimes Unit the following year, I'd be able to read the file and find out. It turns out that the next year was another banner year for murders in the city, and unfortunately it was also where I learned that there was something going on in my head. I wasn't enjoying my dream job like I thought I would, while at the same time being so busy that I couldn't figure out what was wrong, let alone do anything about it.

LANA THE KILLER AND UNREQUITED LOVE

In the summer of 2015, I was approached by the Inspector in charge of the Criminal Investigation Division and asked if I was interested in going to the Violent Crimes Unit the following January. The detectives in that unit were tasked with solving serious crimes against persons. They range from serious assaults right up to homicide. Each detective is also tasked with cold cases to pick away at when there is down time. Of course, I told the inspector I'd happily go. (I may have mentioned in passing a few times over the last couple hundred pages or so that it'd been a goal of mine since the mid 80's.) I'd been on the same patrol team for the last eight years, and it was time for a change. You can never say that any assignment in policing is easy, but I certainly hadn't run into anything that challenged me in quite some time. I'd miss the kids on my team as well as my partner, but I was looking forward to the change. I'm not a fan of working straight day shifts but would sacrifice if it got me to my dream job.

At that time, there were four detectives in the unit, three Sergeants and a Constable. (A second Constable would be joining us a few months after I arrived.) There was a lot of experience in the room as well. Rusty had the record (and still does) for being the primary investigator of more homicides than any other detective in Lethbridge Police Service history. When he got out of K-9, Rusty had gone into Violent Crimes as a young Detective Constable. He was then promoted back to patrol teams, and a couple of years later, was back in VCU as a Sergeant. His partner Luke was an ex undercover drug cop, a guy I'd never worked with before. I soon learned that he was a brilliant investigator. My partner Kory had previous experience in CID in the Priority Crimes Unit when he was a constable. Every one of us had experience in working murders, and the Major Case Management system that we use at LPS that helped keep track of the tasks, exhibits and disclosure for files so big you can't keep everything in your head. It was a really strong unit, and I was really looking forward to it.

One of the added benefits of the job was that our office was offsite. At that time, the headquarters building was going through a major renovation, so we were working out of the Old Court House, a block away from City Hall on 4th Avenue South. We shared the third floor with the Economic Crimes Unit (a Sergeant and two Constables), Domestic Violence Unit (a Sergeant and two Constables), and Priority Crimes Unit (a Sergeant and five Constables). It was a very different (and far more streamlined) setup from the CID I had worked twelve years prior. It was also a great bunch of guys who worked really well together. I was really looking forward to the challenge. I didn't even mind going back into the on-call rotation and always carrying my work phone with me. Every detective in CID was required to take about four on-call weekends per year which was way less than the last time. (I took seven on-call weekends my last year in CID the first time through.) The reason VCU detectives always carried their phones revolved around the types of calls we were required to investigate. If a priority crimes copper got called out Friday night to an assault that turned into a homicide, at least two of us went out with him. It was also a given that one of us would be the primary investigator of the file, letting the young priority crimes detective go back to his work load, or more likely be assigned to us to help with the file and learn from us. (Policing is like that. The older guys are always training the younger guys to replace them one day.) The other thing about being on call was that the selection process for on-call weekends was via seniority. That meant I got to pick my four weekends before anyone else in all of CID. I was that old.

S o, there I was, in VCU, and on-call for my first time that year. It was the second weekend in January of 2016, and I had decided to jump right on that horse and take the first on-call weekend of the year. I figured I'd get one of my on-call weekends out of the way right out of the chute. It was January. Crime doesn't happen in January, right? What could possibly go wrong? You guessed it. I was called out that weekend to begin investigating our first murder of 2016. I found myself going to a relatively affluent neighbourhood on the south side of the city on a crisp Sunday afternoon. Patrol members were on scene at a residence owned by Iris. She was an older, retired woman, who was struggling with some diagnosed mental health issues. (She had caregivers come into her house every day or two to check on her, but she still lived at home.) Her husband was suffering from dementia and was in a facility that could provide him with the care he needed. Iris's daughter Lana lived in Calgary, two hours North of Lethbridge with her husband and kids. Lana and her husband came down from Calgary to visit her mother that weekend and found her dead.

I spoke to the patrol sergeant on scene, and he told me Lana had come to Lethbridge and gone in the back door of the residence with her key when no one answered the door. The house was usually immaculate, as Iris was very strict about keeping a clean house. She would not even let family, or anyone else for that matter, come through the front doors of her residence. The carpet at the landing of the stairs was white and Iris cleaned it so often that it still looked newly installed. Lana told the cops on scene that she and her husband used their key to enter the back door as they usually did. Lana's husband saw Iris first, crumpled in a heap, face up and covered in blood at the landing of the stairs by the front door. He told his wife to call 911 and went only far enough to see that there was no way Iris was still alive. They then went outside to wait for police. They'd provided preliminary statements to the constable there and were then taken to the station for me to come and speak with them further when I was done at the scene.

I called my boss and he called Rusty and Luke out to give me a hand. No decision had been made yet, but I was pretty sure I wasn't going to be the primary investigator on this one. I had only been in the unit a week, and the last time I worked a murder was about eleven years prior. To say I was a bit rusty would be an understatement. While waiting for the back up detectives and Forensic Identification Unit, I had a quick look around the residence. The house was very clean, not just cleaned up for relatives to come over, but obviously always this clean. There were a few things out of place though. There had been a struggle in the living room with some knick-knacks on the floor. The telephone "land line" in the house had been cut. There was a large kitchen knife sitting on one of the kitchen chairs, even though everything else was in its rightful place. There was also one bedroom that had been rummaged through, leaving every other room in the house in pristine shape. Either the bad guy(s) had gone to the room in search of something specific and found what they were looking for, or more likely, the room was staged to appear as a break and enter that went bad.

When I went back to the body, I found Iris face up with a great deal of blood on her face, head, and chest. Her head was in the corner of the landing and there was blood spatter going up the walls in two separate directions. I didn't see it yet because I waited for Ident before I moved anything, but she had over twenty stab wounds to her chest and torso, and the back portion of her skull had also been crushed, consistent with someone repeatedly bouncing her head off of something, possibly the floor. There was also a long streak of blood on the wooden banister as if she'd been bleeding upstairs, had blood on her hand and then slid down the banister where she came to rest, or more likely, someone had tried to clean the blood, and then given up, due to the sheer volume. The stairs up and down (the house was a bi-level split) were backless. You could see between stairs into the basement below. The assault was so violent that when our Ident Unit later checked the basement, they found blood spatter that had ended up on the carpet of the basement about 15 or 20 feet away from Iris's body, having flown through the space between the steps.

After going through the scene with Rusty and Luke, I left for the station to interview Lana and her husband. When I asked Lana if there was anyone who she thought might have done this to her mother, she told me she and her mother had been involved in a minor argument on the telephone the previous Wednesday. She said they argued about some door-to-door salesman that came to her door and told her the furnace was almost shot, and that she needed a new one. Lana claimed she told her mother that they would be down to Lethbridge on the weekend and her husband could check her furnace to see if it needed replacing. Lana told me that her mom become angry at her, claiming she was trying to control her life. Lana thought that it was a travelling furnace salesman that had killed her mother. Implausible, but something that we would have to investigate.

Now, I'm not proud of the next little faux pas, and I've tried to stop, but sometimes it just jumps out and bites me, like it did in this interview. So, I was talking to Lana, and learned that we were the same age. She went to the Catholic high school in Lethbridge, and I went to a smaller school outside of town. I played basketball against her school, and although we didn't know each other, we knew some of the same people. Our conversation was amiable as I spent time talking about other things a bit so that it was easier for her to share some of the more difficult things she'd seen. (After all, she had just found her mother brutally murdered.) That's when it happened, when my defences were down.

I asked her if her mother was on any medication, one of the things the Medical Examiner would need to know when performing the autopsy. She said that Iris was on meds; in fact she had a picture of all the meds on her phone to help her remember the names. She started scrolling through all of the pictures on her cellphone, and I swear she must have had at least a thousand. I watched and waited, and then after two or three minutes, it slipped out of my mouth before I could stop it.

"Come on, killer, I haven't got all day."

I know, right?! I have this stupid speech mannerism that has been a habit since I was a young adult. I say "Hey, how's it going, killer?" and things like that. I don't mean anything by it, and it was certainly the wrong place to use it, but it came out before I realized what I'd said. The funny thing was, she didn't react to it. I know when you begin one of these types of investigations that everyone is a suspect until they've been eliminated, but at the time, I didn't think she had anything to do with it. (I wasn't the only one. About three weeks in, one of the other guys in the unit said, "There's no F#$%in way she did this!") But it is no excuse, even though she turned out to be the murderer, and I called it first. (inadvertently). It was just a hiccup, and I took my share of grief from the boys. Later on when we realized it was her, I looked at the video again and it was a bit spooky. When I said it, the camera picked up what I missed. She looked up from her phone for a second, and the look on her face was like, "Oh crap, they know." Then she realized that I hadn't meant it that way, her face went blank again and back to the screen of her phone.

Anyhow, we all did a lot of work on the file, and over the next few months learned that Lana had a gambling problem. She'd been to rehab in the past, but it never took. Then her parents went to their winter home in Arizona and her mother had a psychological break. Iris called 911 to the Mesa police numerous times in a ten day stretch, the last one being an "OnStar" emergency where she told the operator that she was being held against her will in her vehicle, hence the use of "OnStar." When the police arrived and found her alone, they arrested her, and she was eventually held for psychiatric assessment for 30 days. They released her and billed her over seventy thousand dollars for the hospital stay. Although her healthcare insurance covered the expense, Lana used this as an excuse, and took out a one hundred thousand dollar loan against her mother's house claiming that she needed it to pay the unexpected American hospital bill. (Lana had been given power of attorney over her parents' finances.) When the bank called Iris on that fateful Wednesday to tell her that she was no longer entitled to a program offered by her bank for customers who are mortgage free, Iris realized that her daughter had been stealing from her again. She called Lana and told her that she was going to the police and was also going to have her power of attorney revoked.

Lana drove to Lethbridge that day, went into her mother's house, and then claims that her mother came at her with a knife, where she defended herself by taking the knife away and stabbing her over twenty times. When she went to sit down after the altercation, she heard her mother still breathing, and decided "in for a penny in for a pound" and bounced her mom's head off the floor until she stopped breathing. She then went and cut the phone cord just in case she regained consciousness and tried to call for help.

We know all of that happened because Lana eventually admitted it to Rusty. It just took about six months to get to the point where they had enough evidence to charge her and showed it all to her in the interview. There were over thirty search warrants written including at least one done on our behalf by the Mesa Police Department for health records. We went to the trouble of locating the energy sales people that were going door to door selling their product and had been in the neighbourhood that week. We found and spoke to missionaries who were knocking on doors that week. (I got that task, and spoke to a nice young man from Puerto Rico, who told us where they'd been that day. It brought back a few memories.) It was a lot of work to get all of those tasks in and collated into a readable and cohesive file to help the Crown prosecute the offender. It took about six months, and in that time, we had three more unrelated murders.

****

At this point, I am going to take the opportunity to get even with my good buddy Rusty, the primary investigator of Iris's murder. We get along well, and as such, like to tease each other. After they put this murder to bed, it was so involved and intricate, that they prepared a presentation for other coppers and then delivered it to the entire Service to show how the investigation had developed and what we'd done to solve the crime. Unfortunately, they also shared my faux pas about calling her killer. What's worse is when they'd mastered the presentation, they then took it on the road, to Red Deer, Alberta for the annual Homicide Conference there. (It is awesome. I went the year before.) They also went to Niagara, Ontario for another Homicide Conference to present it there as well. So every homicide cop in the country now knows that I am a halfwit and called her killer in the preliminary interview. So turnabout is fair play.

At one point during the investigation, Rusty and his partner Luke were going to Calgary almost every other day. There were all kinds of tasks that they had to complete up there for the investigation, and one of them was an attempt to find the bloody coat Lana had been wearing when she killed her mother. It was never recovered, but we believed that she had dumped it and a few other pieces of evidence in a field northeast of Calgary, as that was where the GPS on her phone put her shortly after the murder. They valiantly looked for days and days, then they would come back to Lethbridge, and stop at the Tim Horton's restaurant in Claresholm, a town about halfway between Lethbridge and Calgary. The restaurant was going through renovations at the time, so they often stood and chatted in the parking lot to get the kinks out of their legs and backs as a result of the long drive, oftentimes leaning up against the large garbage bin in the lot.

When Lana finally admitted to Rusty what she'd done, he asked her questions about specifics, and one of those questions was where she'd put the coat and other pieces of evidence that we never found. She described the garbage bin in Claresholm at the Tim Horton's restaurant as the dumping point she'd used. The same one that they had leaned against almost every day they went looking. Although they had not uttered a word that could have had devastating results to the investigation because they couldn't control their mouths, they had stood next to evidence, day after day, without knowing that it was there. Not their fault at all, but funny none the less.

One incident happened while I was assigned tasks for Iris's murder where an opportunity arose to tease a new guy that was so heaven sent I couldn't let it pass. One of the hundreds of tasks assigned to the numerous investigators required someone to go from Lethbridge to Calgary and stop at every business along the way that might have video pointed at the highway and was recording the day of the murder. Lana had claimed that she wasn't in, or anywhere near Lethbridge that day, and we had to find some sort of video to show that she was lying. (We eventually found her on video getting gas in Fort Macleod, adding one more nail in her proverbial coffin, but that isn't why I mentioned this.) When you go to another jurisdiction as a police officer to follow up on one of your investigations, it is common courtesy to stop in at the police department or RCMP detachment to let them know you're working in their area and tell them why if you can. Usually you do these types of tasks partnered with someone else. Two brains are better than one, after all.

So, there I was, driving in the small town of Nanton, Alberta going to the RCMP detachment to let them know that we were in their jurisdiction following up on a homicide. I was partnered with a young, handsome copper who came to CID in January just like I had. The only difference was that he had about four or five years of service to my twenty eight. There might also be a couple other differences, like I am a fat old man, and wearing a suit that I've had for years, whereas my young partner was skinny, handsome, and very well dressed. Parker was a great guy and took teasing very well. So we went into the Nanton RCMP detachment and spoke to a records management lady who was older than I am, hard as that is to believe. We told her why we were there and asked to speak to an officer. This woman had seen it all and sat back to watch the entertainment as the copper she called up to the front came to speak to us.

A young RCMP officer, about 26 years old or so, came to the front counter. I was doing the talking, but she wasn't even pretending to look at me, her eyes were locked on young Parker. We told her that we were detectives from Lethbridge investigating a homicide and we would be in her town for an hour or two. We got to talking a bit and learned that this young lady grew up in Toronto, and after university, went into the RCMP where she was eventually posted to her first assignment in Nanton, Alberta. Now Nanton is a great town. They even have this great candy store that I'd encourage you to stop at when you're in town, but it isn't Toronto. The dating pool for this poor young unattached female officer was probably pretty shallow. Not only that but most likely stocked with cowboys who might have worn their cowboy boots without socks, had huge belt buckles and always wore a Canadian Tuxedo (blue jean jacket) wherever they went. I know I'm stereotyping, but I grew up in these parts, so I also know I am not far from the truth. Anyhow, when this young lady took one look at Parker, it might as well have been only the two of them in the room. In fact, it was so obvious that the older records management lady eventually said, "Oh honey, calm down. We can't afford you to go off on maternity leave." I swear it happened! I got to tease young Parker for the next six glorious hours. Then I had a great idea.

When we got back to Lethbridge, I called Jonas, one of the young coppers who used to work for me when I was on patrols. He had been in the RCMP prior to coming to us, and so I asked him to do me a favour, and he agreed. The next day I was at work when I hear a strangled, quiet cry from young Parker saying, "Reeder, come here."

I went over to his area of the bullpen and asked him what was up. Instead of answering my question, he pointed to an email he'd received from Jonas. He told me to read it while he fretted and wrung his hands. My buddy Jonas had emailed young Parker, telling him that he had received an email from a guy that had been one of his troop-mates while training with the RCMP years before. The (fictitious) copper asked Jonas if he knew Parker and if he could get his number. The (fictitious) copper said that he had trained a young female copper in Nanton, and she wanted Parker's number or email address.

Now, I am not very good at practical jokes, mostly because I can't keep a straight face. I start to smile and laugh way too soon. It has plagued me my whole life. A curse if you will. This time, I actually did pretty well. I played the consoling friend who wondered if he was interested in giving her his number and told him the perils of long distance relationships. I held it together until I started to speak about the difficulties of marrying another copper. Who wants to talk shop at home after work, right? I lost it at that point, and the jig was up. Parker still hasn't gotten even with me, come to think of it. I'm not sure if he is one of those guys who doesn't harbour a grudge or is just biding his time. Maybe waiting for him to burn me has been the whole point.

Iris's murder investigation took over six months, involved almost every member of the Criminal Investigation Division, and a great deal of help from the Calgary Police Service. Those guys were great, taking us in and giving advice and assistance any time we asked for it. It was, by far, the most complicated investigation I've ever been involved in, and we all learned a lot from it. As I mentioned earlier, Rusty and Luke did such a good job that it later became a case study that they were asked to deliver at homicide conferences across Canada. It was also later developed into an episode on the CBC Television series "The Detectives". The show was really good but didn't do justice to the complicated and lengthy investigation. It was cool to see something we'd worked on be made into a television show, nonetheless. Thankfully, CBC never mentioned me calling her killer. I know Rusty told them about it, but they left it out. I'm still looking for a way to get even with Rusty for ratting me out to a TV producer.

WIN SOME AND LOSE SOME

There are very few people who've felt the pressure and responsibility (or curse) of being the primary investigator of a homicide. I've had many goals in life, and am constantly adding to the list, but I set two goals for myself when I was a young criminal justice student in college. One was to get a murderer in the box and convince him to tell the truth about killing his victim and why. The other was to successfully investigate a homicide as the primary investigator. I'd already achieved the first goal when I was in CID the first time, when Paul admitted to me that he killed Lyle for making him look bad to his boss. Four weeks into my stint in VCU, the second goal was realized. My first weekend I was called out to Iris's murder, but thankfully not assigned as the primary. When I saw how Rusty did things, I knew I had a lot to learn. I would try to put into practice the things Rusty taught me three weeks later, on Super Bowl Sunday, February 7th, 2016.

I think I was reading a book rather than watching the game when my work phone rang. It was only my fourth week in the unit, and I was already starting to realize that carrying this phone around wherever I went would soon become a major pain, but I answered, nonetheless. It turns out that a middle aged woman had been found in her apartment, dead of apparent stab wounds, and although I wasn't on call, I was asked by the boss to go down and help out the young Priority Crime detective who got the call.

S o, there I was, working the second homicide of the year, even though I still had numerous tasks from the first one yet to be completed. This would soon become an ongoing theme for all of us in CID, and although I'd volunteered and was happy, it didn't change the fact that this was shaping up to be a really long year. I got to the scene and spoke to

Miles, the PCU detective who had been on call this weekend. (The same Miles that I had helped learn to interview years before. He'd achieved his goal of working in CID as well, and here we were at a murder scene together. Even though it was obviously a somber occasion, I was happy to have had a small part in helping him get there as well.)

Miles walked me through the crime scene to show me what he'd found. The murder victim lived in a main floor apartment of a four story apartment building. Her name was Florence, and she was found deceased from stab wounds to her back and left arm. She was in a kneeling position, in a pool of blood that had started to coagulate around her, in the middle of the living room area of the studio apartment. It was Florence's apartment, but she sometimes shared it with her girlfriend, Joleen. Patrols had dealt with the victim and her girlfriend earlier that day for an alcohol and drug fueled domestic disturbance, but there was no criminal offence at that time, and police left with assurances from both parties that they would keep the noise down and go to sleep. Of course, every copper reading this knows how that goes. They *never* settle down and go to sleep. We almost *always* have to go back. Sure enough we did, about eleven hours later, but this time it was to find Florence dead, kneeling in a pool of her own blood. Joleen had been prophetic to those coppers that morning when she said, "Don't worry, I'll take care of her." She was also nowhere to be found.

Florence was found in a kneeling position, sitting on her feet, in her living room area. She was fully clothed with her coat on. There was a large pool of blood that had started to coagulate on the floor to the left side of her body. The two wounds to her back were fairly minor in comparative terms, but the one to her left bicep, we later learned, had severed her brachial artery. Her cause of death was exsanguination (bleeding to death) due to that wound. Because she was still wearing her coat, the blood came down the inside of the sleeve, and pooled on the floor next to the left side of her kneeling body. The fact that the blood had started to coagulate told us that the injuries were at least a couple hours old. Although not located in the apartment, we eventually found the murder weapon. When our Ident guys were processing the scene, the building manager noticed that the wall mounted heater in the foyer near the exit of the apartment building had been pulled partially away from the wall. When he went to fix it, he found a steak knife with blood on it, stuffed behind the heater. The wall heater was down the hall and up a set of stairs away from the victim's apartment, along the fastest route out of the apartment building.

I know what you're thinking. Joleen must have done it. Sure, that thought comes to mind, but you can't put someone in jail on the assumption that they were seen arguing with the victim 11 hours prior to the murder. That whole "innocent until proven guilty" thing comes to mind. We had lots of things to do, and time is always a crunch. If you let one of these cases go cold, they are pretty tough to "warm up" again. Doors needed to be knocked on, people needed to be spoken with, and most importantly, Joleen needed to be found and spoken with. That next morning during our first briefing I must have assigned 60 or 70 tasks to my teammates. This is all while we were still working our tasks for the murder of Iris, that happened three weeks prior. It was a very busy time. (It got worse in April when we had two unrelated murders happen on the same day. Like I said, we were very busy that year.)

Joleen turned herself in two or three days later. She claimed she didn't know anything about what had happened and that when she left the apartment, Florence was alive and well. Joleen claimed that she left at about ten in the morning and hadn't been back since. She told us she'd been staying at an "Auntie's" house for the last few days, and the aunt was the person who told her we were looking for her. When she heard that the police needed to speak with her, she immediately came to the station to talk to us, even though in the previous 60 plus years of her life, with a long and storied criminal history including a previous conviction for manslaughter, she'd never once turned herself in to speak to police when she knew we were looking for her. I know that because the first time I arrested her was 28 years prior, in 1988.

While we were speaking with her at the station, I sent two detectives to the residence where she'd been staying to gather statements and other possible evidence. The Auntie was very helpful. She told us that Joleen had shown up at her house a few days earlier, in the afternoon sometime. She was drunk and had blood on her pant legs and shoes. In fact, she told us that when Joleen went to the station to speak with us, she'd "borrowed" and worn the Auntie's shoes. (When we asked Joleen whose shoes she was wearing, she claimed that they were hers and that she had been wearing them when she moved out of the apartment.) While the two detectives were still at her house, the Auntie pointed out all the property that belonged to Joleen, including her shoes. There was visible blood drops on the tops of the shoes and laces.

One of the many judicial authorizations (search warrants, production orders, etc.) we wrote for this investigation was for the landline telephone belonging to the victim. We saw that a call had been made on that line to Joleen's sister at about 1:30 in the afternoon, three and a half hours after Joleen claimed she left the apartment. More importantly, if you factor in the blood

221

beginning to coagulate around the body when the victim was located at about 5:00 pm, it put her time of death at about one or two in the afternoon as well. (That is obviously just an educated guess. Those TV shows where the Medical Examiner tells you that the person died between 12:15 and 12:30 are pure fiction. There are too many variables to get that precise, unless you saw someone alive at 12:14, and then found them dead at 12:31.) When we spoke to Joleen's sister, she told us Joleen left a message at 1:26 pm on the day of the murder, crying and asking for a ride. The sister deleted the message but there was a time stamp on her phone as well as the phone records from the search warrant. We obtained a statement from the sister telling us about the message and its contents. Things were shaping up, but we weren't quite there yet.

We sent the blood from the knife and the shoes away for DNA analysis, and then got a warrant for Joleen's blood so we could have a standard sample of her blood to compare to the unknown samples sent to the lab. We sent samples of the victim's blood to compare as well. We then tried to see if Joleen knew where the murder weapon had been hidden. (Something only the murderer would know.) I asked our Tech Crimes Unit to go set up a covert camera at the scene that would record the hallway where the knife had been dumped. Then I had a uniformed copper bring Joleen in, so we could execute a warrant to collect a sample of her DNA. I talked to her at great length, and in a purposely adversarial manner. I let her know, in no uncertain terms, that when we found the murder weapon (without telling her that we already had), we would compare her DNA to the DNA that was sure to be found on the weapon and prove that she'd done the deed. This is called a "stim" to stimulate an action by the perpetrator. I hoped that Joleen would go back and check where she dumped the knife, to either move it or just check that it was still there, capturing her on camera, checking on a knife in the place only the murderer would know. Great plan, right? Except there was a problem with the camera for the first couple of days. No fault of anyone's, just proof that Murphy's Law is still alive and kicking.

So we waited for the DNA. Even with the DNA returning to show that the blood on the knife and Joleen's boots belonged to the victim, it could be argued that she lived with the victim, so there would be cross contamination of DNA on almost everything from that residence. (For example, the blood on a shoe could be explained by helping the victim with a nose bleed days prior to her death.) This was one of those cases that short of the accused giving a statement taking full responsibility for the murder, we'd have a mountain of circumstantial evidence, and then need to prove the statements she did give us were lies. (Like the telephone call from the landline in the victim's apartment to her sister, almost four hours after Joleen claimed she left the residence, or the fact that she wore her Auntie's shoes to the station when she turned herself in but lied by claiming they were hers.) In jury trials, it's often about "provable lies" rather than the "gotcha" statement from the accused. In today's environment, it's difficult to get a statement admitted into evidence without the defence attacking it on numerous grounds from deceit and trickery to oppressive behaviour by the cops. For example, when I interviewed Paul about murdering his buddy Lyle 12 years prior, it had taken seven and a half hours to get him to admit to what he'd done. Today, that might be considered oppressive by a judge or a jury. On the other hand, when they hear fifty lies that the accused gave to police, lies that the cops have proven to be lies, a Judge or a jury is more likely to believe that the dirty, lying liar is also lying about their innocence.

A couple months later, we got the results back from the DNA lab. The blood on the knife and on Joleen's shoe belonged to the victim. (The chance they gave that it would be anyone other than the victim's blood was twenty seven sextillion to one. That is 21 zeroes, so we were pretty confident that the blood belonged to the victim.) We arranged one more piece of the puzzle prior to arresting Joleen again and bringing her in for an interview. The vernacular for this investigative tool is called a "cell shot".

There's a pool of trained undercover coppers in the province who can be called upon to do certain tasks in other jurisdictions. The scenario we came up with went something like this. The U/C operator was a young woman from Edmonton who'd gone to a party with her boyfriend. While at the party, her boyfriend had consumed so much alcohol, he passed out leaving her to fend for herself. She was attacked by a man at this fictitious party who tried to rape her. Our girl would then claim that she'd bottled him in the head until he was unconscious, thus stopping the assault. We then put this young undercover copper with that cover story in the same cell that was wired for sound with Joleen for the next few hours. We wanted to see if Joleen would tell our operator what she'd done to Florence. When this was all arranged, the pieces in place, we arrested Joleen for murder, and brought her into our station. We put her in a cell with the young undercover copper and left the two alone.

Over the next few hours, we recorded the idle chatter of two complete strangers sharing a distasteful experience. Then I went in and took the operator out and let her rest for a bit and hydrate and have a snack if she wanted one. When I took her out I told her that things had changed, as the guy she'd assaulted with the bottle had taken a turn for the worse and might not make it. The Edmonton Police Service undercover operator then asked me to give her more information so she could call her lawyer again. We put her back in about an hour later. She and Joleen eventually struck up a more substantive conversation, and our operator shared the scenario. Joleen was silent for a long time, and then she told the undercover cop that if she was attacked or the guy had tried to rape her, that she needed to tell the cops. If it was self defence, they needed to know that.

Finally we took Joleen out of her cell and tried to interview her. She refused to talk to us at all. She wouldn't even say she didn't do it; she just wouldn't say anything at all. We tried three different interviewers, and she was having none of it. We put her in a room with the Auntie whose shoes she had claimed were her own, and that was the only time we got her on tape saying anything incriminating. Joleen got mad at her Auntie for not covering for her when she told us that Joleen had lied about owning the shoes. Even after all the attempts to get her to give us a reason why, to give us some mitigating facts, she remained silent. We had enough provable lies to show that she was deceptive through the entire investigation, and now we had her giving advice to someone else to admit to the assault if it was in self-defence. Advice that she would obviously follow herself, if what she had done to Florence had been in self defence. We charged her with second degree murder.

A year or so later, a jury found her not guilty by reason of self-defence. I still struggle with that for obvious reasons. Two of the stab wounds were in the back of the victim, we proved she lied about so many important things, and most importantly, she gave someone else advice to talk to the police if it was self defence and yet she didn't follow her own advice. The only solace I have is the fact that she admitted to the killing (proving we got the right person) and she did more dead time (pre-trial custody) than she got as a sentence for her first murder.

****

One sad but sort of funny thing happened while we were investigating Florence's murder. (Funny from a cop's perspective, so those of you that aren't cops and don't want to be offended, skip the next four paragraphs now.) The majority of witnesses we had in this case were either homeless or one (marginal) step above homeless, usually couch surfing at friends' houses. Two witnesses died between the time we took their statements and the trial date. (That definitely isn't the funny part.) One of the guys I was looking for to give a statement was someone I'd known for years. He'd started working for the city in the parks department a year or two after I started with the police. He was a young guy who had a wife and a couple of beautiful kids, and he was doing really well. He was supporting his family and loved his work. Every time we saw each other we stopped and chatted for what seemed like hours. Then someone very important to him died. He started drinking to quell the pain, and then his wife took the kids and left him. He lost his job, and then his home shortly thereafter. I would still see him on the street and still talk to him like the old days, and he really seemed to enjoy our chats, but he'd fallen down the rabbit hole of addiction and all that entails.

I spent about three fruitless weeks looking for him, when I came across him by happenstance. I was with my buddy James, a member of the Forensic Identification Unit. We were in his personal vehicle at the time and had stopped at a local business when my witness just happened to walk by. I called him over and we started talking. After the "how are you doing" discussion, he gave me the information I needed about the investigation. After that we chatted like old times for about fifteen minutes. He then hit me up for a couple of bucks, but I told him I had no cash on me. James interrupted us at that point and gave him five bucks that he had in the console of his truck. He thanked us and was on his way.

When we came back to work the next morning, we found out he'd killed himself. He'd gone to the dollar store, tendered a five dollar bill to buy shoe laces, and then hung himself with them. I'm not going to lie. I was pretty sad about the whole thing. This guy had taken a wrong turn after a difficult time in his life, and things just compounded, until he thought there was no other choice but to hang himself at three in the morning in a bank ATM lobby with shoestrings bought with his last five dollars.

Even though this was a sad event, I still couldn't resist teasing my friend James about his unknowing assistance in the suicide of my witness. The receipt for the shoe strings he hung himself with was found in his pocket, along with the exact change from the fiver that James gave him. I know it probably makes me a bad person, especially since this was about the suicide of an acquaintance of mine, but I couldn't resist. Cop humour is something that you can't really understand unless you've done the job for a while. (Inappropriate humour, I later learned, is an indication of PTSD. As mentioned in the beginning, there will be a whole chapter about my issues coming up.) James thought it was just as funny as I did, so I guess he has issues too.

Even though I was working in VCU, and as a result, was doing inordinate amounts of overtime, I was still getting called out as a negotiator as well. One call that happened around that time was very interesting for a bunch of reasons. There was this kid who was driving around the city one night, obviously looking for cop cars, and then doing outrageous acts with his vehicle to try to get them to chase him. (I later asked him why, and he told me that he wanted the cops to kill him.) Lethbridge Police Service policy prohibits us chasing a vehicle where the sole offence is a provincial statute like speeding. (I often tease my buddies about the "good old days" where we used to pursue everyone to their fiery death. Thank heavens we don't do that any more.)

This kid was driving a fairly new vehicle and after the second or third unsuccessful attempt at getting coppers to chase him, the sergeant working the street that night had dispatch contact OnStar and see if the owner of the vehicle in question subscribed to their service. It turns out he did and so they waited until the vehicle was heading back to the downtown area from the west side of the city, using the east lanes of Whoop Up Drive. This is one of the longer stretches of road in the city that connects the east and west side by a bridge that spans the Old Man River. Once on that stretch of road, you're committed. There are no exits until you get to the top of a large hill on either side of the river. At our request, OnStar shut the vehicle down as he was going down the hill. The vehicle came to rest on a bridge deck spanning the Old Man River with two or three police cars right behind him. There he was, barricaded in his car, refusing to exit. When coppers approached the vehicle, they saw that our boy had an SKS rifle (Chinese knock off of a Russian AK 47), with the barrel in his mouth, the stock between his knees and his finger on the trigger. The Tactical Response Unit was called, and I was the only negotiator that they could get to come out.

So, there I was, sitting in a patrol vehicle in the eastbound lanes of Whoop Up Drive at about two o'clock in the morning, with a young copper that'd been trying to talk our boy out of the car for about 20 minutes or so. A second negotiator was unavailable, so I kept Aaron as my secondary, while I talked to the kid in the car in front of us, by cellphone. The kid was really polite and appreciative of our efforts but was pretty intent on killing himself. He was hard to understand at first until I asked him what was in his mouth, and he told me that it was the barrel of his gun. We started up that Behavioural Change Staircase by just trying to build rapport with the kid, using active listening skills and at the same time trying to figure out how we got here. I had been a negotiator for over fifteen years by this point, and this was clearly one of the most "truly" suicidal persons I'd ever spoken with. (That includes people that are one foot on and one off of the train bridge I've spoken about earlier.) Usually when the trained negotiator gets there, everyone else that has had conversations or interactions stop all communication with the person in crisis and defer to the negotiator. (There needs to be a clear, concise message from one person to the subject in crisis, and that's very difficult to do with more than one person speaking.) Aaron had built some rapport with the kid already, and there was no secondary negotiator coming out, so even though I did the lion' share of the speaking, I asked Aaron participate as well. Even though Aaron was not a trained negotiator, he was really good. He'd worked undercover drugs at one point in his career and you could tell he thought fast on his feet. He was also a genuinely compassionate dude. He cared as much as I did about this kid and wanted to get him out of the car, safe and sound. The way the kid was talking at the start, it wasn't looking good.

About an hour into the conversation with the kid, I noticed that he was enunciating his words much better. He'd obviously taken the gun out of his mouth. Aaron and I remember this next part differently. I'm pretty sure I asked him this, but Aaron is pretty sure he did, so I'll just say that we asked him where the gun was, since it was no longer in his mouth. He said he now had it pointed at his stomach. We became somewhat animated at this point, letting him know that he could hurt one of us if he pulled the trigger. We were in one of the vehicles behind him. He immediately apologized and moved the gun. That is when I realized he'd progressed up the Behavioural Change Staircase further than I'd previously thought. He cared about me and my partner and changed his behaviour as a result. I knew it was only a matter of time to get him to come out. I had my doubts this would end well until that point.

At the end of these incidents, we usually try to interview the person that was in crisis. The goal is to see why he chose to surrender, what things we'd said that set him off, and what things we talked about that convinced him to come out. I asked Aaron to go do that, so he could learn from the experience. The kid said that there wasn't any one thing that made him change his mind. He just figured after a while that it wasn't the time to kill himself yet, so he didn't.

About 6 months or a year later, I was interviewed by a guy named Patrick Burles, who was a local reporter with Lethbridge News Now. The article wasn't just about this incident, but rather about generalities of how a Negotiator does his job, the concept behind it, and the fact that we care about these people we are talking to. That wasn't the cool part. When I checked on some of the likes on Facebook, I saw that the kid we had talked out of the car that night had obviously read the story and had liked it. He only clicked the like button, without identifying himself other than his name, but I knew who he was. I also know that I haven't heard his name since. There are not many jobs where you have a part in saving someone's life, let alone having photographic evidence. I have a great picture taken by one of the EDU guys using their bomb robot. It shows the kid on the phone with me and the rifle in his mouth, only a trigger pressure away from death. I talked him back to his senses, helping him to save his own life. Every now and then we get a win.

COLD CASES

By the contents of the last two chapters, you probably think that murders were the only thing we investigated in the Violent Crimes Unit. Even though the unit had investigated ten murders in a fifteen month period, we were responsible for a lot more than that. There were drive by shootings, stabbings, other serious assaults, including one horrific sexual assault that just about did me in mentally. We were also assigned cold cases that we were responsible for when we had any "down time". The unit was also required to attend training courses when available, to make us better investigators, and better resources for the police service. When young coppers had questions about their files, we were supposed to be there for them. Another part of the job was to develop and teach members of the service about how to do their jobs more efficiently, and with the latest techniques. For example, one of my tasks was to prepare a two or three day course for members of the service on how to investigate sexual assaults. I didn't get a chance to do that before I was re-assigned, but I was later designated as a subject matter expert (or "SME") for the training unit and was tasked with teaching a modified two day course to the recruit class of 2017. We had a lot on the go, and I loved it.

A couple of the interesting cold cases I was assigned happened long before I became a copper. Julie Derouin went missing from her home in 1980 or 1981. (It was reported to us in 1981.) I can't get into too many details because, unlike all the other cases that I have talked about in this book, this one is still under investigation. Another one is a robbery at a gas station that happened while I was on my mission in the mid 80's where the seventeen-year-old employee was shot in the back of the head. He lived, but the bad guy left, thinking he had killed the kid. Reading updates and investigative techniques used over the years by various different investigators assigned to these files was an education in and of itself. It also came crashing home to me how much more important formal education had become in the policing world over the years. This is definitely not to cast aspersions on those investigators who went before me, but it was definitely a different world. So was the way police did things.

One example screamed at me when I first read it. It was a shooting that happened in the 40's. The case had been solved, but tactics and practices then were clearly different (and wildly dangerous)! The way they apprehended the shooter was significantly different than the way we would now. It seems that there was an intoxicated fella walking down the street by some older houses on the north side. He decided to start shooting into the doors of houses as he walked by. The police were called. (I don't even know if people had telephones in their houses back then or not, but we were informed somehow.) I do know that back then in Lethbridge, there was only one police car on the street at any given time, and that was driven by the sergeant. The rest of the men, other than the copper assigned to transport prisoners, walked the beat. So, this shooting call came in, and the copper got the call from a call box. (No radios back then, just phones in boxes next to a pole with a blue light on it. When you were being called, the light lit up, and you walked to the closest call box and got the location that you were dispatched to and what was happening there.) The copper was told to wait for his sergeant who would be there shortly, so they could go to the call together. The plan they came up with was interesting, to say the least. As they rolled up, the constable rolled down his window, and then the sergeant drove right up next to the shooter. The constable then reached out, grabbed his gun hand with the gun still grasped firmly therein, and pulled it into the car. It worked and no one was hurt, but I can assure you, we would not do something like that in this day and age. When we talked about it in the bullpen our first response was thinking it was funny (and a bit foolish) but then one of the guys brought up how brave it was to do something like that. They had no tactical team, and none of the tools we have at our disposal, instead they had to rely on speed and courage.

We also had the responsibility of assisting other police agencies if they needed something done for one of their major crimes. I was asked at one point to interview a subject who was suspected of being involved in two pedophilic sexual assaults that had occurred years prior, in a small town in Saskatchewan. I called the suspect and asked him to come and see me. He agreed, but never showed up. I called him again and asked him to come in and see me. He said he was sorry for missing the first appointment when I brought it up, and then agreed to come down to see me that afternoon. Again, he failed to show. The next day I called, and a woman answered the telephone. When she found out I was the guy who had called her husband the last few days, she apologized. She told me her husband had onset dementia and would not be able to help me with what he did last Tuesday, let alone forty some years prior. I was able to get a copy of his medical records and talked to his doctor, who confirmed the diagnosis. I then called the RCMP officer back and told him the bad news. He wanted me to interview him anyway. I told him I wouldn't. Even if the guy miraculously remembered what happened, with his diagnosis, he certainly wouldn't be convicted. He was pretty adamant, and so I told him to tell his boss what I'd done and call me back if there was anything else I could do. He never called back. (This investigator also made the mistake of sending me his entire file, including notes from his supervisor on the file for the last four or five years, telling him to get on it, or he would not be transferred to his next assignment until he did.) Had he made the request when he first opened the investigation, things might have worked out. As it is, I assume that he closed the file due to lack of evidence. I'm sure that didn't please his victims.

Part of the job in VCU was to go to all seemingly suspicious sudden deaths, and that year, Luke got a doozy. He was asked to attend the river bottom where a dead body had been discovered. The scene, and especially the body itself, were pretty gruesome. Skip down a couple of paragraphs to avoid the gory details.

Attempts had been made to slash the inside of both thighs, apparently looking for the femoral arteries. When that didn't work, his throat had been cut right to the spinal cord. It was pretty horrific. There was a pair of vice grips with a safety razor clamped in the jaws of the tool lying next to the body in amongst the blood matted fallen leaves, and a retractable carpet knife near his hand. There was also a suicide note in his pocket, confirmed to be in his hand writing that said what he was planning on doing and the reasons why. He had tried to cut his femoral artery by digging at his thighs with the vice grip with the safety razor clamped in it. That didn't work so he took the carpet knife to his neck. The first cut to the neck was a hesitation cut. He got about a quarter of the way down his jaw line from his ear and realized that he had to go lower and deeper. The next cut was on the neck line, and ultimately successful. He cut right to the bone. The poor man had an intensely troubled life, suffering from such serious mental health issues that his family had seen this train coming for years. We definitely thought we had our fifth murder of the year with that one, until Luke found the note. We teased him a lot that the note appeared to be suspiciously similar to the investigator's scruffy handwriting. He took it pretty well.

While all of this was going on, we were still responding to major files, while trying to find time to finish the ones we got the week before. It was **NEVER** this busy when I was in CID years prior. Part of the stress comes from the pressure to solve a violent crime. If a drug file or a fraud goes unsolved or a mistake is made it's still a bad thing, but there's much less of a feeling that you have let someone down. We were doing this for the families of the victims, and at the same time, actually speaking for the victim, who can no longer speak for themselves. Not one member of the unit had to be reminded why we were there. The amount of "self-applied" pressure to succeed was enormous, sometimes helpful, and sometimes not. We were harder on ourselves than any boss reviewing a file or questioning our decisions. Every specialty unit that I'd been assigned to over the years was that way to an extent, but this was different. Guys were coming in on their own time to work on a file or to help another guy out, sometimes without even billing the service for the overtime.

The other thing I soon noticed but really knew all along, was that the city had changed. We were in fact, a city now, and not a large town or a small city. We had big city problems. I got called out once that year to a double stabbing where it was clear to me that it was a domestic dispute that got physical. Both parties had carved each other up pretty good. It was nothing life threatening, but bad enough that we were called out to take over the file. In my first stint in CID I would have spent hours, if not days and numerous attempts to cajole the information I needed out of one of the two victims to be able to lay a charge. This time I didn't.

There were two reasons for that. Part of it was that I'd matured as an investigator and realized this file was never going to be successful in court, as I will soon explain. The other is that neither victim wanted my help. I had plenty of files where the victim wanted and needed me or couldn't speak for themselves, so someone had to. These two half-wits had probably stabbed each other, fighting over a meth pipe or the tv remote. But they claimed they were both stabbed in retribution for their undying love for each other. It turns out that the man was a well known member of one gang in Lethbridge, and the woman was the mother of her paramour's chief adversary in the underworld, the opposing gang if you will. (Think Crips and Bloods, although if either of these two boneheads were to be dropped off at any corner in East LA, things would not go well for them.) Either way, they claimed that they could not be apart and so like the Capulets and the Montagues, they were willing to stay together, come what may, because love was more important than a simple stab wound. The gang affiliations were true. I just couldn't wrap my brain around the fact that either side cared that much about this. It had just enough truth to it though, to prevent me from swearing under oath that I believed it was domestic related and could be nothing else. I wrote it off. I saw her a couple months later and asked her if she wanted to tell me the truth about what happened, and she claimed that she already had. I said, "Ok, Juliette." But she didn't get the reference.

The first time a judge ever denied a search warrant I'd written also happened while I was in this unit. The first time in over 30 years that this had ever happened to me! I guess there always has to be a first time. I'll give you the scenario and let you decide whether it was me over-reaching, or evidence that things had changed.

S o, there I was, called out to a home invasion on the north side of the city, where not only had the caller been assaulted and then stolen from at gun point, but his dog had been shot and killed by the perpetrators. Now, those of you who aren't cops have to understand that the chances of a stranger walking into your home, shooting your dog, and taking your stuff are so slim as to be almost a statistical anomaly. Those types of incidents are very often as a result of the criminal activity (usually drugs) of both parties, and almost always, the victim and the bad guy know each other. It's also most likely that some, if not all of the items stolen by the bad guy go unreported by the victim, because they are usually things that the victim shouldn't have in the first place, like drugs or guns. You get the picture. That said, you have to go to every file with an open mind. This one file might possibly be that statistical anomaly.

The victim in this case told me he was watching TV at home with his family when a couple of bad guys came into his apartment through the unlocked door. They demanded all of his money, and when he said he didn't have any, they shot his dog with a .22 calibre rifle that the victim said had been sawed off to be the size of a large handgun. They then searched the house for money. As they were searching, the home owner jumped on the back of one of them and began hitting him, which caused crook #2 to come to the aid of crook #1. After he got the home owner off the back of his friend, the two bad guys fled. He claimed that he'd never seen either person before and had no idea why they'd targeted him, and that they hadn't stolen anything.

I asked him simple questions like if he even used weed. (Hinting that maybe the guys came here looking for his stash.) People don't normally shoot each other over weed anymore, but it opens the "drug door," at which point I can dig a little deeper. He claimed that he did not use weed, never bought it before and would never sell it. As if by providence, someone knocked on the door as I asked that very question. I asked him to ignore the door while we talked, and he agreed. The person turned out to be persistent, and kept knocking, so I went and answered the door. I wasn't wearing a uniform, but I had my gun and badge hanging from my hip, and the guy who stood there recognized me as a cop right away. He muttered, "Sorry, wrong address." He turned without answering any of my questions and tried to leave, so I went and stopped him and asked him why he was there. He told me he was just there to buy a little weed and didn't want any trouble. I let him go and went back and had a lengthier discussion about lying to police even when you are the victim. The victim still stayed with "I don't know anything officer, and that guy must have come to the wrong address."

At that point, I could have probably talked him into giving me consent to take his cellphone to download the content. I may have intimated earlier that I am a pretty good talker. I could have spent more time and probably gotten what I needed, but there were two problems with that. The first was that when you give police consent to search something, you can change your mind at any time, and in this case, demand the phone back. The other was the fact that he was a dirty lying liar, wasting my time by lying. Shooting someone's dog, not to mention having an illegally altered firearm and then using it in the commission of a violent crime was way more important in my mind than selling a bit of weed, especially in Canada. I'd learned over the years though, that criminals will lie when the truth would suffice. It is one of my pet peeves. I seized his phone and told him that I was going to get a warrant for its content, making everything on it free game, including his client list or other incriminating things that might indicate illegal activity on his part, and more importantly, I would keep the phone until trial, or a judge orders me to give it back to him.

When I wrote the warrant, I spoke to a buddy of mine who was one of the sergeants in the Combined Forces Special Enforcement Unit (integrated drug unit) and told him what I had. This is a guy who had been designated by courts on numerous occasions as an "expert witness" on certain areas of the drug trade. He laughed when I told him about the guy coming to the door to buy drugs from the house while I was there. He then gave me a few paragraphs that I could use in my warrant application showing that I had spoken to an expert witness on drug related offences, and that these sorts of home invasions are most often drug rips. Moreover, they generally know each other and communicate with each other, usually via text about their grievances prior to inflicting violence upon each other. I was asking for permission to search the phone in order to identify the person or persons who were texting our victim and who had most likely been in a text dispute with the victim prior to forcing entry to the residence and then shooting the dog.

The judge denied the warrant, saying I couldn't prove the owner of the phone was a drug dealer. That file also remains unsolved because the victim still claims that he doesn't know who did it, and he's not a drug dealer and has no idea why someone would come to his door while the police were still there to purchase drugs. Poor dog. Another shooting that I went to later on was a little more intense.

****

So, there I was, going over to the headquarters building from our current office in the "old courthouse", to assume a file we were taking over from nightshift. The original responders were going home at the end of their shift but were waiting to brief us on a drive-by shooting and what they had done about it to that point. We learned from two very tired, almost punch drunk constables that during the night, two drug dealers well known to us, had been shot at in a lane behind a gas station on the north side of the city. We got all the information we could from the two coppers and sent them home while we took over the file. We first interviewed the two victims who claimed they didn't know of any reason on God's green earth why someone would want to shoot at them. They professed to be paragons of virtue, innocently walking home when unknown ruffians set upon them, without warning or justification, firing 5 or 6 rounds from a handgun at them. After talking to them, my partner and I agreed we should ignore the "innocent victim in the wrong place and time" theory, and go out on a limb, and narrow our focus on the probability that this was a case of drug dealers arguing over drugs, money, or clientele or a mixture thereof.

This is still technically an open investigation, so I won't get into how, but we learned there was a strong possibility the drug dealer who'd been seriously dissatisfied with his two employees, had ordered enforcement action. What's more, we also found out that, although a resident of Calgary, the boss was currently staying at a third "employee's" house, here in Lethbridge. We decided that we needed to talk to everyone inside, and probably seize their drugs as well. Because of the type of file, and the likelihood of armed bad guys and large amounts of drugs, we called the Tactical Unit, and for once, I didn't have to be the negotiator. I wasn't there, but I don't think they even called in first before they kicked the door. It was a non-announce, night time authorized search warrant. Judges don't grant those often, so that tells you what threat level we assessed these knuckleheads to be.

When we kicked the house, all those found inside were transported back to the station, where we took over interviewing them. Unfortunately, there was no gun located in the residence, but the huge bag of fentanyl that we found in the tank of the toilet was enough drugs to charge someone with possession for the purpose of trafficking. Two people we were most interested in that were found in the house were the home owner Solomon, and a "friend" of his from Calgary. I tried to interview the idiot from Calgary, and it went nowhere fast. He was just in the wrong place at the wrong time, that sort of thing. Solomon on the other hand actually talked to me. Like one human to another. It was refreshing.

I could tell that he was scared, and he knew he was going to jail, but I let him in on a little secret. Not even most murderers in Canada go to jail for life. He could rebuild his life if he started making right choices and getting rid of baggage and the other things and people holding him back. He didn't know it, but I had an ace up my sleeve. I knew his father who emigrated to Canada in the 80's from eastern Africa. He'd owned a novelty shop in the downtown core when I was a young copper. Back in those days, you could spend more time with citizens and just talk, instead of going call to call. I would get out of my car and speak with his dad from time to time. He had shared with me the reason that they emigrated. They were Christian, and it was hard to be faithful in his homeland. A lot of our conversation revolved around repentance and what it takes to clear and center your life back to where you want it to be. Solomon did some crying, and then he did some confessing. He didn't know anything about the drive by shooting we were investigating, and I (sort of) believed him. He claimed that the drugs were his, even though we both knew (without saying it) that they belonged to the big wheel from Calgary. He was remorseful and worried about what his neighbours would think of him because of the Tactical Unit entering his house using flash bangs and other distraction devices. I even believed that part.

At the end of the interview, especially if it is going well, I usually ask the bad guy if there is anything else on his or her conscience that they might want to clear up. That way, nothing will get in the way of their attempts to climb out of the lifestyle they've found themselves in. This is an attempt at helping them have a truly clean slate when they get out of prison, but it can also help clean up outstanding or cold cases. I wasn't overly surprised when he said there was something he needed to talk about. He told me that the spring before our drive-by shooting, he'd been involved in a home invasion in another city, with at least four other guys (who he claimed he only knew by

236

their street names). They went to a competitor's home and, while brandishing a firearm, hoped to relieve him of his guns, drugs, and money. The problem was the other guy wasn't as intimidated as they thought he would be. Two rounds from the .45 calibre handgun were discharged, one round hitting the home owner in the leg, and the other hitting his assailant who was wielding the gun. I knew that Solomon was purposefully editing the names of the guys he'd committed this crime with, and minimized his own involvement, but he did put himself as a co-conspirator of a home invasion and shooting. I congratulated him on his courage and told him I would contact the cops in that jurisdiction and let them know what was going on.

I contacted the RCMP in the small city in British Columbia that Solomon said the crime had occurred. They did indeed have an open file, and even knew the identity of some of the players. The copper told me that she would talk to their Crown Prosecutor to get warrants for Solomon's arrest for the home invasion and shooting sworn out right away. I sent her a copy of the statements I'd obtained and anything else she needed. The drive-by shooting in Lethbridge that we were originally called out to investigate ended up going nowhere. It turns out that every person involved (including the victims), were suffering from an acute case of "pants on fire" syndrome. We found out later that the bigger drug dealer was ripped off by our two victims and so he had another of his employees take a few shots at them. We are still unclear as to whether it was his intent to have them just scared or killed. They straightened up and started towing the party line thereafter so our drug dealer from Calgary was happy.

Sadly, Solomon's story doesn't end there. He didn't fight extradition to British Columbia and pled guilty to his involvement in the home invasion. The problem was, other charges were not brought against the co-accused persons quickly enough. By the time the trial was ready to go ahead against the shooter, Solomon had already done his time, and his mediocre at best attempts at getting his life in order were well and truly over. When the preliminary hearing for the shooter went ahead, Solomon gave evidence saying he was the only one there and didn't know why these other guys got charged. He claimed he had paid his debt to society and had nothing else to say on the matter.

I found out that a month or so after he lied in court for his co-accused, an off-duty RCMP officer stationed in Saskatchewan had taken his girlfriend to Waterton Lakes National Park for some kayaking and hiking. She didn't know it, but it was also his intention to ask her to marry him. His plan was to go out on the lake in the kayak with her, and when they got to a particularly beautiful spot, he was going to propose to her. The problem was that about halfway to his planned spot, their kayak ran into what he first thought was a log. Upon closer inspection, they saw that it was Solomon's bloated and very decomposed body. The off duty Mountie postponed his plans to propose.

The last I heard; Solomon's death is still being investigated by the RCMP Major Crimes Unit for Southern Alberta. I am not sure if they consider it a homicide or not. (There is very little doubt in my mind Solomon was murdered.) It is kind of sad. I liked that kid. I know he wasn't shining me on in the interview room when he said he wanted to be normal again. He didn't have to say a word about the home invasion because I didn't know anything about it. For that one moment in the interview room, he really did want to change his life. Like everything else in life, when exposed to temptation and other worldly pressures, those good intentions sometimes go awry. He just back-slid when he went to prison. Drugs are a millstone around the addict's neck. His family can be proud of the fact that at one point, he had the courage to try and change. It isn't much, but it's better than thinking their son was a hardened criminal whose every waking moment was based on the enslavement of others through selling addiction. Unlike the other man we arrested when we did that search warrant, Solomon, at least for that short period of time, truly made some effort to change.

UNEXPECTED BUT NEEDED CHANGE

I was in the Violent Crimes Unit for one year. On December 21st of 2016 I was told that I would be transferring out of the unit and assigned to the Community Engagement Unit. I had only worked in a non-operational function for a grand total of five months over the last 28 years of my career. Not only did I not want to go, but I also wasn't prepared to go. I had no idea how to lead the School Resource Unit, the Community Policing Unit, or the Cultural Diversity Unit. I didn't even know what those nine constables did from day to day. I was not a happy man, but it probably saved me, even though I didn't know I needed saving. It turns out that the new Chief of Police was making changes. I was being replaced with a constable in VCU. In fact they were restructuring the unit so that instead of three sergeants and two constables, they put one sergeant in charge of it, and put four constables as investigators. There are positives and negatives to that decision, and I won't give you my opinion, because it is just that, my opinion. What I did know was that I was going somewhere I hadn't asked to go.

The other thing I didn't realize was that I still wasn't doing well. My stay in VCU had done nothing but exacerbate the issues that I was having, but the pace and pressure hid the problem, at least from me. It wasn't just the pace or the investigation of the deaths of other human beings. Every file we had involved a person being violent toward another. The one that affected me the most was not even a murder, although it probably would have been if it had occurred twenty years earlier. (Medical science is a wonderful thing.) A young lady was just walking to work one morning when she was attacked from behind by a complete stranger. She was struck in the head with a metal pipe and sexually assaulted. The perpetrator struck her so hard that he must have thought he'd killed her. She was unconscious during her attack, or at least she couldn't remember what happened. After sexually assaulting her, the perpetrator stuffed her into a garbage container like a piece of trash. We were all deeply affected by what had happened to this beautiful young lady and by extension to her family as a whole. That year we started a collage of pictures of the victims we were working for on one of the walls in the bullpen. Hers was her wedding picture, and it made us all motivated to find her assailant.

I remember one of my tasks for this horrific assault was to view and identify people from a video. In it, I saw the offender go up to another well-known criminal, and as they spoke, the new guy began to take his shirts off. He had three or four shirts on and gave the offender the one closest to his skin, then walked away. I saw the offender then take the shirt that he'd been wearing and put it in the trash at the homeless shelter. It's the first time I'd ever hoped to go to the landfill and crawl through smelly, rotting trash to see if I could find a piece of evidence. I was actually disappointed to learn that the garbage in question had already been raked and spread out, so they had no idea where to start looking for the shirt. Even if we found a bloody shirt in the trash, there would be no way to link it to the offender short of DNA and the lab wouldn't take it unless we could prove the shirt belonged to the offender. An impossible task, but one we were all willing to do. That poor girl's life changed that day in a permanent way, and so did her young family. The offender got twenty years in jail for the crime, but it will bother me until the day I die. When I got to the Community Engagement Unit, it was obvious that I was not handling my memory of investigations like that very well.

This new job had a steep learning curve, but I dug in as best I could. I struggled with things like quarterly reports and yearly reports, and I had to re-learn how to communicate with community partners. I recall one conversation I had in early February with an addictions counsellor that may not have gone as well as I would have liked. How did I know, you might ask? Well her crying after I opened my mouth and said one sentence was the give away. She had a great relationship with my predecessor and they both thought alike. I won't cast aspersions on the sergeant I replaced, because she was really good at the job that I was now assigned. When Claire, the addictions counsellor, asked her to write a request for a grant from the Provincial Government, my predecessor did an excellent job. When we got the money, my predecessor assigned one of the School Resource Officers to the task of running this program. Once a year we would select three or four kids from each high school to come to a daylong retreat where we helped them come up with plans to show leadership in their schools. The problem with the program was that it simply wasn't a police function, not even before I had been given direction to change things up. This was school counsellor territory, not copper territory. So, I went to the retreat, where I met Claire for the first time, and told her the bad news just like I had learned over the last 28 years how to talk to co-workers – short, succinct, and to the point, without a great deal of emotion.

"So, Claire, we won't be doing this program next year. We'll come and help you with the retreat, but we can't do the planning. My officers have too many other things on the go and this doesn't quite fit into the mandate that I've been given."

I wasn't rude and didn't raise my voice. I just laid out the facts. I was used to people asking me questions for clarification or reasons why, but that's certainly not what I got. She started to cry. That is when I knew I was in a different world. How was I supposed to know that you couldn't talk to counsellors (and regular citizens for that matter) differently than you would with fellow coppers? It didn't change the way I looked at things, in fact I'd been told by the boss that he felt we had strayed too far into the counselling world ourselves and he wanted me to centre the ship again. I just needed to use a bit more tact. I think I built the relationship with Claire to the point where she would speak to me again before I was re-assigned two years later, but I'm also pretty sure she was happy when I left.

The new directions of the unit caused a bit of push back from a couple of the members working for me, but for the most part, they were okay with the changes the Chief asked me to accomplish. One of the easiest things to do was tell the members, especially in the School Resource Unit, that larger criminal offences like sexual assaults, would not always get an automatic transfer to another unit for investigation. The entire criminal process for those types of investigations should revolve around the victim. Why take it out of the hands of the copper who the victim would see on a daily basis for the next three or four years in their school? It made no sense to give it to someone who might see them twice or three times total, and only with regards to that one thing. Most of them agreed with this notion, as long as they were given the time and training to do the work. Most of the SRO's were trained in interviewing children and just needed time and direction from someone who knew how to investigate those types of files. I guess I fit the bill and was soon teaching again.

A couple of those investigations will stay with me. Most major sexual assaults that a School Resource Officer will investigate are not one kid doing it to another. Those happen, but (not to minimize the result) they are less complicated. The ones that are more complex are usually historic, pedophilic, incestuous sexual assaults. One of my young coppers was called to a junior high schools for just such a call in my first year. It turns out that this young twelve-year-old girl had recently moved to Canada from her step-father's home in the U.S. They moved back to Canada when her Canadian mother divorced her American step-father for slapping one of her sons. In any event, this girl was in health class hearing the spiel about good touch versus bad touch for the hundredth time, when all of a sudden it hit her. Her step-father had been raping her since she was four years old. She started to cry, right there in the class while the teacher was speaking. A counsellor quickly took her from the room, then called her mom and the police.

This poor kid described the barn where it happened on her step-father's land in the rural South Eastern U.S. and went on to say that he had continued raping her even after the divorce. When he came to Canada to visit his kids with the woman he divorced, he assaulted the victim here as well. This was a complex and multi-jurisdictional investigation that the year prior would have been transferred to me or one of my buddies in VCU. The young copper was all for keeping it he just needed help with the nuts and bolts. He was a really good (I mean REALLY good) child interviewer, but he wasn't as sure of what to do with information he had. I won't discuss too much further about it because it is still open. It turns out that the victim's mother was a very angry woman. (Who could blame her?) She contacted the suspect at his home in the U.S. and told him that she knew, and the police knew, and he was going to go to jail forever. (She may have also added that if he didn't, she would probably kill him herself the next time she saw him. Again, who could blame her.) Understandable emotion, but unfortunately this gave him a heads up that the cops down there were looking for him as well. In the U.S. they have a different idea about how to sentence people convicted of sexually assaulting four-year-old kids and crossing international borders to commit that type of offence. He was a dual American/European Union citizen and sold everything he had at a pawn shop and fled the U.S. We got warrants for him in Canada, but the U.S. also has warrants for the guy. When they grab him up, the Americans will probably give him to us after he has served his 250 years in jail.

Another particularly bothersome sexual assault that first year was of another twelve-year-old girl who was sexually assaulted by her father while her step mother watched and did nothing. I have long ago stopped trying to figure out why people do the things they do, especially to children, but my goodness, it gets to be a heavy burden to bear. The copper who took this file was a really good child interviewer. She got some excellent detail from the child as to what was on TV at the time of the offence, what she was wearing and other simple little details that a person who struggles with the truth would also struggle with "remembering". The victim was also adamant that the step-mother took no part in the actual assault but was "just in the room" when she was assaulted by her father. In fact the kid liked the step-mother, thinking of her as a person who was stuck in the same situation, without any control of her own. The question then came from the investigator; do we charge mom?

As a primary investigator, it is your job to control the speed, flow, and direction of the investigation, while at the same time going where the evidence leads. You have to think from both a tactical and strategic viewpoint. Does the step-mother bear some culpability for allowing the assault of a young child to occur without doing or saying anything? Would it make more sense using the mother as a witness instead of a co-accused so that the conviction of the subject does not rest solely on the evidence presented by a twelve-year-old girl in court? These are very difficult decisions to make and usually hinge upon the degree of criminality of the potential witness/co-accused. In the end, after giving her the options, the investigator chose to interview the step-mother after explaining her rights to her and telling her what she might be charged with.

During the warned statement, the step-mother gave us the information that we needed, denied any participation, and claimed that she was scared for herself and the child if she'd tried to intervene. More importantly, she corroborated many of the things the victim told us, like what the child had been wearing, what was on TV and what they ate that night for supper. Because she remembered many of the same details as the victim, and the investigator was smart enough to think to ask those seemingly inane questions when interviewing the victim, it went further to proving the veracity of the child's statement. I know we are supposed to believe the victim, and we start every investigation of this kind from that position. That said, it always helps when attempting to convict the bad guy, to have confirmation of the story from a witness. When that witness provides details that the victim also provided, it becomes more believable to a jury or a judge. It also helps a great deal when that witness confirms things that appear to not be germane to the investigation. It shows that the twelve-year-old victim's memory was accurate. When the investigation is done well, the bad guy often pleads guilty, and that's what happened in this case. He got three years. Although I was no longer in VCU, I still had a hand in teaching a young copper the skills required to successfully investigate a pretty horrific crime. There was an up side to the job.

One of the things I did not anticipate was the "feel good" stories that I saw and heard during that two year assignment. They are so few and far between on the operational side of policing (or were there, but so obfuscated by the sheer volume of evil that you see in operational policing), that you forget that we do things other than just put people in jail. It took me going to the Community Engagement Unit to remember an incident that happened to me and a friend of mine when we were relatively young coppers.

So, **there I was,** with about ten years on the job, working a night shift with one of my best buddies from college. Tyler was one of the three guys I spent almost every day in college with. Every Tuesday we'd go to "The Barn", a pub on campus that had "Toonie Tuesday" special. You got a beer (in my case a soda) and a burger for two bucks. The four of us would sit and play hearts for hours in that place. When Tyler applied to go to the Schools Resource Unit after about four or five years on the job, I told him I thought he was damaging his chances for promotion. (The only way to get in to CID in our day was to get promoted.) He told me that he didn't care about that and wanted to try something new that might challenge him a bit. (Tyler was way smarter than I am and needed a challenge.) He was successful and spent five years as an SRO. When he got out of that unit he went to patrols, and two or three years later, we were back on the road, working a nightshift together.

That night Tyler and I were standing in front of the old Coalbanks Tavern on 5th Street South. It isn't even a bar anymore. It's since been converted to low income housing, but that just shows how old we both are now. As we were standing next to the lane by the Coalbanks, we both heard a guy from that dark alley call out "Officer Tyler!" This guy started walking toward us and he was about 6'2" and at least 200 lbs. He was a young adult but a pretty big dude. He looked at Tyler and said to him, "You don't remember me do you?"

Tyler looked at him for a moment, and then shouted out the kid's name. They hugged, right there in the middle of 5th Street South at about two in the morning. The kid then looked at me and he said, "Six years ago, this guy literally saved my life" and then he brushed a tear aside. I stood as silent witness as this 20-year-old young man talked to Tyler about years gone by. They made promises to catch up, and the kid left. Tyler's voice cracked as he told me when he was an SRO, the kid was literally being fed soda crackers under a locked bedroom door. His parents kept him locked away for hours at a time. Tyler found out about it and got the kid out of the situation. The kid went to a foster family in another province, and he was now a college student, and doing okay. I was so proud of my friend. Going to a gun call or arresting someone in the act of hurting another person was heroic stuff, but this was more. This young man, and whatever kids he might have at some point, and all of his current and future friends will all hear the story of Tyler saving his life, not because he was answering a radio call, but because he went to a kid's house when he hadn't been showing up for school and helped the kid out. (You may recall this was the very reason I'd decided to do this for a living so many years before. Being on the pointy end of the spear for so many years made me forget that.) What's more important, promotion or saving that one kid's life? I've been promoted and I know the answer to that.

****

One of the younger coppers working as an SRO probably did the same sort of thing during the first year he was in the unit working with me. Scott is from my hometown; in fact I went to high school with his older sister. He even learned French when he went on his mission to France. He was at one of the elementary schools on the west side, and a young first grade student was pointed out to him as a child who might be at risk. Scott went over and talked to the kid, who had a distinct aversion to coppers. Because the kid didn't want to talk to him, Scott went easy, and just sat and ate breakfast with him. (The school provides breakfast for some kids who come from less privileged homes.) After about a week of being there for the kid, the little guy began to open up a bit. Scott learned he was homeless, living in the river-bottom in a tent with a relative. This was the beginning of the school year, so it would only get colder before it warmed up again. Scott did what he could to get other agencies involved in getting this kid and his family out of the tent and into someplace a bit more permanent. He became a fixture in this young child's life. I could see from day to day how helping the kid affected Scott. I am glad that I've had the career I've had, and the places I've worked. I know I've helped people along the way. I do sometimes wish however, that I would have taken three or four years of my life and worked in the schools program when I was younger to see immediate and obvious changes you can have on the lives of children, as well as see the long term effects of helping a kid out of a bad spot or just doing the right thing.

Some things were a little more out of my comfort zone, but I learned to adapt and probably surprised some people. I can think of one incident that helped others realize that I was not just a broken down old detective. One of the units I was responsible for was the Cultural Diversity Unit. That includes teaching recent immigrants the differences in Canadian laws and those from the country they left behind. (Things like domestic violence laws are different in second and third world countries, for example.) Another thing we do in Community Engagement is to help engender trust in the police and the government in general. It's a difficult task considering the places some of our new citizens come from, or some of our homegrown citizens who might be marginalized like the LGBTQ+ community. A part of the job entailed helping to coordinate the policing activities during Pride Month.

So, there I was, called up to the second floor to one of the executive board rooms where some representatives of the LGBTQ+ community had come to ask for help in the coming Pride Month festivities. (Things like possible participation in the Pride parade and other similar activities.) When I walked into the room, I saw a guy I hadn't seen since I was probably in 11th grade. He was a couple of years younger than me, but his younger sister and my younger sister were best friends for years, and our families lived next door to each other. I'd lost track of him so long ago that I didn't even know he lived in Lethbridge. We recognized each other at about the same time and met in the middle of the room and gave each other a big hug, asking how each other's families were and all that. That's when I learned that he had been divorced and was now involved in the LGBTQ+ community. I didn't care, he was a good guy, and we continued our chat for so long that others were basically waiting for us to shut up so they could start their meeting.

After the meeting, I got approached by one of the Inspectors who was in the room. He told me that he was somewhat disappointed that the meeting went the way it did. He actually thought that because of my religious beliefs I wouldn't be able to do a good enough job representing the service with that community, and he had been looking forward to me being uncomfortable. I just left without comment. I guess there are all kinds of intolerance and perceptions that might not be founded in fact. My old friend was one of God's children and loved by our Heavenly Father just as much as I was. I'm not gonna lie, I wasn't very impressed with that Inspector who'd known me for years. To think that of me, even if he'd concealed his preconceived notions of me and my faith as a joke, was disappointing.

****

It was also while I was in this unit that things came to a head, and I was diagnosed with Cumulative Post Traumatic Stress Disorder. I'll get into how that diagnosis came about later on, but I will say one other thing about this portion of the job that I hadn't wanted. The two schoolboards (Public and Catholic) had excellent heads of counselling services. I didn't usually interact with specific counsellors in schools, my constables did. I usually interacted with their bosses. We talked quite often and went to meetings together about once a month. When I was diagnosed, I told them both, sort of as an apology for anything I might have done over the two years we had worked together that might have seemed less than caring. Both of them clearly already knew. (This made me sad, because it was obvious to everyone but me.) They were very helpful not only with the job, but on a personal level as well.

You heard it here first, and I will never admit it if you tell anyone else, but I should've gone to that unit sooner. Apparently there are still good people out there who like the police and don't commit crime! I'd just been immersed with citizens who were either victims or predators for so long that I'd forgotten that very important fact.

BACK WHERE I STARTED

At the beginning of 2019, after two years of working entirely outside of my comfort zone, I was finally granted parole and transferred from the Community Engagement Unit back to Patrol Division. In fact, I'd been moved back to the patrol team I'd spent eight years of my life as the Team Sergeant prior to my move to Violent Crimes, good old A Team. (There were four patrol teams of about 20 guys and girls that had to be designated somehow. A to D seemed the easiest.) Even though I didn't like the CEU job much, I learned a lot of things that I might not have, had I not been sent there. When lateral transfers for constables come available (every fall), there is a posting that lists the job criteria and skills required for the applicant to be successful. There is also a requirement that the applicant have written support from his or her sergeant and staff sergeant with comments included on whether or not they meet the required skills. Sergeants and staff sergeants had no such application process for lateral transfer. The administration put you where they want you, usually without asking your opinion or consent.

I'd been guilty for many years of telling young coppers that going to the School Resource Unit wouldn't help, if their goal was promotion. I learned when I went there that it was, in fact, real policing, only a different side of the same coin, and very hard to quantify. How can you prove how many crimes you prevented from occurring? I learned a lot of interesting things about the job and about myself, but the most important thing I learned was that there were citizens out there who actually were good people that wanted us to succeed. I'd forgotten that. I realized I'd become too stiff and rigid and seemed to be angry all the time. My two-year sojourn in CEU helped me to soften and remember about the time when I was a nicer person. I just needed to find out how to get at least part of that person back.

I was very happy with the transfer and to be able to work with my new partner, Rusty. He and I'd worked together in VCU, and he'd been transferred back to teams. We would be working together again as the two team sergeants on A team. My new staff sergeant was Mack, the defecation magnet I'd trained over twenty years earlier. The Constables on the team had varied experience and years of service, but none had issues that would cause a sergeant to pull his hair out. Combine this with the fact that at least a third of them were there when I left, and another third I had worked with before in some capacity or other, made for relatively clear sailing for the "twilight" years of my career, right? Sure it would.

Another good thing about A Team was the current home of the beloved (or scorned) Brown Nose Award. It had kept going in my absence and was still changing hands between guys committing one boneheaded play after another. I may have mentioned before that the award had been going since long before my time. It was so old that the majority of the Constables on the team had not been born when this started in 1983. (That wasn't a difficult feat, considering half of them weren't born when I started policing in 1988.) The good news was that members were still making boneheaded plays like I'd done when I was their age. All you have to do is read the citations for each award in the notebooks that went with the award. I was first mentioned in 1988 for my poor attempt at growing a "cop mustache." It's right there in black and white! Which gets us to our next war story.

S o, there I was, the acting staff sergeant for the set of night shifts when the last recipient wanted to hand out the award for some stellar police work. The sergeants and staff sergeant are never told prior to the presentation who the recipient was or what he or she had done to deserve their peers' notice. That would be unfair and ruin the surprise, especially if the award was coming our way, which had happened from time to time. It would appear that I would dodge it this time. It turns out that during a very cold winter night, with lots of snow, ice, and wind to deal with, the fellas responded to an intrusion alarm at a local dentist's office in the downtown core. We'd been having problems with this particular building for a couple of years. It had a perfect alcove behind it where homeless people and intravenous drug users would congregate and sleep through the night, or at least use their drugs out of the sight of citizens or a passing police car.

On this cold and stormy night (I've always wanted to use that line in a book) the two very young fellas assigned to the call got there and immediately saw that all the windows and doors seemed intact. All appeared to be secure that is, until they saw a young, well known homeless fella coming out from the side of the building. When they asked him what he was doing there, he immediately confessed, saying "I just broke into this building" or words very similar. Well, quick as you please, these young coppers grab hold of their perpetrator, and bracelet him up, and congratulate themselves on a job well done. The problem is, they couldn't find the point of entry or exit from the building. One of them even gathered up enough courage to climb onto the roof and look for a point of entry through the roof. He didn't realize the amount of snow and ice that had collected up there, or the power of the ever present wind in Lethbridge. He nearly fell off. This young copper then said something along the lines of "If I can't climb up here sober, there is no way that drunken half-wit could make it up here."

They called a much more experienced member to come over and have a look. Now this was a guy that'd spent five years in the Property Crimes Unit, investigating things like break and enters. He was in that unit when I was in VCU, and he is a rock solid copper, and a good investigator. If anyone could recognize a break and enter, it would be this guy. So he got there, walked around the building to see if he could find a point of entry, and then called dispatch to see if a key holder was coming. When they told him they were still trying, he told them to cancel, because it wasn't a break and enter. He then told the two young fellas to write our bad guy a ticket for trespassing (being on private property in the enclosed space behind the building) and drove away. The two young, overly trusting coppers were thankful he came by, wrote the ticket, and drove away, leaving our break and enter artist to find his own way home.

The next night we all learned that there had in fact, been a break and enter to the dentist's office the previous night. Someone had climbed on to the roof and gained entry to the building by the air conditioner somehow. Once inside, the bad guy was crawling in the space above the suspended ceiling, until his weight was too much for the tiles, and he fell through, breaking some of the ceiling tiles, and close to breaking his neck. (It was the common belief that if he'd been sober when he fell through the roof, he would've been seriously hurt.) When he ransacked the place for a bit and found nothing of value, he decided it was time to leave, but was interrupted by two fine gentlemen in uniform. He knew the jig was up and was one of the few crooks who learned to be honest, especially when caught in the act, and to take responsibility and show remorse. When you did that, the cops, and judges went easier on you. That is, if they believed you in the first place. I'm sure as he walked away with his trespassing ticket, he thought to himself,

"At least I tried to be honest."

Our two recently bamboozled, but now humbled public servants, went out that night to find the miscreant and charge him accordingly. The both of them took their ribbing with good grace and didn't even give their more senior advisor up as the guy who should've known better. (A mitigating factor in the severity of their varied sins.) The storied Brown Nose Award could only go to one person, so the more senior of the two members who originally attended lucked out. He later confessed that the only thing that bothered him about getting the award was that he didn't even write the ticket. He gave that up to the young probationary constable who was with him, as a reward for nearly killing himself when he slipped and nearly fell off the roof, instead of taking the safe route that the crook had obviously taken. He got the award and didn't even get the stat for it. He was somewhat mollified by the fact that he was told during the presentation that the ticket would have to be withdrawn as it was not an accurate assessment of what had occurred, and more importantly, if the crook pled guilty to it, we weren't sure that it would count as double jeopardy for the break and enter charge they laid. It was a blessing to see the fellas still providing great fodder for the Brown Nose Award. Hopefully it continues for another 37 years.

****

Any copper will tell you that there's a distinct difference between dayshift and nightshift calls. Dayshift calls are sort of like "My neighbour pissed me off last night, but I was tired, so I went to bed and now I need you guys to come and solve the problem". Night shift calls, especially those that come in after midnight, are as a result of someone calling us because "they need the cops right now!" Don't misunderstand, the occasional dayshift can be really bad, and nights can be more humdrum, but at the risk of over generalizing, most calls seem to shake out that way.

So, there I was, working a nightshift and responding to a call of a "crazy naked girl climbing a 50 or 60 feet high fir tree, at two in the morning." After I got on the radio and cancelled half of the male members of the team who'd volunteered to attend, some from the other side of the city, I started to head that direction to help out the two that had been assigned. The two coppers assigned to the call were both really sharp. One was our first female Tactical Unit member, and the other had just spent a three year stint in the Violent Crimes Section. (She was the constable that replaced me when I left. She became one of the best sexual assault investigators in the Service.) In any event, as I rolled up, I saw both of these strong, capable women looking up a huge fir tree where I could see a young woman, wearing not a stitch of clothing, almost at the top, trying to climb higher, all the while talking to herself and totally ignoring them.

As I approached the scene, I heard one of my coppers say, "Oh no!" and then observed the very naked crazy girl fall to the ground from the top of the tree. It was almost comical how both of my coppers reacted. They were close enough to the bottom of the tree that when the girl started to fall, they both put their arms out, as if to catch her, as she bounced from one limb to the next on her way down. They also seemed to arrive at the same conclusion at the same moment that trying to catch her was a really bad idea. They both pulled their arms back at almost the exact same time. (It kind of looked like a basketball player going for a loose ball headed out of bounds and then realizing that the ball had last been touched by the opposing team and pulling their arms away to ensure that the refs could see that they had not touched the ball.)

Naked girl was lucky she hit the occasional branch on the way down. She was high enough up (between 50 and 60 feet) that the fall would have almost certainly been fatal, but the tree limbs slowed her and cushioned her fall enough that although winded, scraped and bruised, she appeared to have survived the fall intact. While we waited for the paramedics, we tried to talk to the girl. She was clearly under the influence of a narcotic, probably crystal methamphetamine, a drug that had become a scourge on the street since I'd last worked on patrols. She was talking in a nonsensical fashion, about generals in wars that she knew, reciting their names and what they commanded. Her eyes kind of focused on me and said, "General Reeder", and then kept on talking in a nonsensical fashion. I didn't recognize her at first, but then realized that she was the very troubled sister of one of the guys who'd worked for me for many years. Even in her drug addled state she obviously recognized me and said my name, promoted me from sergeant to general, and then continued her rant. When she mentioned my name, it scared all three of us at first until it dawned on me who she was. (My coppers gave me the gears about knowing the crazy naked girl, but that's the price of fame I suppose.) She was taken to the hospital to get the help that she needed.

****

The year 2020 started out like any other. There were some team transfers like any other year, and the leadership on the teams was moved around as well. Rusty got promoted to staff sergeant and Bill was transferred to the difficult job of being my new partner. He'd spent the last year in administration but before that, we'd been detectives together in CID. He'd been in the Domestic Violence Unit while I was in VCU and was an excellent investigator. More importantly, he was hard working, conscientious and an all around great guy. You may have noticed a pattern here. I'd now been a sergeant longer than I was a constable and for all but three and a half of those seventeen years, I've had a partner to work with. I've been so lucky through that entire time that there was not one guy that I didn't like, respect, or get along with. Bill was no different. I've been very blessed.

The new members of the team came from different areas within the Service. Some came from CID, some from different teams, some from Admin, but all of them were hard workers. The team gelled quickly and that was a good thing. We needed to stick together because for some reason this year, we were chronically short of manpower, and then COVID-19 hit. No one on the team got sick, but we had to change how we responded to calls and even to what type of calls we would responded. For the entire summer, we only dealt with crimes in progress and crimes against persons as a priority. A special unit was created to deal with the non-priority police calls that could be dealt with over the telephone. It helped some, but most people that call the police expect a copper to show up at their door, not to deal with matters over the telephone. We made it work. We were short, and we were tired, but we managed to survive the year, having each other's back, and finding humor and happiness where we could. Team members still won (or got found out, and then shamed with), the Brown Nose Award. We still went to calls, and every now and again we went to them at a higher rate of speed than your average citizen. Why, just a few months ago, I got a photo radar ticket in my PC, going to a call to back one of my teammates up at a house fire. I hardly ever go really fast anymore, but this time was different. Seth called to help get people out of a burning house. He and his partner had already saved the lives of 13 people by the time I got there.

I may've mentioned earlier that I loved to drive fast when I was younger. I may've even admitted that my licence was suspended for loss of demerits when I was 19 years old. I used to tell my friends when I was in college that the real reason I wanted to be a cop was so I could "drive fast in a car I didn't own." These things are sadly true. I also mentioned early on that going to a collision where a young man lost his life, cured me of speeding just for the thrill. I very seldom speed when I'm in my private vehicle. I seldom speed in my police vehicle without justification, and we hardly ever pursue vehicles anymore. That wasn't always the case. When I was a young copper, you were encouraged, dare I say bullied, into driving fast to prevent offenders from getting away. We chased every vehicle that didn't stop for us, and nothing but common sense, or a mechanical break down would prevent us from pursuing the offender to their fiery death. (I say that in jest, but just barely.)

I distinctly remember the moment I realized I was mortal and should use the brain the good Lord had given me. I was only on the job for a couple of years. It was about three o'clock in the morning and there was absolutely nothing going on. A cannonball could've been fired down Mayor Magrath Drive without hitting a thing. It was summer, and I was sitting by the side of the road with my window down, eating a sandwich, when I heard a car coming toward me at a high rate of speed. I was parked facing the wrong way, so when the vehicle flew by me, I didn't get a radar reading. (I was perpendicular to the road he was travelling.) It was a new (late 80's) red Corvette with Texas plates, going at least 100 kilometers per hour in a 50 zone. I pulled out to stop him, and the chase was on.

I was in a late 80's Chev Caprice and they went really fast. (Not as fast as a Vette, but still fast enough to kill you before you knew what you'd done wrong.) It was an unmarked car, so it went faster than the patrol cars. I wasn't belted in. (We seldom wore our seatbelts back then.) I was concentrating on trying to catch up to the Corvette that was now accelerating pretty hard, while at the same time doing all the things we're supposed to do in a pursuit. (Broadcasting clear, concise information like the speed and direction we were travelling, the road and weather conditions, including other traffic.) This one was easy. We were travelling in a straight line, south on Mayor Magrath Drive, without another car in sight, and the weather and road conditions were excellent. I didn't realize how fast I was going until I noticed the light standards. They were strobing past me so fast that I felt like I was flying. I looked down at the speedometer and it scared me.

I can't remember if those car speedometers back then went up to 200 or 220 kph, but I *do* remember there was a small peg at the bottom of that circular dial that you could reset the trip meter of the odometer with. My indicator had gone all the way around the dial and was lying on that peg. I was going faster than my speedometer could measure. It suddenly hit me that if I got a flat tire, I would die a horrible, and probably painful death, all because a guy was speeding. I immediately took my foot off the gas, called on the radio that I was discontinuing the pursuit, and to contact the border, as the vehicle was most likely heading there. I got the usually taunts for being a wimp but catching a guy speeding was not worth my life, and I've tried to remember that to this day.

254

Contrary to public belief, when we are caught on photo radar, even in a marked police vehicle, we have to prove how we were in the execution of our duties, or we get the ticket. I have been caught on photo radar a few times, but it has always been deemed as justified. Once, many years after the speeding Corvette, I had to explain why I was doing 165 kph in a 60 zone at two o'clock in the morning on University Drive. It was easy when I told the traffic sergeant I was going to back up an RCMP member who was by himself and responding to a shots fired call in his jurisdiction. That wasn't ego. I was going as fast as I thought was safe, to potentially save another copper's life. I also got one on Christmas day a couple of years ago, while going to a domestic dispute in progress, where the man had assaulted the victim and was leaving. I caught him on the front lawn of the house. It was worth it, and the traffic sergeant agreed, I was going to a violent crime where there was a reasonable possibility of apprehending the offender by my prompt attendance. Which brings me to a few months ago when I was going 105 in a 50 kph zone, captured for posterity on a photo radar camera, to help Seth save some folks at a house fire.

So, there I was, in the north part of the city, walking out to my car from a local convenience store after having purchased a snack. It was about one o'clock in the morning, and the city was pretty dead, even though we'd experienced no less than five arsons that night. We'd caught one offender in the act, and solved three of them, but two more happened after that, and a lot of my coppers were out shaking bushes, trying to drum up the second pyromaniac. The first unsolved one had happened near the homeless shelter around the time that an unruly client had been removed. A second fire was discovered a few minutes later a few blocks to the south of the shelter, under a highway overpass. Most likely started by the same person, heading south after being kicked out of the shelter.

A short time later, Seth and his partner had been dispatched to a disturbance between a mother and her son on the south side of the city. Although Seth was training his partner, she was so close to being able to go out on her own that he claimed he didn't need any backup. Three or four minutes after he and his partner arrived, Seth called for backup because the house they'd responded to was on fire. They needed assistance in evacuating all of the occupants. Although I was way north, I stepped it up, to go give a hand. (That is how I got the photo radar ticket.) By the time I got there, Fire HQ was rolling up as well, and they didn't need me for more than scene management, but I saw about 12 people out in the front of the house. The owner of the single family dwelling had made four illegal suites out of it, and there were a total of 13 people living in the house that Seth and his partner had woken up and safely escorted out.

It turns out that a resident of the house and her son had become embroiled in a very heated argument (excuse the pun) over whether he'd be allowed to stay at her house in his intoxicated state. He'd been kicked out of the homeless shelter because of his drunken and unruly behaviour and that behaviour continued when he got to his mom's house. At one point during the de-escalation of the argument, Seth was in the kitchen area, and smelled something burning and opened a door to a mud room off the side of the house. When he did, he saw flames shooting up about as high as the door. That's when he made a life saving decision. He closed the door, depriving the fire of oxygen, and evacuated all of the residents of the house instead of trying to put it out himself.

The fire department soon put the blaze out. It was pretty obvious from where and how it started, that it was another case of arson. Seth and his partner did a great job of interviewing witnesses and determined that the intoxicated son who had been arguing with his mother had started the fire. He'd been the only person to go into that mud room during the time frame when it could've started. When he was arrested, we learned that he'd been kicked out of the shelter (around the time that the first unsolved fire started), and then walked south to his mom's place, (right past where the second unsolved fire started). Unfortunately, we couldn't prove he set the first two, but he was charged with arson and endangering the other 12 people in that residence.

Before we cleared the scene, the platoon chief of the fire crew on-scene sought me out and wanted to tell me how proud I should be of the guy that discovered that fire. He said that the natural reaction to seeing a fire like that would be to try to put it out. It was just too big to do that; Seth had made the right choice. He closed the door to deprive it of oxygen and tried to get everyone he could to safety. The platoon chief told me that Seth saved the lives of at least some of the 13 people who had been evacuated from the house before the fire department got there.

I have been so fortunate over the last 33 years to have worked with young men and women like Seth and his partner. These fine human beings put aside their own fear and comfort, to do a job that most wouldn't, no matter what the pay. They seldom receive thanks or appreciation, and especially in the last few years, are viewed by many with scorn, contempt, and mistrust. They're accused of ineptitude or worse, by the very people who call for their help. Those same people will go back to heaping scorn and derision on them, sometimes before they even leave, dissatisfied with how the problem they created was handled by the people they called because they couldn't solve it themselves. I'm thankful and consider myself blessed every day I go to work to just rub shoulders with men and women like Seth. These fine men and women have the courage and conviction to choose to do the right thing, even when it's uncomfortable or unpopular. They do it for that very reason; because it is the right thing to do.

CUMULATIVE PTSD

I don't sleep well. What I mean by that is, sometimes I sleep three hours, then can't get back to sleep, and other nights I sleep too much. I haven't spoken to a friend outside of the job for at least five years, other than the occasional text. I've thought a lot about why and realize that I've been the one to purposely distance myself from those who don't understand what I do for a living - not because of some elitist notion, but because I want to avoid embarrassment. My humour is not appropriate anymore. I find myself telling stories, usually of things that happen at work. My friends with no frame of reference, either think I am a boor, or those that can compare from the way I used to be, feel sorry for me. (At least that's the way it feels). The last time I got a call from someone near and dear to me for many years (and coincidentally, my cousin), was to get legal advice. I don't blame them. I've analyzed how I interact with others and I'm sure I make people feel pretty uncomfortable. I've withdrawn from them, so they don't have to feel that way. We used to have people over to our house for dinner parties, and I had friends who I would hang out with on my days off. That sort of diminished over time until I don't have anyone who isn't a cop that I consider a "go to" friend.

The biggest change in my life, however, is that I don't leave the house. **Ever.** During my four days off, it's not uncommon for me to go get groceries and stay home for the rest of the stretch. I'm still a staunch believer in my faith, and yet I haven't been to a church meeting in over four years. None of this affects me at work. I'm just as outgoing as always, but I'm an introvert to the nth degree when not working. This is antithetical to my personality and how I grew up. How did this all happen? It certainly didn't happen all at once, but rather a slow creep that finally turned into an almost siege-like mentality. I've known for a few years that I wasn't the same person I used to be, but I would just rationalize the changes by saying to myself that people change as they get older. I even missed visiting with my grandfather for years while he was in a retirement home. I didn't realize what I'd done until I went to his funeral and saw how it affected my young son. I realized as he cried at the funeral, that I'd robbed him of some of the lessons I'd learned from the one man in my life who was constant and taught me the responsibilities of being a man. All because I couldn't leave the house more often. I've tried to teach those lessons to my son and find myself woefully inadequate in comparative terms. To my eternal shame, I probably saw him maybe five times in the last few years of his life. I finally realized something was going on with me while in court giving evidence on the stand for the preliminary hearing of a triple homicide. (An interesting place to have a personal epiphany.) It took a couple more years and a caring friend to act on my behalf to get me help. It's a long story, but you've put up with my stories so far, so here are the last few, and how I realized that I needed professional help.

So, there I was, giving evidence at the preliminary hearing about a rather heinous crime, a triple murder. I was asked to testify as to what I had seen and then interpret from the evidence, what might have happened in the apartment that night. Strictly from a cop's perspective, it was really cool for a couple of reasons. First off, how many times do you give evidence in court about a triple murder? More importantly, I was being asked to give my opinion on my interpretation of the evidence. The Crown was asking me what I believed happened that night, as if I was an expert in interpreting evidence. It had never happened to me before. I've also never had a defence lawyer actually get up and object to my testimony. Twice! The judge overruled the defence both times and I was allowed to continue with what I'd seen and what it meant to me.

That night I was one of the two team sergeants working and sitting in the staff sergeant's office chatting about life. The staff sergeant and I'd been friends since college, and most of what we talked about had nothing to do with the job. Then the call came in where the complainant claimed they could see what he believed to be three dead bodies through the window of an apartment. The other sergeant was a really good friend, and relatively new to the acting sergeant role. He acknowledged that he was enroute. I knew him so well that I could tell by the tone of his voice, he thought the complainant was wrong, or possibly on crack. A triple homicide in Lethbridge? Not likely. Then he got there and confirmed it was true. I left immediately from the staff's office to backstop my friend James. He'd never been to a scene this big and important before, let alone been tasked with controlling it. When I got there I saw that he'd done everything he was supposed to do but was also relieved that I'd come to check and make sure he was alright and to backstop some of his decisions. He had a young copper posted at the door limiting access and making note of those of us who went in or out, when, and why. He told me he had a second copper at the back entrance to the place as well. I took another teammate with me to clear the apartment even though James had already done just that. I wasn't doubting him. I'd been to many more murders than he had, some as a patrolman, and some as a detective. Experience matters in these things, and James knew that and wasn't offended.

The apartment was a split-level affair, with stairs leading up and down from the entry. The side window to the apartment showing the bottom level had no curtains, allowing us to see into the main living area. Three bodies covered in blood could be seen lying on the floor in the living room area. There was also a large (and I mean really large) amount of blood on the floor and walls. There were puddles of it on the floor where the bodies were and a great deal of spatter on the walls. I went in gun drawn, but unsure if it was necessary. Others had already cleared the place, but one is never really sure. We had to be careful about where we stepped and aware of our surroundings the entire time we were in that apartment. There was so much physical evidence, I was scared we would contaminate that one piece that would solve the murders.

I got to the first body and found a young twenty something man, lying face up in a pool of his own (and others') blood. I crouched down and saw he'd been dead for at least a day, probably longer, and then started to count stab wounds on his chest. I stopped at twenty or so, but there were plenty more. It was also obvious that someone had tried to move the body by dragging it toward a smaller room, because I could see the slip and slide marks with footwear impressions in the pool (almost a lake) of blood. The second body was another young adult male who also had numerous stab wounds to his back. (He was lying face down) with the same drag marks, showing that someone had tried to move him as well. The third body, a young adult female, was closer to the area where the couch and coffee table were. She was lying face up, and also had innumerable stab wounds all over, including at least twenty stab wounds to her upper chest, most of which appeared to be post mortem. (The knife doesn't come out as easy as it goes in. It usually has to be pulled a bit harder, and the skin and fatty tissue act as a sort of clamp, holding onto the knife as the offender tries to withdraw it, drawing that tissue up with it to a small degree.) Most of the fatty tissue visible on her chest was yellow with no blood, leading me to believe that those wounds were possibly post mortem. She'd clearly been on the couch, probably asleep (or passed out). We later learned that she had an extremely high blood alcohol content and was possibly unconscious when she was killed. You could see on the couch where her head had been because of all the blood. Her body had been moved from the couch and the offender tried to drag her from that area to the small room where he'd intended to put his two other victims.

My partner and I went up the stairs to clear the rest of the house, and I noticed a small bedroom with a mattress on the floor and a small fuzzy Disney blanket on it, with a "My Little Pony" lamp in the room. That ramped things up even more. I had everyone search the apartment again for a possibly dead or injured child. I reminded them to look in closets and larger cupboards because an injured and scared child might hide in places an adult couldn't get. When no other bodies were found, I started to worry that there might have been a child taken, dead or alive, from the apartment. It was bad enough that this was a triple murder, but there was the possibility there might also be a fourth victim, potentially kidnapped.

The three victims had to be positively identified. That means by way of picture ID, or preferably by a family member identifying the decedent. There is a horror story about improperly identifying people at a car accident in a neighbouring jurisdiction. Two girls were in the same car that was involved in an accident. They were really badly injured, and one died. Either the coppers didn't identify the body well enough, or there was a communication screw up. One girl was transported to the Medical Examiner's office in Calgary under name "A" and the other to Calgary Foothills Hospital under name "B." Coppers went to notify the parents of both girl "A" and "B" about what happened, and where their daughters were. Hours later, the cops realized their mistake and had to tell the parents of the deceased that the child they were sitting next to in the ICU was not their kid, and that theirs had died. Making a positive ID is a pretty important thing. We knew who the three victims were, but they hadn't been "positively" identified yet. Even so, I had to go talk to Lola, the mother of two of the young people dead in the apartment. We had to see if she knew where her grandchild was.

I've known Lola for many years as a result of previous interactions with the police when she was younger. She lived two blocks away from her daughter, so my partner and I went to see if she knew where her grandchildren were. We knocked on the door and when she answered, it was obvious that we had interrupted her sleep. (It was five in the morning.) Without any preparation or lead in, I asked her if she knew where her grandchildren were. She said, "They're right here." Then she gasped and asked me where her daughter was. I had to tell her that there'd been "an incident" at her daughter's apartment but we were not yet sure who was involved, and some people had been found deceased inside. I even used the example about the misidentified girls as to why I couldn't be sure who was dead. I didn't want to give Lola inaccurate information about her children for something this important. She knew what I was saying and broke down. (As an aside, I saw her at a convenience store while with my wife about six months later. Lola walked up and hugged me, surprising the heck out of me, and really surprising my wife. I guess I was diplomatic enough that I hadn't hurt her feelings when I asked her if she knew where her grandkids were.)

So, back to giving evidence in the preliminary hearing. So, there I was, on the stand for a few hours, describing the scene. The subjects had been stabbed over 480 times in aggregate. The offender had broken four knives. Imagine how angry you'd have to be to stab three people to death, then continue to stab their dead bodies until the knife broke, get up and go to the kitchen to get another knife, then go back and continue until the second knife broke, go back to the kitchen to get another one, then go back and continue to stab them some more, until the knife broke again. . . Well you get the general idea. As I was answering the questions of the prosecutor and was nearing the end of my testimony, I looked up from the crime scene photos used to refresh my memory (as if I will ever forget) and saw that Lola was sitting directly behind the prosecutor. She was quietly but inconsolably sobbing. It was at that point that I got teary eyed on the witness stand for the first time in my life. It wasn't that I had some huge outflowing of emotion about what Lola was going through, or what it might've been like in the apartment that night, or even what was wrong with the murderer who'd done what he'd done. I was crying because I felt **NOTHING!** I was in my professional mindset and just responding to the questions and answering them without editorializing or showing emotion. I realized at that point what this job had done to me. If a copper wore his emotions on his sleeve, it would soon be a ripped up sleeve, with a scared and damaged arm therein. This job had slowly stolen my ability to feel, and the realization of how it'd changed me, caused my tears to fall.

****

You might think that at that point, I would've become a bit more introspective, or maybe even gone to see someone about what was going on in my head. You might think that, but it was also around that time I was transferred to the Violent Crimes Unit. I'm from the generation of coppers who think that if the Service found out you needed counselling, or that you might be having problems, it would mean the death of your career. I thought I was just fine. I also thought I might lose the position I'd worked to attain for years if I started seeing someone for the simple fact that I didn't have emotion while on the stand. We were supposed to be that way. "Just the facts ma'am" and all that! I happily went to Violent Crimes, but with a secret sliver of worry in my heart. Then we had four murders in the next four months. I was too busy to think, spit, or go blind. I know now that I didn't bring my "A" game when they put me there, but I didn't realize that I wasn't one hundred percent. Major case after major case happened, not allowing me a moment to think about what might be wrong. I recall another particular issue around June of that year that should have been another clue that things weren't right.

S o, there I was, finally in a position to complete the court package, including writing the case report for my homicide. I say "my" because I was the primary investigator of the case. The DNA was back from the lab and now we had all we needed to prosecute. The murderer had been arrested and processed, it was time to finish the paperwork and get it into the prosecutor's hands and move on to the next file. One little problem existed. I couldn't finish the report. I had all the information I needed, and writing was my hobby. I kept trying, but I'd get to a certain point in the report, and nothing more came. I couldn't figure it out, but I knew something was wrong. I was coming up on a deadline, and still nothing. I went so far as to delete the first eighty pages and start again. I got to the same place and still stopped just like the previous time. I even printed out two case reports of other detectives, (almost five hundred pages), and took them home to study writing styles so that I could emulate them. That didn't do anything but kill about 70 trees. I was frustrated and angry with myself, which made it worse. I finally sorted it out when one of my partners in VCU reminded me how long I had been on the job. It wasn't meant rudely, but rather as a reminder that I'd done this sort of thing many times before. I should just stop thinking about it and do it. So I did. It was a great wake up call, and I was done in about two days. If I'd been thinking straight, after seeing all these clues, I might've realized I needed help.

****

At the end of that year, the Service restructured the unit, and instead of three sergeants and two constables, supervised by a staff sergeant, they decided to have four constables in the unit as investigators, with a sergeant as the supervisor. I'd sort of seen the train coming and had hoped to be put in charge of the unit. I thought at the time that this was where I wanted to retire from. Instead, they transferred me to the Community Engagement Unit. The job was straight days, and very little pressure like I'd been used to over the years. I won't re-hash how the job was, because I described it earlier. Suffice it to say, I was not happy, and I am sure some of my community partners wanted a more engaged and interested police partner. I also had a lot more time to think about the things that might be wrong with me, and it sort of sent me into a tailspin. It all came to a head in the spring of 2018 when I was sitting having a BS session with one of my friends, Wes. He was the traffic sergeant and we had been partners as team sergeants a few years before I went to VCU. He knew me really well, and it turns out could tell that there was something wrong with me. Most importantly, he had the courage to do something about it.

So, there I was, in my office chatting with my friend Wes in a rather animated fashion about an investigation that one of my constables had been helping a patrol member with. Truth be told, I was more than a bit angry. One of the young probationary constables on a patrol team had come to us to ask for our assistance in identifying four school-aged subjects responsible for a wilful damage offence on the south side of the city. The young copper knew who the driver of the getaway vehicle was but couldn't get that driver to tell her who the four offenders were. One of my constables knew the driver because she'd been her school resource officer for four years or so. Kallie went in to interview the girl, who eventually gave up the identity of the four offenders she'd driven to the crime scene. At the end of the interview, Kallie asked the young girl "What happened to you? You used to be so happy and easy going. We got along so well, and now you are cold, distant, and so obviously unhappy. You would have never been involved in something like this before." Kallie wasn't that shocked when the young girl broke down in tears.

It turns out that the girl had been sexually assaulted by two men from another jurisdiction. She'd gone to someone she trusted who was a trained psychiatrist. That person told her not to go to the police, and that he would help her with counselling. She was instructed to go back to the scene of the crime once a week and "cry it out." That's it! This counsellor she had received the advice from was also one of the counsellors the police service used on occasion when needed. (Like when our Tactical Support Unit is in a six or eight hour standoff with a barricaded person who is displaying signs of mental health crisis. I'd never done it, but this guy was one of the professionals we were supposed to call if we needed some insight as to how to proceed further.)

As I was venting about this incident to Wes, I blurted out, "I probably have

PTSD, but there is no way I would go to that person for advice about my mental health and well being!" (I may have been a bit more colourful in my language. Don't tell my mom.)

Wes looked at me for a second and then asked me in passing, "If it was someone else, would you go?"

I said that I would probably go and then we went on with the story. I didn't think anything more about it until I got an email from Human Resources the next morning, telling me I had an appointment with a counsellor that same day if I was willing to go. I told Wes I would, so I did. Wes knew me well enough to know that I wasn't the same guy I'd been when we were partners. He had the courage to do what he thought was best, gambling that I'd take the gesture for what it was. He is a man of courage and conviction, and I am indebted.

****

So, there I was, sitting in a psychologist's office. He was a really nice guy that you would never think a copper would open up to. He asked me what was going on in my life. I thought that was a relatively benign question, so I gave the rote response back. I was a bit guarded at first but then started to warm up to the guy. He never asked me about a specific thing on the first meeting, but he asked me questions that forced me to be introspective and honest with myself. I knew there was something going on in my head and so I told him about the first time I thought there might be something wrong with me, when I was giving evidence on the stand for that triple homicide. That started the ball rolling, and I opened up.

He asked me how else the job had affected me over the years. He asked about my relationship with my wife, how often I went to church and got out of the house. He asked about my non-cop friends. He asked about how much I slept and a host of other health questions. I started to realize why I was seeing these problems in my life. They'd been there for a while, but I'd been too busy to notice. I'm not saying that CEU isn't busy, but it's a different kind of busy. I was no longer on the "pointy end of the spear" and therefore, less keyed up and worried about the next major file that came down the pike. Worrying about the four budgets I had to deal with now was considerably less stressful or troubling to me than worrying about bringing a murderer to justice or reading a cold case from the 80's and trying to apply new techniques and technologies to possibly solve the case.

My wife and I were doing just fine, but she was suffering from some pretty difficult health concerns of her own, so she wasn't on me about sleeping too much or not going to church in the preceding years because her sleep patterns were as bad as mine and she hadn't been able to go to church for years either. I'd just been through a particularly busy and stressful year in VCU. I'd been called out to a murder ten days after getting the job, where a daughter stabbed her mother to death, then bashed her head in, "just to make sure". Three weeks later I was at another one, where I was now the primary investigator of that murder, while still trying to complete very important tasks for the three week old murder that was still very much an active investigation. I recall working a full day, then going to Calgary to execute a search warrant on a house, then getting back to Lethbridge at about two or three in the morning, then going home, catching a few hours of sleep before going back to work at seven that morning. I didn't have time to think about what was wrong with me. Then I got transferred to a job I didn't want, that operated at a different pace than I'd been used to, in an environment where I was uncomfortable. I had all the time in the world to think about what was wrong with me now.

Brad asked me why I hadn't been to church, and if I was still a believer. Apparently inappropriate humor is another giveaway as to someone with PTSD, but I only found out after I told him this story. I told him what I thought was just a funny story at the time, but how past the line it really was. I'd embarrassed myself so badly and offended someone so horribly that I didn't want to be in a position where that would happen again.

****

So, there I was, at church one fine Sunday morning. I was walking into the chapel from the foyer where I happened upon one of the sweetest ladies in our ward. She is one of my wife's best friends and I don't think she even knows how to curse, let alone the requisite vocabulary to do so. If you look up the term "Molly Mormon" in the dictionary, there is a description and her picture as an example. I know it is a bit of a pejorative, but it is not meant as one. She is just so genuinely sweet and nice that I am embarrassed and ashamed about what happened next. You see, the week before that fateful Sunday morning in the foyer outside of the chapel, the five of us in VCU were sitting around the bullpen talking about different homicides we'd responded to over the years. If you have stuck it out for the first 300 pages, you might have already realized that I am a bit of a storyteller. I told them about a murder that had occurred in Lethbridge before any of them worked with the Service; a woman had been killed by her husband. He'd recently been released on parole for a murder he was convicted of 20 years earlier. For some unknown reason, he decided to kill her and then kill himself. He drowned her in their bathtub, then froze her body in a freezer in their garage. When the body was frozen solid, he cut her up into eleven pieces with a chainsaw and buried her in the back yard. He then killed himself by carbon monoxide in the garage. Even though that happened at least 25 years prior, and I was not the investigator, I remembered it and shared it with the fellas. So I had this story in the back of my head when this sweet, lovely lady asked me how my wife was doing. My response was typical, in that it was not thought out at all as it passed my lips.

"Oh, I killed her, cut her up into eleven pieces and buried her in the backyard." I quipped, thinking I was the funniest guy in the world, right up until I saw the look on her face and the tears start down her cheeks.

I was mortified. Even though I tried, how does one apologize his way out of that one. How could she understand? I go to these types of calls, so normal people don't have to see these sorts of things. I am the shield that protects them from the ugly things of the world. My copper buddies would have thought I was hilarious, proving that this job does that to most of us. I haven't been back to church because I didn't want to offend others. They're in church to be edified and find comfort from the cold and dreary world, not be reminded of it by the blowhard who can't tell the difference between appropriate and inappropriate humor.

****

How can you explain to people who genuinely want to help you, when they can't understand what you've seen? They may watch a TV show, or even see something on the news, but they've never been to a crime scene and smelled the coppery smell of blood and other bodily fluids mixed with the tang of spent gunpowder. They haven't gone to a sudden death where the person's been dead for so long that the body no longer smells until you move it, and the worst smell in the world hits you in a wave. They've never wished the dead person had a friend or family member who might have been interested enough in their lives to drop by once in a while. The ones that've been dead that long are the saddest, and then it hits you. **You've ostracised so many friends and family that you might be found the same way one day!**

They've never been to a car accident where a truck has rolled and then come to rest on what used to be the driver's head, crushing it flat. They've never dealt with a kid who was messing around with a blasting cap and accidently set the explosive off while it was right next to his genitalia. They've never tried to talk a guy out of killing himself, even though he's gone to the trouble of tying a noose around his neck, attached the other end to his sturdy bed frame and then sat on the edge of his third story window, contemplating jumping out. They've never had to explain to someone that their son shot himself in the stomach with a rifle in hopes of gaining sympathy from the girl who just broke up with him, only to use a weapon of such high velocity that the exit wound is the size of a basketball. Then have to console the mother who found her son with the hole in his back and three holes in her window - one from the bullet, and two others caused by sections of his spine.

They've never had to admit a prisoner they knew from church, into the short term holding facility, only to find that he held a knife to his wife's throat because she couldn't be allowed to leave him. They've never found the remains of a person who fell out of the box of a moving truck on the highway, only to be run over by the next vehicle behind, causing his head to do the same thing that a ketchup packet does when you stomp on it, or try to identify, let alone investigate a dead person in the coulees with only 7 bones left, after the coyotes got to him. They've never had to learn by experience to spit their gum out before going to investigate a stinky sudden death, because you know from experience that eventually the gum takes on the flavour of the smell in the air.

How do you describe what it feels like to be the breathalyzer technician taking breath samples from an impaired driver who just killed a police officer (that you happen to know), and then listen to him joking about his burning semi-truck and trailer unit on the highway. Others have no frame of reference for the feeling you get when responding to a 911 call at three o'clock in the morning of a screaming child, and then find a four-year-old inside a camper in the backyard of a house, the doors barricaded from the outside so the parent can go partying. At least they left a space heater on in the camper to keep her warn from the frigid November air, even though pillows had fallen to cover the heating elements. (I'm still thankful we got there before something worse happened.) How do you explain what it's like to ask a terrified woman with a knife protruding from her chest to identify her assailant, all while she fearfully asks if she is going to live. She didn't. My friend Mitch had to comfort her and try to get her to identify her murderer before she died. I haven't even mentioned the four police involved shootings that I've been witness to, or peripherally involved. (The first time I ever gave evidence in court, was the fatality inquiry into an officer involved shooting.) Thankfully I've never had to pull the trigger, but a couple of my friends have, and I've come pretty darn close a time or two.

These, and thousands more stories like them still remain with me and my co-workers. You probably won't ever have to see, hear, smell, or feel any of these things. Someone needs to, and we have agreed to. **We do it so you don't have to.** The police truly are a shield to most people of this cold and dreary world. We are a life raft, or at least a bit of flotsam to cling to when you've fallen into a sea of uncomfortable or dangerous situations. We will be there to ensure you are as safe as we can, even if it's to sacrifice ourselves for you. In the tactical world we state the "priorities of life" when planning a tactical intervention. They are, number one, the citizen and/or victim, number two, the police and number three, the perpetrator. We voluntarily and willingly put the value of *your* life above our own.

This job has changed me, in some ways for good, and has damaged me in others. Over the years, I've broken my right hand twice and my left hand once. I broke my right ankle and did serious damage to the ligaments that still cause pain. I've bruised the meniscus on both knees and came close to losing my right eye. I had a heart attack at 38 years old, partly due to the stresses of this job. Finally, I've been diagnosed with a mental health condition that probably wouldn't have even been a thought, if I'd decided to be a mechanical engineer or a welder. At the same time, I've enjoyed the camaraderie of a brotherhood that wouldn't exist if I'd chosen one of those other careers. One of my buddies on the job once said it best when he was the MC of the wedding of a co-worker. "Cops are a funny breed. We might hate one another, or perhaps have a bitter argument with a co-worker, but then potentially kill ourselves five minutes later to get to that person we quarreled with to try and save them." Truer words have not been spoken, and if you extrapolate the "priorities of life" mantra that we use in the tactical world, we put ourselves in harms way in order to save you, even though we might never have met before.

As my time serving and protecting you comes to an end, I'm so thankful for the prompting I got that day in Quebec City in 1985. I'm no longer that idealistic 21 year old missionary, thinking he could save the world, but writing this has been cathartic as well. I've come to realize that I've actually helped the occasional person over the years. How many jobs can you say at the end of a shift that you talked a guy out of shooting himself, and then see a picture of him with the gun in his mouth and the cell phone in his hand while you were talking to him to show you how close it came. How many other jobs give the satisfaction of getting someone to admit the truth about why they killed someone, giving the victim's family the truth about what happened, and making society just a bit safer when you've done your job right, a job not many can do, and most wouldn't want. I used to think a lot about the incident I described where the young man came up to my friend

Tyler in front of a bar so many years ago and said, "You saved my life!" I think that most cops have one or two of those stories, but the noise of all the really bad experiences drown out those positive memories. I didn't realize how loud the bad experiences were, and how many good ones had been muted, until I wrote some of them down.

This has been a great career, and I've done some really cool things. I've had the opportunity to meet or exceed every goal I made when I started. (The only goal left is to make it to retirement, and that's just around the corner.) I've been involved in some really interesting investigations and had the opportunity to meet and rub shoulders with some really good men and women. I've even had the chance to save the occasional person along the way. Even though I'm not the same person I was when I started, and I'll have to work on fixing some of my issues, I would make the same career choice again. The book is entitled "*So, There I Was...*" and I have recently realized something after writing this all down and sharing it with you. I am so thankful that I **was** there.

So, There I was… 34 years wearing the badge

ABOUT THE AUTHOR

Mike Reeder was born and raised in Southern Alberta. He began policing in 1988 in the city of Lethbridge, Alberta, and after 34 years of service, retired in 2022. Mike was blessed with the opportunity to work in a wide cross section of policing over the years. As a constable, he was assigned mostly to general patrol and traffic duties. In 2004, Mike was promoted to the rank of sergeant where he went on to serve in many other areas of the Service, including the Criminal Investigation Division, Recruiting and Training, Community Engagement, and Patrol Division. He also served 18 years in the Tactical Support Section as a crisis negotiator. He admits that his favourite job over the years was as a patrol team sergeant. He loved the opportunity to teach, mold and mentor young "coppers". Mike has been married to the love of his life for over 34 years. They both agree that raising their son has been the best thing they've ever done. Mike is looking forward to spending more time with his family and travelling a bit. He may even write another book or two.

Made in the USA
Monee, IL
29 November 2021

83441531R00155